The events described here are all true to the best of my recollection.

A number of names have been changed to protect the safety of those concerned, or by request, or to prevent embarrassment.

Continuum

The Tower Building, 11 York Road, London SE1 7NX
80 Maiden Lane, Suite 704, New York NY 10038

www.continuumbooks.com

First published 2006

British Library Cataloguing-in-Publication Data
A catalogue record for this book is available from the British Library.

ISBN: 0-8264-8502-2

Typeset by Kenneth Burnley, Wirral, Cheshire
Printed and bound in Great Britain by MPG Books Ltd, Bodmin, Cornwall

Titanic Express

RICHARD WILSON

continuum
LONDON • NEW YORK

For Charlotte,
with love and apologies

Don't you really feel – I mean,
and just be – let's be totally honest.
Isn't a person a person goddammit?

President Richard M. Nixon,
24 September 1972

Prologue

The water's fixed but the electricity's playing up, so most of this letter has been written by candlelight. We went outside earlier and the frogs were chorusing away. There was a lightning storm in the distance, and the sky above us was incredible – you've never seen stars till you've seen an African night in a power cut.

No gossip this end. There's one cute-to-middling NGO guy who lives in Kigali, but the last time I saw him he was covered in spinach. We had one of those awkward social greeting situations – to kiss or not to kiss and if so, how many. I went for two, then he went for three, then I went for four but he had stopped and then he's so tall that I couldn't reach him. I went to do the same for his friend, who didn't recognize me and thought I was being forward. Admittedly I was wearing a hat but it did have my name on it! Cultural morasses are obviously not confined to Rwandans . . .

Some truly terrible things happened in this country – everyone I speak to has lost someone close. The only way I can justify being here is to let everyone start over again with a clean slate. I can't speculate what they did in 1994/5, or even where they were. I can't tar everyone with the same brush, and anyway these people need a teacher. Some were adults during the genocide (I think that my oldest pupil is 28) but a lot were kids and even if they did take part they weren't responsible.

We did sex education this term, which was fairly excruciating. One of the boys, who's a bit of a troublemaker, asked me, 'Do women ejaculate?' ('No.') 'But don't they spurt at all?' (All round the class girls are going 'Spurt?!!') I decided not to understand the question – if they don't know by now then they can't be very good lovers, but I can't say this in class!

PS – Congratulations on the pay rise – when are you coming out to see me?!

PPS – I spilt some mosquito repellent on the paper – sorry!

— 1 —

As we stepped off the plane, it felt like a kind of transition. Catherine and I had flown through the night, over Italy and the Mediterranean, Libya and Sudan. It was morning now, and Uganda's plateaus rose like steps as we began our descent to Rwanda. Until this moment I'd barely set foot outside the cool confines of Northern Europe, let alone south of the equator. For 24 years the Developing World had been a distant and dangerous place, something on TV, somewhere other than Here. Now I was standing in the middle of it.

The distant figure on the observation tower, waving manically before we were even on the tarmac, could only be Charlotte. She had persuaded Catherine to come, and Catherine convinced me. All I had to do was give her the money for my airfare and turn up. This was the way things often worked with my sisters. As a child, Charlotte would buy all her Christmas presents in August and then ask if I wanted to 'go shares'. Of course I did. Having sisters was one of the things that made my life gloriously easy.

It was Thursday 13 July 2000, and my life was gloriously easy. I'd left home and I was living in the coolest city in the world. After a long and humiliating period of singledom I was in a relationship which, by my standards, verged on the long term. And I had a job that paid well without asking too much of me. Perfect.

My older sister, in contrast, seemed to enjoy making life difficult for herself. Charlotte had gone to Rwanda ten months ago, and I still didn't really know why. After 'sweating blood', in her words, to finish a microbiology PhD, she was well on the way to the research career that she'd always said she wanted. She had an action-packed social life and a boyfriend who seemed to make her happy. And she'd decided to up-sticks and spend two years with 'Voluntary Service Overseas' in the ruins of the world's most vicious civil war.

3

Rwanda was high on my list of places-never-to-go. I remembered the harrowing reports – Hutus killing Tutsis, Tutsis killing Hutus, massacres and reprisal-massacres, attacks on UN peacekeepers. Not even children were spared. It seemed far worse than Northern Ireland, another place I wouldn't dream of going to. Charlotte insisted that Rwanda had been peaceful for the last three years, but this didn't seem like such a long time. Why take the chance? What if trouble flared up again?

Kigali's ageing airport terminal reminded me of Broxbourne railway station, and the toilets were similarly disgusting. Catherine and I queued nervously to show our passports to the sullen-looking man with a gun. Beyond customs, next to a stuffed gorilla and a sign saying 'Welcome to Rwanda', was Charlotte Lucy Cameron Wilson.

'I can't believe you've come!' Charlotte was grinning broadly. Her campaign to get us to visit had begun shortly after she'd left. Things had changed so much since the war, and Rwanda was so beautiful, she insisted. Furthermore, I'd promised to go and see her when she was studying in Paris, and never did. But the crunch point was that she had decided to work abroad for two full years without a break. So unless I flew halfway across the world to visit her, I wouldn't be seeing my sister until the summer of 2001.

Not so long ago I'd have told her where to stick it. Off to be poor and penniless in a Third-World war zone? Ha! What a stupid idea. See you when you come back then. Charlotte was, it seemed to me, the bossiest, stubbornest, most irritatingly manic person I'd ever met. Frequently on the edge of workaholic burnout, dangerously lacking in self-awareness, she was a freak, and she'd driven me up the wall when we were growing up.

But she was also the most generous, gregarious, good-hearted and energetic person I knew. If she was a freak, so was I in my own way. Her freakiness made her interesting. I couldn't help liking her. And if she'd driven me up the wall as a kid, I'd chased her across the ceiling and down the other side again.

Irritating Charlotte had been my primary source of entertainment until my early teenage years. Repetition seemed to work the best. I could annoy her just by breathing. The trick was to inhale, hold your breath for as long as possible, preferably until your face has turned pink, hold your breath for just a little longer, then exhale as noisily as you can. 'Haaaaaaa . . .' – AND repeat. If Charlotte retreated to her room, I would sit at the top of the stairs, bouncing a rubber ball off her door, onto the landing, into my hand and onto her door again.

Thud THUD . . . Thud THUD . . . Thud THUD . . . Thud THUD . . . Thud THUD . . . Thud THUD . . .

'Aaarghh! *You LITTLE SHIT!*'

My timing was impeccable, my patience inexhaustible. Every so often Charlotte would beat me to a pulp, but it was worth it for the times I got away, happy and fulfilled at a simple job well done.

Yet the games, and my sister's violent retribution, became boring after a while, and we started slowly to become friends. It was Charlotte who took me to my first music gig, when I was fourteen and she was two years older. In my last years of school, visiting her at university was a welcome escape from home and the moronic suburbs. When I came to study in London, we met up regularly, swapped music and went to each other's parties. I was proud of my increasingly glamorous sister, who knew all the good pubs in Hammersmith and who half my friends seemed to fancy. When I started working and she was the penniless student, I took her out to dinner from time to time. She would vent frustrations about her alcoholic supervisor and I about my disastrous love life. We still argued, and we could still annoy each other to the point of tears. But we had few secrets and nothing was unforgivable.

Having Charlotte around added colour to my life, and when she left for Rwanda, some of that colour faded. Her letters were a consolation, though. They were not so much prolific as relentless. Mixed with the minutiae of her life in rural Rwanda were vivid descriptions of the landscape, and the legacy of the 1994 war. And alongside the typically quirky anecdotes were less typical reflections on the choices she'd made and the challenges she faced.

Kigeme, 20th November 1999

I'm not 100% sure whether I'm doing the right thing by being here. I know it's good for me, and I'm having a great time, but I'm not convinced that I'm any great shakes as a teacher. The reason we're here is that a lot of teachers were killed in the genocide. The question is whether I'm just *propagating an unstable and unjust society by teaching the elite. From my (limited) vantage point I think that there are a <u>lot</u> of unresolved issues here.*

In a strange way Charlotte's doubts reassured me. So often in her life she'd seemed so sure that her way was the right way. But it felt as though she was doing this with her eyes open. In the photos she sent back, she looked happier and more poised than she'd been during her last few, stressed-out, PhD years in London. I still wondered about the wisdom of what she was doing, but I was intrigued by it, and I didn't want to go for two years without seeing her.

Charlotte was trimmer and more relaxed than when we'd last been together, but as stubborn as ever. Although Catherine and I were exhausted, we weren't going anywhere until Charlotte had bartered mercilessly over the taxi-fare into town. She was earning Rwandan wages, she told us, unlike most of the foreigners employed here by Non-Governmental Organizations (NGOs). She resented the assumption that she was rich just because she was white, and was determined not to pay over the odds.

Kigali was hot and dusty, yet surprisingly green. The road was lined with small shacks, and many had their own patch of land for growing vegetables. Goats grazed on the grass beside the airport. Further along, some of the larger buildings were nothing more than burned-out shells, hulking relics of 1994.

'Msungu! Msungu!' At the city's chaotic, open-air bus park, everyone seemed to want to sell us something. We quickly crammed into a white minibus that took us out of the city, across a palm-covered plane and into the green hills of Gitarama province. Rwanda *was* beautiful, notwithstanding the Celine Dion music blasting out from the front of the bus. Every so often we saw a grave by the side of the road, but I tried not to stare. Charlotte had warned us that Rwandans were sick of people treating their country like a freak show.

My last trip abroad had been to New York, more than 18 months earlier. The friend I'd been visiting had gone down with flu soon after I arrived and I'd spent most of my time exploring the city alone. One cold December evening I'd walked across the Brooklyn Bridge and been awestruck as I caught sight of the immense, glittering beauty of the World Trade Center by night. Rwanda felt about as far from New York City as it was possible to be.

After an hour, we were dropped off at the beginning of a mud track. Half a dozen bike boys were waiting.

'Charlotti!'

These laughing teenagers were on first-name terms with my sister, and seemed to regard her as a source of some amusement. For 100 Rwandan francs each, they pedalled us and our bags the last two miles through the leafy fields. A small crowd of kids ran after us, exuberantly piping 'Msungu!' at the tops of their voices.

'Oui, c'est vrai: msungu', I laughed as we wobbled by, trying out my rusty French for the first time in years.

Charlotte had already told us about *msungu*, the Rwandan word for 'white person'. Wherever she went, people would point and shout it at her. After ten months this was driving her nuts, and she couldn't let it go. Each time someone shouted 'Msungu!', she would shout back 'Banyarwanda!' ('Rwandan person!'). The bike boys found it hilarious. But I quite enjoyed being a *msungu*. I was only going to be here for a week, after all, and I'd never been an object of curiosity before. As we got closer to Charlotte's village, more and more people greeted her by name. She seemed to be something of a local celebrity.

Sainted Shyogwe, as Charlotte called it, was caught in a two-way tug-of-love between the Anglican and Catholic Churches. Her school, and the house she shared with another VSO volunteer, belonged to the Anglican faction. Charlotte's was one of Shyogwe's better houses, a large, modern bungalow that wouldn't have looked out of place in the English suburbs. Only the fact that termites had eaten part of the wall in one of the rooms gave away that this house was made of mud.

It had been a very long trek, but sitting in Charlotte's kitchen, I at last felt able to relax. My sister was an excellent cook, and Charlotte's kitchen was always a good place to be. We ate a late breakfast of dry bread with marmalade, avocado, pineapple and fresh, Rwandan coffee. Avocadoes were so cheap here that Charlotte had taken to spreading them in place of margarine, and it worked surprisingly well. While Catherine took a long nap, we drank more coffee and talked through a warm, woozy afternoon.

Charlotte had thrown herself into this life with all her usual gusto, and her doubts about coming here had faded as her confidence grew. She talked enthusiastically about her work, and her hopes for her students. Last year they hadn't had a science teacher; this year they at least had her. If just one of them went on to become a doctor, she told me, then her posting would have been worthwhile. Faced with a lack of teaching materials, Charlotte had written her own worksheets, duplicating them by hand with an archaic carbon-copier. And she'd come up with a way of teaching the motion of molecules by getting her class to stand in circles and throw rolled-up pairs of socks around the classroom.

Charlotte's religious convictions, which in London marked her out as something of a freak, were quite normal here. She went to the Anglican church every Sunday, even singing with the choir. She'd made a lot of friends in the last few months and was never short of visitors.

Every so often one of Charlotte's students would knock on the door to return textbooks and pick up the grades from their final exams. Tomorrow would be the last day of term and the kids, boarders from all over Rwanda, were going home for the holidays. Although they were thought of as children, many were in their twenties, finishing an education that had been interrupted six years ago by the war. Charlotte didn't know where they'd been, what they'd done, who was Hutu or who was Tutsi. She was careful not to ask. She had to be careful about a lot of things.

Gitarama province saw some of the worst violence, and many had died in Shyogwe itself. A few months ago, Charlotte had arrived home to find her neighbours holding a religious ceremony around a pit latrine, just a few yards from her front door. Her bemusement turned to shock when she was told that this was a memorial service for two women whose dismembered bodies had been thrown into a pit during the war.

In the evening, the sun set so fast it was as if someone had snatched away the daylight.

Less than 48 hours ago I'd been at my desk in London W1, staring at a screen full of numbers. There'd been endless jokes about my choice of holiday destination. One colleague thoughtfully advised me to keep a pocketful of pennies handy at all times. If I found myself in a tight spot with the impoverished masses I could fling the cash up in the air and make my escape while the locals scrabbled through the dirt for my small change. I'd left the small change at home. I'd always been told that a job like mine was what Real Life was all about. But here in Shyogwe, it was my own comfortable life that seemed unreal.

I'd wondered why Charlotte had come here, but now I started to get the point. Her work was hard, even harrowing at times. The conditions were basic, the remuneration laughable. And she was happier and more at ease than I'd ever seen her before. It seemed as if she'd finally found a challenge to match that relentless energy of hers.

But this was not a peaceful place. Cowering beneath my mosquito net, I thought again about the women in the pit latrine. Who were they? Had they lived in this house? I wondered who'd slept in this room six years ago.

'What are you doing here?'

The angry voice in my mind's ear had an African accent.

'Do you think you can just walk in, like a tourist?'

It took me a long time to get to sleep.

The next morning was fresh and bright, and I woke up early. There was a goat tied up on the patch of land outside Charlotte's living-room window, and smoke rose from the farmsteads on the hills behind the house. Shyogwe seemed peaceful again. But I was still spooked. So many people had died in this peaceful place, and I had almost no idea why. Charlotte talked about a genocide, but what did that mean, really? I interrogated her over breakfast.

'It started when the president's plane was shot down, in April 1994. He was a Hutu, and the government blamed it on a Tutsi-led rebel group, the Rwandan Patriotic Front (RPF). But some people say it was rival extremists within his own government, who wanted an excuse to kill Tutsis.'

Hutu and Tutsi spoke the same language, and had the same customs, Charlotte told me. But Rwanda's Belgian colonial rulers had believed that the Tutsis were racially superior. They forced every Rwandan to carry an identity card, rigidly defining their ethnic group. Hutus were excluded from power, while Tutsis governed Rwanda on Belgium's behalf. By the time of independence, in the early 1960s, the Tutsis were a despised minority.

Earlier in the year, Charlotte had been discussing with her class the differences between countries around the world. She asked what it was that made Rwanda different. 'Le genocide', replied one of her students, provoking grim laughter from the rest.

There had been periodic massacres of Tutsis ever since the 1960s, but what happened in 1994 was different. Even before the president was killed, the government was characterizing Tutsis as 'rats' or 'cockroaches', fifth columnists, one and all, for the RPF rebels. Gangs of machete-wielding, Interahamwe militia had been trained throughout the preceding months, and blacklists of Tutsis drawn up. The killings began within hours of the assassination. The ruling party's radio station urged Hutus to 'exterminate' their Tutsi neighbours. Wiping out Tutsis was nothing more than 'bush clearance', they were told – a service to the community. Once the violence started, the UN quickly pulled out, leaving the Tutsis to their fate.

One of Charlotte's colleagues at the school, Bonaventure, had confided in her more than most. He felt that the genocide had been allowed to happen because people were just too willing to do what they were told. Above all, he wanted his students to be able to think for themselves.

The international community stood by and did nothing as the killings escalated, speaking sagely of 'bloodletting' and 'ancient tribal hatreds'. But thousands of Rwandans, including many Hutus, joined the RPF, who stepped up their attacks from bases in neighbouring Uganda. By the time Kigali was captured, 100 days after the genocide began, nearly 1,000,000 people were dead, one in six of the population. Armed, for the most part, with sticks and knives, the Interahamwe had killed more, per day, than the Nazis. The new RPF government declared that 'we're all Rwandans now', discouraged any further talk of Hutu and Tutsi and set about rebuilding the country. More than 100,000 people were now awaiting trial for their involvement in the killings. Charlotte would sometimes see these *genocidaires* working the fields in their bright pink prison uniforms.

This, at least, was the official story. Only the extremists denied that a genocide had taken place – but there were plenty of rumours of reprisal massacres against Hutus. Charlotte found it hard to believe that ethnicity was no longer an issue here, when everywhere she went she was addressed as *msungu*. Was this new government really dealing with Rwanda's ethnic divisions, or pretending that they didn't exist? Charlotte was haunted by the thought that violence might return to Rwanda. Like her friend Bonaventure, she encouraged her students to ask questions, and even challenge her authority.

Charlotte had invited Bonaventure to join us for dinner that evening. She seemed fond of him and it was good to know that she had friends in Shyogwe. His English was excellent, his familiarity with English culture less so. 'So, you are Charlotte's sister?' he said, jovially, on meeting Catherine. 'But I think that you have eaten much more than she has!'

The next day was Saturday, and time to head back to Kigali. Azzi and James, two of Charlotte's friends from university, were arriving today. Tomorrow we would all be travelling together to Lake Kivu, in the west of Rwanda. We took another hair-raising ride on the back of the taxi-bikes along the track to the main road. On the minibus to Kigali, a Rwandan child stared at us in wonder, reaching out to touch my hair before being chastised by his mother. Two women at the back of the bus also seemed intrigued by our presence. Though the conversation was in Kinyarwanda, every tenth word they said was *msungu*. Our bus driver seemed to be another Celine Dion fan, and we had the soundtrack from *Titanic* all the way into town. The film had been a runaway success here, according to Charlotte.

We arrived in Kigali around noon, and had lunch in the 'Traveller's Rest' cafe. I found a battered copy of an English-language newspaper. The top headline was a story about Rwandan and Ugandan troops clashing in the Congo over the control of a diamond mine. Every other page had a salutation from one local business or another 'To Major-General Paul Kagame on the auspicious occasion of Liberation Day, 4 July 2000'. Azzi and James arrived three hours late, after a marathon bus journey from Kampala, and we set out for our guest house. While most of Kigali's roads were tarmacked, the pavements were rubble and the going wasn't easy.

'There are no killers in Rwanda!', shouted an unkempt, shoeless Rwandan man as we made our way through one of the poorer neighbourhoods. We passed the heavily fortified US Embassy. After the terrorist attacks in Nairobi, traffic around the Kigali Mission had been diverted, and huge barriers erected to prevent suicide attacks. The British Embassy, by contrast, barely seemed to be defended at all.

The guest house was a former missionary centre, some way from the city centre, and the white compound had a peaceful air about it. From here Kigali looked as I imagined ancient Rome might have done, columns of smoke rising from the small, red-roofed farmsteads scattered across the city's hills. Catherine, Charlotte and I shared a three-bed room, with Azzi and James taking the one next door. Darkness fell quickly again as we changed.

Charlotte was planning to meet up with some of the other VSO volunteers that evening. Many of them were going back to the UK for the summer and this would be the last time she saw them for a while. We waited outside the guest house for a minivan into town, and before long one pulled over. The two young guys in the front waved away our money. Charlotte explained that it was common in Kigali for people to pick up foreigners simply as a good turn.

From the centre of town we took a taxi to one of Kigali's swankier hotels, where the VSOs were meeting. The main section had been taken over by some kind of Red Cross party. Gleaming, white four-by-fours crammed into the car park, and plush tables were laid out in the open air. A troupe of traditionally clad Rwandan dancers had been hired to entertain the guests. It seemed reminiscent of the colonial era, and there was something distasteful about an aid charity spending its money with quite so much abandon. One corner of the hotel was still Red Cross free, and there we met what seemed like about half of VSO Rwanda, a friendly bunch. I ordered vegetarian macaroni cheese. The vegetarian element seemed to be that they only included a *small* amount of ham.

Back at the guest house, I looked at the book that Charlotte had lent me. It was strange to read about Rwanda's recent past so close to where the violence had happened. Kigali was where it had all started. President Habyarimana's plane was shot down over the airport where I'd been just a few days before. It seemed that every imaginable form of depravity had been visited on Rwanda's Tutsis. Some of the worst violence had taken place in Kibuye, on Lake Kivu, where we were going tomorrow.

We were up early the next day, and the city was already busy. Our guest house was next to one of the poorest quarters of Kigali, but Charlotte insisted on walking us through it rather than getting a taxi. There were bullet holes above the door of the building on the corner of the street. Most of the houses here were little more than corrugated iron shacks. We waited some time before a bus arrived, while the whole neighbourhood stared, and cries of 'Msungu!' resounded from the rooftops.

In the Kigali bus park it was even worse. We were mobbed as we looked for the bus that would take us west to Kibuye. 'Msungu! Msungu!' – people trying to sell us trinkets, or simply begging, crowded round.

'*Sin twa* Msungu! Ni twa Charlotte!' was my sister's stern, only slightly pompous reply – '*My name's not* Msungu! My name is Charlotte!'

I tried to avoid the stares. Most were friendly at least, but one guy had a different air about him.

'Ou vas-tu?' he demanded to know – 'tu', the word you use with good friends or people you want to insult.

'Kibuye' – I tried to be polite at least. 'Kibuye?', he replied, mimicking my accent. Then, sneering, 'C'est grave; les batutsis . . .'

'Oui, je sais', I said, not sais-ing at all, and turned away. 'C'est grave' – it's a strike? No, that wasn't it. He was gone by the time I realized what he'd said. 'C'est grave' – it's serious. 'Les batutsis' – the Tutsis. Kibuye had been a Tutsi enclave, and thousands had been killed during the genocide.

We at last found the bus to Kibuye and got on board. And waited. The vehicle was almost full but it wasn't moving. 'Msungu! Msungu! Donne-moi de l'argent'. We were quickly surrounded by beggars. One boy stood by my window, showing his disfigured hands. Another opened the window and thrust his open hand towards me. Charlotte was adamant that handing out money was the wrong thing to do. It would only encourage the idea that white people had endless cash to give away, that problems could be solved by the *msungu* rather than by Rwandans themselves. But for me, sitting in a bus park surrounded by very obviously impoverished people, things didn't seem that clear cut. They were poor, and they were not going to stop being poor any time in the near future. The money I had in my pocket was more than most would see in a whole year. A small amount could make a huge difference to any one of them. I knew that, and they knew that. I wondered what they must think of us, as we sat inside our bus, giving nothing away. Did they understand that we didn't want to encourage the idea that Rwanda's problems could be solved by white people rather than by Rwandans themselves? Or did they just think we were mean, selfish *msungus*, like the UN staff who'd abandoned Rwanda in 1994, and the NGO workers stuffing their faces in swanky hotels?

The bus was full now, but we still weren't going anywhere. Neither were the beggars who surrounded us. A Rwandan guy gave one of them a couple of notes. Our fellow passengers looked disapprovingly at us. Two more people were squeezed onto the overloaded vehicle. And still we weren't going anywhere. Were they doing this deliberately? The beggars continued to beg, and we continued to wait. We had been sitting there for what seemed like 40 minutes. One more woman pushed her way into the crowded minibus. I now had only half a seat, and couldn't sit upright without squashing myself against the other passengers. Finally the bus started to move.

'Near . . . Far . . . Whereeeeever you are . . .' – it was Celine Dion, again.

High in the hills, the border between two provinces was marked by a tall, leafy arch over the road. There was a checkpoint here and we all had to get off the bus. As we queued to show our ID I felt distinctly uncomfortable. These soldiers had guns and we didn't. If they decided to cut their losses and rob these *msungus*, there would be nothing we could do about it. The soldier who checked my passport looked at me with some curiosity, but we were allowed on our way.

Charlotte had more or less forbidden us to take photographs in public. After the genocide, when the foreign media invaded Rwanda, the cameras had been everywhere, and many Rwandans were still very sensitive about it. Now Charlotte hissed at me if I tried to take pictures of the landscape we were passing. I read my book, and tried to find a more comfortable position. A little further and the road turned into a work-in-progress. Our bus slowed to manoeuvre its way around workmen and surfacing vehicles, and the ride suddenly became a lot more bumpy. There'd been no road to Kibuye before, Charlotte explained, because it was seen as a Tutsi town.

Some of the men working on the road were Chinese, which seemed odd to me – no more odd though, on reflection, than an English person teaching science in French in a Rwandan school. The rest of the journey was long, cramped, uncomfortable and frustrating. By the time we reached Kibuye I'd acquired a stabbing cramp in my ribcage, incurred the wrath of my older sister by sneaking a couple of photos of the landscape and had as much of Celine as I could take. We rounded one more hill to a spectacular view of Lake Kivu, shimmering blue in the afternoon sun.

Across this calm, inland sea was the Democratic Republic of Congo, where a full-scale war was raging. Close by, a Russian-made, military helicopter was coming noisily into land. Ahead in the road, a large crowd of men was walking towards the town. They wore the pink pyjamas of *genocidaires*, and there were soldiers with them. So these were the Interahamwe. The people who'd plunged machetes into the heads of children, who'd gang-raped women and left them to bleed to death. These were the people who'd slashed the hamstrings of their victims and then gone to have lunch before returning to finish them off. At least, this is who the government said they were. I stared as our bus passed through the crowd. One of the pink pyjamas stared back with a dull curiosity. 'What did you do?' I thought, wondering what he must think of me.

In the centre of Kibuye we at last emerged from our cramped bus. Hotel touts mobbed us, but Charlotte had been here before, and knew the guest house she wanted to go to. Kibuye also had bike boys, who eagerly agreed to pedal us up the hill. It was hard going, and before long the sweat was pouring off my driver's forehead. It seemed wrong to make him do so much for such a derisory sum of money. I clambered off and walked the final stretch. At the top of the hill, our bike boys tried to charge us double the going rate – RF200 instead of RF100 – 40p each instead of 20p. Charlotte insisted that we shouldn't give an inch but I'd had enough of being bossed around. I generously gave my bike boy an extra 20p, to my sister's disgust, and we made our way into the guest house.

The pain in my ribs wasn't going away. We were all exhausted, and irritable. Night had come by the time we emerged for dinner. Under a gazebo, beside the immense darkness of the lake, we drank Rwandan, Primus beer, ate freshly caught fish and humiliated each other with embarrassing childhood stories. I told Azzi and James about the time Charlotte wanted a pet duck, helpfully impersonating Charlotte, aged 12, wanting a pet duck. Charlotte told them about me when I was 14 and thought I needed fillings but didn't. By the end of the evening we'd managed to annoy each other thoroughly. Catherine, wise as ever, stayed out of it.

Charlotte and Catherine got up early the next morning, and swam until they were two distant dots on the other side of the bay. I was put off by the knowledge that hundreds of corpses had been thrown into this lake just a few years before. I stayed by the shore, chatting with Azzi and James, and reading more horror stories.

Later, I decided to explore the little area around the guest house. I followed the path through the bushes until I caught sight of a Rwandan man walking towards me, carrying a huge machete. I jumped and headed back. What was I thinking? He was just a gardener.

Walking up the hill from the shore back towards the guest house I met two friendly, matronly, Rwandan women.

'Mwirirwe', I said – the greeting Charlotte taught me when I first arrived in Shyogwe.

'Yego', replied the larger of the two ladies. 'Mwirirwe'.

I smiled and nodded. 'Mwirirwe', she repeated, then prompted me; 'Yego'.

'Yego' – I was learning. 'Mwirirwe – Yego. Amakuru?'

'Amakuru?' I repeated, parrot-fashion.

'Nimeza!', replied the two Rwandan women in unison.

'Mwrirwe, Yego, Amakuru? Nimeza.'

'Yego' simply meant 'Yes', Charlotte later explained. 'Amakuru?' was 'What's the news?' and 'Nimeza', 'The news is good'. It seemed ironic in a place that had seen so much bad news.

The sun was dazzling now, and Lake Kivu's waves sparkled. This vivid, blue expanse filled my vision all the way to the horizon. It was hard to believe that such violence had happened in this beautiful place.

In the evening, the sky slowly turned to gold as we watched the sun set over the lake. A solitary fishing boat made its way across the bay. After dinner we played cards and drank Primus beer until late. The stresses of yesterday were gone now. We seemed to be the only people staying here, and it was nice to have had a break from being *msungu*. But my job had only allowed me a week's holiday. I would have to fly home in less than three days.

We left the next morning to return to Gitarama prefecture. The bus back was less crowded than before, but just as bumpy, and there was no escaping Celine. A couple of hours into our journey, and high in the hills, our bus was forced to a halt. One of the front tyres had burst. We were in the middle of a small, remote-looking village. People here didn't point and shout 'Msungu!' as they had in Kigali and elsewhere. The tiny children who crowded nervously round the vehicle acted as if they'd never seen a white person before. Their eyes widened even more when Charlotte spoke to them; 'Bité' – the greeting you use with small children. The oldest child, who looked about six, summoned up the courage to reply – 'Bité'.

'Witwa wiki?' Charlotte asked. 'Ni twa Immaculée', replied the child, sweetly. James, less constrained by sisterly regulation, decided to get out of the bus to take a picture. At the sight of this huge, white person walking towards them the children panicked, each trying to hide behind another as they backed away.

We arrived in Gitarama in the late afternoon. Returning to Shyogwe, we met Charlotte's housemate Leonora. A likeable, down-to-earth Englishwoman in her early 60s, she'd joined VSO after retiring from teaching. The next day we got a lift into Kigali with one of Charlotte's colleagues, the school bursar, tailing a Primus beer lorry much of the way. It was a welcome relief from the public buses. The bursar was an affable, talkative chap. Like Bonaventure he spoke good English. He translated the Primus slogan on the back of the lorry: 'Keeping the family together'. As we passed through the marshy valley on our approach to the city, he proudly pointed out what he said was the source of the River Nile.

We reached Kigali around lunchtime and ate a buffet lunch in an outdoor café. There we were joined by another VSO volunteer, an unsmiling Welshman called Gryff. Gryff had just returned from the Democratic Republic of Congo, the place where the war was raging. He seemed very proud that he'd gone there against the advice of the VSO Programme Office. I took an instant dislike to him. What alarmed me most was that Charlotte talked gleefully about going with him next time, 'without telling Fran', the Programme Director. As if straying into a war zone was like walking on the grass without permission. I couldn't understand it. Wasn't Rwanda dangerous enough?

We spent the rest of the afternoon walking around Kigali. I realized there was probably a reason that you didn't see many whites in the poorer districts of this city. Even going down the street was hard work with dozens of people mobbing you. I didn't blame them for it; I just didn't enjoy being in that situation. But Charlotte seemed to take it as a challenge – why *shouldn't* she be able to walk through these areas without getting hassled?

And so we were dragged through the slum districts yet again, with Charlotte sternly chastising anyone who asked her for money. But was it so presumptuous to think that she might have money to spare? Could these people really be blamed for trying? In a country where the average wage is less than $300 a year, surely anyone who can even afford to fly to Kigali is rich. Many of the people Charlotte spoke to were offended, even perplexed, by her vehemence. It seemed deeply insensitive to lecture such desperate people about social niceties.

Back at the guest house I told Charlotte that I thought her attitude here was reckless. Catherine and I were both worried by what she'd said about travelling to the Congo. Charlotte tried to sound reasonable and placatory, but it was as if her brain couldn't connect with what we were saying. We didn't understand the situation, she insisted. She had local knowledge. VSO was overcautious. Going to the Congo was fine if you knew what you were doing. Burundi was fine too, so long as you stuck to Bujumbura. What frightened me most was that she seemed so willing to put her own safety at risk to prove a point.

I wondered if she'd been desensitized by being close to so much violence, and perhaps by nagging fears about security in Rwanda. Maybe she thought that by putting herself in an even more dangerous situation, she would feel relatively safer when she got back to Shyogwe. Or perhaps Gryff had brought out some childish, thrill-seeking, let's-play-chicken-with-war-zones side in her that I'd not seen before?

Charlotte and I got up early the next day and took a taxi to the airport. She insisted on buying me breakfast, and we ate together on the concourse overlooking the runway. I wondered what it must have looked like here the moment that Habyarimana's plane was shot down. Over our yoghurt and tinned peaches I apologized for getting so annoyed with her the previous day; I was just worried about her. Charlotte assured me that she'd be fine. During the Rwandan genocide foreigners were only attacked if they tried to get in the way: but why put your head into the lion's mouth just to prove that it's tame? I wanted her to promise me that she wouldn't go to the Congo, or to Burundi. Charlotte said that she'd be careful, but she didn't make any promises. Yet she seemed to have taken on board what I'd said, and I knew that Catherine would also be speaking to her about it. I'd done as much as I could. I had a feeling that she'd be OK.

I told Charlotte I was glad that I'd come here, even though I'd been reluctant at first. Glad, even though it had been hard work. It had been good to see her, and I was proud of what she was doing here. We watched my plane as it came into land, and then went downstairs so I could check in. I said goodbye, and walked out onto the tarmac. From my window seat, I looked for Charlotte on the observation tower, but she wasn't there.

—— 2 ——

Date: Thu, 27 Jul 2000 01:32:34 –0700 (PDT)
From: =?iso-8859-1?q?Charlotte=20Wilson?= <clc_wilson@yahoo.com>
Subject: Greetings from Mwanza!

I'm here on Lake Victoria waiting for the train to Dar Es Salaam. It is really nice to get out of Rwanda, it's a lovely country but it can get a bit oppressive at times. It is INCREDIBLE how much difference it makes just crossing the border. I've been here for 3 days and haven't been called 'msungu' once – or had a crowd of kids standing round watching my every move. You can draw a parallel between the people and the landscape here. Tanzania is open and uncompli-cated, whereas Rwanda, though very pretty, is enclosed, hilly and hard going at times.

There were no smiles on the train back from Heathrow. I looked round at the faces. Just by being here these people had opportunities that would never be open to most Rwandans, and yet they seemed far more miserable and preoccupied than anyone I'd met in the last week. Charlotte, Catherine, Azzi and James continued their travels, through Rwanda, Tanzania, Kenya and Uganda. I returned to my flat in West Norwood, to my comfortable job and my increasingly uncomfortable relationship. To London and its beep-beep-beeping sounds. I finished the book that Charlotte had lent me, and started another, Fergal Keane's eyewitness account of the immediate aftermath of the genocide.

In the summer of 1994, just before my 'A' level exams, our English teacher had shown us a graphic documentary about the liberation of Auschwitz. 'I hope this will help you to keep the next couple of weeks in perspective', he'd said. It did – and yet, I'd had no idea that another holocaust was going on, at that very moment, in Rwanda. The British government of John Major had been one of a number that had systematically blocked UN efforts to intervene. It was the Rwandans themselves who had driven out the *genocidaires*, and the RPF liberators of 1994 were now in power. A new, multi-ethnic government was rebuilding the country – and my sister was a part of it. I'd never been more proud of her.

Date: Wed, 23 Aug 2000 01:10:26 –0700 (PDT)
From: =?iso-8859-1?q?Charlotte=20Wilson?= <clc_wilson@yahoo.com>
Subject: (no subject)

We made it back to Shyogwe in just one day, which was a trek. Catherine left last Thursday. It was great to have so many visitors and for such a long time. It's also good to be back here. Though I haven't minded the complete absence of being called 'msungu' it is nice to be where people know you. It's not as if nothing happened when I was away, either. Two of my friends have had babies, and we went to the naming ceremony for one of them, a little boy called Hope.

I was haunted by the memory of the bus park. In my world, people complained about the price of petrol, train cancellations, the fact that there was nothing good on TV. Forever lining our bank accounts. Forever barging past each other to get a seat on the 18.38 to West Croydon. I was still one of those people, but I was beginning to look at my life in a different way. If I was honest with myself, there really didn't seem to be much point to my comfortable job. It was easy, granted. The money was good. They made very nice cakes in the canteen. We were all 'Partners'. It was nearly impossible to get fired. Some of my colleagues had been watching those screens-full-of-numbers for 25 years, enjoying the cakes, the Christmas parties, the perks and the automatic pay rises. Telling the odd joke about the starving millions in Elsewhere-land. Complaining about how much tax they were paying.

Shyogwe, Thursday, 31st August 2000

One of my friends from the choir, Foster, has just been diagnosed with AIDS. I get so worried about HIV and so frustrated because from a biological point of view it is so easy to stop people from becoming HIV positive. Do you think that the campaigns have worked in the UK?

I got a bit annoyed because someone said that Foster was stupid. I'm sure he's no more stupid than most young people round here. I just worry about my students – some of them are off sick 50% of the time. Lots of girls were raped and gang-raped during 1994 and could have contracted HIV then. I'm just revamping my sex education and microbiology lessons for next year. I hope I've got the guts to show them how to put on a condom – I think I have a moral obligation.

While Charlotte engaged with poverty, disease, ignorance and the legacy of genocide I was engaging with a computer system for ordering carpets and table lamps. I tried to be enthusiastic about work but it wasn't easy. I'd spent much of the last two-and-a-half years looking for creative ways to persuade my colleagues to take tea breaks. I'd become adept at producing ASCII-art pictures of mugs, teapots and cupcakes and not much else.

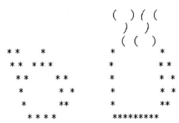

Shyogwe, 29th September 2000

Our term has finally started. It was meant to start on Tuesday but of course we didn't actually begin teaching till Wednesday. Today I'm expecting a visit from Fran Roots, the Programme Director, and Penny Lawrence, VSO Overseas Director. They're going to come and watch me teach and then take us out for lunch. In the evening Leonora, myself and

*the Head are invited to an exclusive club in Kigali for a reception to
welcome Penny Lawrence and the new volunteers.*

In my tea breaks I plotted my escape. Anything else would do, I
supposed, so long as it was worthwhile, risk-free and, naturally, comfortable. There were risks involved in staying, of course. If you
chopped a Partner in half, you could determine the exact number of
years served by counting the rings of cake. Five more years and I'd be
too fat to get out through the bars.

Thursday 12th October 2000

Dear Mum,

*I want to discuss the possibility of extending with VSO for another year. I
feel that I'm doing quite a good job at the moment and if I stayed another
year I would be even more effective. Also I think I'd get more out of the
experience. I'd probably still come back for about a month next summer.
What do you think? If you need me to come back or even if you'd really like
me to then I will.*

Monday 29th October 2000,
Centre des Mamans Sportives, Kigali

*On Wednesday morning I was coming back after break when the head
collared me and said that we must ring Kigali. We did, and they said that
I was needed at the Ministry of Education <u>now</u>, for a month. I walked into
my class and had to tell them that I would leave for an unspecified amount
of time for an unspecified reason. Then I got on the first taxibus to Kigali.*

*I was taken to the Centre des Mamans Sportives, still not knowing what
was happening. It turns out that I am here as the biology 'expert' to help
write the syllabus for Health Sciences and Agrovet sections. I'm doing the
translation from French into English, as very few of the experts speak both
languages.*

*I'm staying with a Canadian VSO couple, Glenna and Whybo Otten-
breit-Born, who live about 20 minutes away from the conference centre.*

They were very nice because I turned up on their doorstep without warning the first night and they offered to let me stay the whole month.

On Halloween, my girlfriend Emma's friendly, tortoiseshell cat had to be put down. One moment here, the next gone. Her firm, final 'miaow' cut out so abruptly it was as if she'd been switched off. A week later I moved flat, and a week after that Emma and I broke up. But the split was destined not to last and by the time Charlotte's sympathetic email arrived we were together again. Charlotte, though, had news of her own.

Date: Fri 9 Nov 2000 15:04:37
From: =?iso-8859-1?q?Charlotte=20Wilson?= <clc_wilson@yahoo.com>
Subject: (no subject)

Hi Rickerella! I now seem to be going out with a 6 foot 6 Burundian ex-monk, also called Richard. Just hope it doesn't all end in tears. I have to admit that it freaks me out slightly to be with someone who has the same name as my brother – I have to pronounce it the French way. I think you'll like him when you meet him, though.

I didn't think much of it. My sister had been single for barely six months of the last eight years, so it could only have been a matter of time. And of course it would have to be an unfeasibly tall, ex-monk from Burundi. They'd originally met in May, when Richard was working at the same school as one of the other VSO volunteers. They'd stayed in touch, and got to know each other better when Charlotte was seconded to Kigali. He sounded like an interesting guy, but none of us had any inkling of what was coming next.

X-From_: clc_wilson@yahoo.com Mon Dec 11 07:28:20 2000
Envelope-to: margot@wilson.fsnet.co.uk
Delivery-date: Mon, 11 Dec 2000 07:28:20 +0000

Dear Mum,

Richard and I have decided to get married in the summer when I come over.
I know that this is a bit sudden but I'm sure that when you meet him you'll
realize why I've chosen him. Don't worry – I am not about to disappear to
deepest darkest Africa forever. We are still planning to come back after I've
extended for a year. Of course I want you to give me away and Catherine to be
my bridesmaid. I will try and ring you ASAP so we can talk a bit better, but you
are the first to know.

Charlotte emailed me the same day – she was marrying Richard and
she'd definitely be extending in Rwanda for an extra year. Not
knowing what else to say I sent back a one-word reply. A couple of
days later I wrote and told her I was sure she knew what she was
doing. I was proud of her work in Rwanda and if she wanted to stay
another year then she should do. 'Rikki's final thought', I told her, was
'follow your star, do what seems like the right thing to you and have
fun because you deserve it.'

Subj: Re: Big News!
Date: 12/17/00 10:44:17 AM GMT Standard Time
From: clc_wilson@yahoo.com (Charlotte Wilson)
To: Rcameronw@aol.com

Hey Rikkitikkitavi,

Thanks for the answer, I have been really touched by everyone's replies. I can't
wait for you to meet him, one of the many reasons we're getting married is that
we spend hours and hours discussing things – philosophy and religion. It does
make for very little sleep, but I hope that we'll be able to spend more quality
time together soon. After all we'll have decades to discuss things in the future.

Richard doesn't play an instrument or sing, but I taught him the flute a bit last
weekend and he picked it up really quickly. He's a great dancer, so he's got a

good sense of rhythm. I'll try and write you a proper letter over Christmas, but I hope you have a great festive season. I'm definitely following my star even if it leads me to places that aren't part of the conventional road to happiness – but then, when was I ever conventional? I am happier (apart from being away from my family) than I have ever been in my life and having a fantastic time.

OK, the man himself wants a word!

I've seen your photo, the one where you're enjoying a pint. I'd like to meet you and talk more face to face. I'll be the first person to welcome you and your girl-friend to Bujumbura in July. (No he won't, I will – C!) Yes I will!

Alors, petit frère, sois fort dans ton travail.

The other Richard . . .

I'll be near a landline on the 3rd Jan, from 3pm GMT, 5 pm our time. You'll be able to call as late as you like as I'll be the only one there.

Lots and lots of love
Charlotte

Busy with work, I made a mental note to send a proper reply before the end of the year. Emma, who hated Christmas, decided to spend the holidays working in a homeless shelter in London. The rest of us had a relaxing few days with family in Bristol. On Christmas Eve, Catherine and her affable, American boyfriend Carl announced that they too were getting married. In the space of a month, both of my sisters had become engaged. I quite looked forward to having one brother-in-law from the richest country in the world and one from the very poorest.

A couple of weeks before Christmas, our mother had received a long, thoughtful letter from Charlotte.

Just been introduced to the Bishop of Shyogwe, darling. He's much more cosmopolitan than the parish priests. He was away all last year – someone threw grenades at him so he took a sabbatical to study theology in Strasbourg. Due to a mistake I made with 'sa' and 'son', he thought that Tom and Steve at Byimana were getting married. I've not spoken to anyone at Shyogwe about homosexuality, apart from Bona, briefly, who denies there is any. The bishop acknowledges that it does exist here, but thinks this is due to an increasingly libertine society and Western influence. I said that surely it was better for someone to express that side of themselves than to force themselves into an unhappy marriage. The bishop said that unhappy marriages aren't such a big deal in Rwanda because people live as part of the community instead of in little units, as they do in Europe.

I sometimes wonder whether Europeans don't have an impossible 'happy ever after' view of marriage. Adultery and polygamy seem to be tolerated much more here. The important thing is to have a father and provider for your children. I know that if I love someone then I can remain faithful to them all my married life. The thing that bothers me is could I love someone for decades? I know that I can judge whether someone is right for me now, but how can I predict how he will change? Sometimes I think that I'm being silly, because I know that I will love my family until I die (and after), no matter how you change.

Richard's coming tomorrow and I have only twelve more lessons to teach; hooray! I'm in a very good mood – I think even the students noticed it. Each time Richard and I meet we spend hours and hours discussing things. It's a bit like when I first met Mike – except that Mike was a fundamentally unhappy person and I could never touch that fundamental sorrow, I could only scratch the surface. That depressed me too much, eventually.

Richard is both a balanced person and interested in the big questions of life, which I think is rare. The most interesting people ask 'Why are we here?' but I have rarely found that these questions make them happy. I think that Richard isn't unhappy because he believes in God. Faith of any kind would probably do, but it is nice that we're both Christians. With most of my friends back home I can never talk about my faith, because it's inappropriate to the company I'm in. That is one of the nice things about Rwanda, I can express it when I want to.

I hope you're not too worried by what I was saying about fidelity and love – I was talking about rural Rwandans, which Richard most emphatically isn't. He's part of the Bujumbura elite and has had a lot of contact with Westerners through the Dominicans. I think we enjoy talking to each other so much because despite our different cultures and differing viewpoints, we have a lot in common. On change nos idées.

Lots and lots of love,
Charlotte

PS - Everyone here is saying that Africa should send observers to ensure that the US elections are free and fair!

I went back to my system testing on the Thursday after Christmas. It was 28 December. The heating had broken in the office and despite my extra jumper I spent the day freezing and looking for distractions. Most of my colleagues were still off with their families or families-to-be. Over a late lunch I had coffee with my mother, who was in town to spend her Christmas vouchers. The cold got to me, and I spent that evening at home in my own little world, pottering around morosely with some music software I'd been given for Christmas.

A stone had been thrown into a pond that day, and as I slept, the ripple widened. There were details to be examined, names to be checked, protocols followed, authorities notified.

The next day I tried to get back down to work and checked BBC Online to see what was happening in the world. Africa was on the front page: '16 die in Burundi massacre' – Hutu rebels had attacked a bus on its way from Kigali to the Burundian capital Bujumbura. I shuddered – it was all a little too close to home.

Throughout that morning, the ripple reached wider. Faxes were sent, phone calls made. Photographs were sent via email. Confirmations were passed on.

It was another quiet day, but there were more people in the office. I spent the afternoon talking about card tricks and Christmas presents, then at 5.30 the phone rang. It was my mother. She was using her Serious voice, but sounded quite calm. She had something to tell me and wanted me to come home. I wondered if the dog had died or something. I wasn't just going to come home without knowing what this was about.

'It's Charlotte and Richard. They were in Burundi. They were on a bus. It was attacked, by Hutu rebels.'

Now she was making me nervous, and the way she was stringing this out annoyed me. I really wasn't expecting her to say what she said next:

'They've been killed, Richard.' The ripple had finally reached me.

—— 3 ——

Charlotte Lucy Cameron Wilson was born on 4 June 1973, in Milan, northern Italy. Her parents, Margot and Peter, were teaching English in one of the city's many language schools, and Charlotte was their first child. She was a happy baby, and her parents doted on her. Two years later, feeling that they'd been away long enough, Margot and Peter decided to return home to England. I was already on the way by then, and in September of that year Charlotte acquired a little brother. Her feelings on this were mixed from the start. She now had competition for her parents' attention, but she also had a new playmate. One of my earliest memories is of Charlotte taking a handful of bath bubbles and crowning me Prince Edmund of Narnia. She must have been about four at the time.

In 1978, our sister Catherine was born and it was my turn to get jealous. Charlotte was more than happy to play the role of 'protector', especially as it gave her an excuse to rough me up every once in a while. In the summer of the following year, my father began to get mysterious pains in his stomach. By the time we moved to Hertford-shire in September, he had been diagnosed with leukaemia.

If I was told that my father was dying, I either didn't understand or blanked it out. The following February, the hospital decided that there was nothing more they could do, and sent him home. A few days later I was surprised when my mother came downstairs, picked me up in her arms and told me, shaking with tears, that Daddy had died. He was 34.

I put down the phone. It didn't make sense. Charlotte was dead, but nothing seemed to have changed. I shut down my computer and walked out to the lifts. On the ground floor, I swiped myself through the revolving doors and out into the bitter cold of the street. It was the same journey I'd made hundreds of times before, and nothing seemed to have changed. At Warren Street station, the people were just as busy as they always were, just as keen to get through the ticket barriers, just as caught up in their own thoughts. But Charlotte was dead. The indicator said that there would be a train to Walthamstow in two minutes. Charlotte was dead and it didn't make any sense.

Who had killed her? I didn't know. Why had they done it? Because people kill people? Because that's the kind of world we live in? Did I want to go along with that? Did I want to be a part of this new, ugly, stupid, arrogant world where Charlotte was dead? The train was arriving. For a fraction of a second I thought about jumping in front of it. And then the thought was gone.

I stumbled into the carriage, found a seat and tried to think rational thoughts. Did I believe that something like this could never happen? I can't have thought that we were immune. I had to deal with this logically, get it into perspective, limit the damage. The important thing was to make my way home, and see what kind of state my mother was in.

I'd arranged to meet some friends in the Marlborough Arms at six. Catherine and Carl, who'd been shopping in town, were also coming. At Seven Sisters I tried to phone Catherine but her mobile was on voicemail. I left a message asking her to call Mum as soon as possible. Emma's phone wasn't answering either. I got through to my friend Anthony and told him I was going home because Charlotte was dead.

Most of all I felt a kind of numbness. I avoided the eyes of strangers. My tears, when they came, were tears of bewilderment as much as anything else. Was I crying because I was upset or because crying was the thing to do, now that Charlotte was dead? On the overland train I phoned James, one of my oldest schoolfriends. But what was there to talk about? Charlotte was dead. Maybe if I told enough people enough times it would start to seem real. I got off at Southbury and tried calling Catherine again, but still all I had was her voicemail.

It was explained to us that Daddy's spirit had gone to heaven. I took this to be somewhat akin to going to Devon, another mysterious, far away place. Death, it seemed, was a bit like moving town. While I wasn't happy about what had happened, my four-year-old mind accepted it. But Charlotte, old enough to feel the full impact of our father's loss without any of the emotional resources for dealing with it, was transformed.

Pictures from that time show Charlotte as an intensely angry child, her face glowering behind cumbersome NHS glasses. She took refuge in the books that Daddy had read to her. There was no death or dying in Charlie's chocolate factory, just rivers of confectionery and tribes of friendly Oompa Loompas. In Narnia, gentle Aslan returns to life triumphantly, just when it seems that the White Witch, aided by the treacherous Prince Edmund, has succeeded in destroying him. But in Hoddesdon, Hertfordshire, the White Witch had won. Daddy had been killed by Loo-key-mee-uh and he wasn't coming back.

Just as it was Edmund, not Aslan, who deserved to be killed at the hands of the White Witch, Charlotte hissed that she wished I had died instead of Daddy. But it was Loo-key-mee-uh she despised most of all. At the age of six, Charlotte swore revenge. She was going to become a scientist, and find a way of defeating the disease that had killed Daddy.

I stumbled on, down Southbury Road. Charlotte was dead, and someone had killed her. 'Shot twice, in the chest', my mother had said, giving more detail than I wanted. How could they have done it? How could they have looked her in the eyes and shot her? And how presumptuous were these 'Hutu rebels', to think they could award themselves the right to steal a life? To steal *this* life. And to think there was no price attached. I'd been to Rwanda. I could go to Burundi. I had money. A bit of that can go a long way in Central Africa. A lot of people around with not much to do and nothing to lose. Maybe I could just let it be known there was cash on offer for anyone who tracked these bastards down and wiped them out.

And of course I knew that life wasn't that simple. Sure, I could probably find someone who'd take my money and go out and kill Hutus for me. But how would I really know that the right people were getting 'got'? Did I want to risk having innocent people killed? Even if the right people *could* be found, did I want to see them dead? Would Charlotte want that?

Daddy's death hung over us like a shadow, but it was the impact on those around me that affected me most. Time was divided into the golden age of 'when Daddy was alive', and the grim, impoverished afterwards. Our mother was shattered by the loss of her husband, whilst all the time pretending that she was OK. She was determined to keep going without help from friends or family, but every so often the mask would slip and she would scream about putting us all in an orphanage.

At school, Charlotte was meticulously studious, at home meticulously tidy. Her teachers were warm in their praise, though some were concerned that she seemed so isolated. Was it inevitable, in Hoddesdon, Hertfordshire, that this angry, traumatized girl would end up being bullied mercilessly?

Charlotte had few friends in the first years after the death of her father. For the most part she seemed to prefer the company of books. Some of the boys teased her about her glasses, her middle-class accent, her studiousness. Her response was to glower ever more disdainfully from behind those NHS glasses, to read even more books, to enunciate her consonants ever more clearly. There was no getting away from it – Charlotte was 'posh'.

Being posh in 1980s Hoddesdon, Hertfordshire, was a crime unforgivable. The fact that we were a single-parent household, had a black and white TV and no car and bought our clothes from Oxfam didn't stop us from being posh. It just meant that we were 'gippos' too. Posh gippos in 1980s Hertfordshire. As the teasing got worse, Charlotte became more angry and defiant. Yes she *was* posh, we all were. While I tried to argue, and Catherine tried to avoid the question, Charlotte embraced the label. We were *posh*. We went to church and sang in the choir. Sometimes we even sang in Latin. We did our homework, went birdwatching and listened to classical music. We read C. S. Lewis and J. R. R. Tolkien. We had supper, visited the lavatory, didn't use the word 'ain't' and said 'yes' instead of 'yeah'. We switched off lights to save the environment. We switched off the television when we left the room. In Hoddesdon, Hertfordshire we were as posh as posh could be.

My friend Sean rang as I was walking down the Great Cambridge Road. I told him what I knew, which wasn't much, then turned off the phone. It still didn't seem real. It probably wouldn't feel real for a while. The important thing in the meantime was to stay rational. We'd been here before, in a way, with the death of my father. We would get through this, awful though it was. Nothing could undo what had happened, but we still had a choice about how we dealt with it. We mustn't let ourselves feel powerless.

At my Mum's house I unlocked the front door and pushed it open. The lights were on, and my mother stood alone in the dining room. I hugged her awkwardly. She seemed so small. 'We've just got to look after each other', she kept saying, as she cried. I remembered the last time, when *I'd* been the small one, and I cried too. Angry, bitter tears. It seemed so hopelessly cruel. How could they do this to her? This mother of mine, who'd brought up her three children single-handed. Now to see her eldest child's life thrown away so casually. Had they even known what they were doing, these murderers? How many lives they were wrecking? How arrogant, how self-infatuated, how *fucking self-indulgent* it all was?

We waited for Catherine to come home. Her phone still wasn't answering. Mum had been out for most of the day, walking the dog through the Lea Valley Park. She'd got back around four. Not long afterwards two police officers had knocked on the door. Charlotte had been killed yesterday. Her body was identified by the British Ambassador to Rwanda, who knew her through VSO. The attackers let one woman go, telling her to tell the government 'we're going to kill them all and there's nothing you can do'. Charlotte had apparently been singled out and shot. The others were forced to lie face down on the ground and killed together in a group.

Catherine and Carl got back an hour or so later. My sister's phone needed recharging and she hadn't got any of our messages. She'd gone to the pub expecting to see me, and it was Anthony who'd broken the news to her.

Catherine was angry and tearful from the moment she walked through the door. 'What *the fuck* was she doing in Burundi?' But she couldn't bear to hear any of the details. Carl, ever the gentleman, stepped outside into the cold and closed the door behind him. I went out and called him back.

We phoned family first. I wanted to speak to my Uncle James. He, more than anyone in my life, had filled the gap that my father, his older brother, had left two decades ago. Now I too had lost an older sibling. It was good to hear his voice, even if my thoughts were too muddled and unclear to say anything very meaningful. I got off the phone and tried to compose myself. I wanted to try and do something – anything – to mitigate the awfulness of all this. VSO had phoned earlier and told my mother that the BBC would be 'breaking the story' at 11pm. Perhaps if I could save some of Charlotte's friends the shock of seeing this first on TV, that would help in some way. At least it would give me something to do.

Charlotte had stayed here in my mother's house for the last few months before she left for Rwanda, and we quickly found her address book on her meticulously arranged desk. It was Friday night, not the best time for getting hold of people. The first person I spoke to was Amanda, Charlotte's university friend with whom she'd spent a year in Paris. She was in a noisy bar somewhere and could hardly hear me. I told her what had happened, and said that I'd wanted her to hear it from us first.

'Yes, thank you. Erm, well, goodbye then.'

She sounded as if she didn't quite believe what I was saying. On to the next person. It felt like a job, a routine. Something to pass the time. All I had to do was go through the names in the book, one by one, and talk.

'Hello, is that Mark? Yes, this is Richard Wilson. Charlotte's brother. I'm afraid I've got some bad news . . .'

It was simple, straightforward. In a strange way it took my mind off everything else. But I felt as if I was spreading some kind of disease. And was I doing this for Charlotte, for her friends or for myself?

Catherine couldn't bear to listen and went upstairs. Carl went with her. Mum made a cup of tea. I tried phoning Emma, but she still wasn't back from that evening's stint at the homeless shelter. I wasn't looking forward to telling her. Now that Charlotte was dead, the whole thing with Emma felt like far more trouble than it was worth.

I turned on the television and began flicking channels. There was no mention of Charlotte on any of the news channels. I watched and waited. Still nothing. Didn't they think this was news? Catherine and Carl stayed upstairs. Mum went to bed. I carried on flicking. Nine o'clock came and went, nine-thirty. The sitcoms, the dramas, all seemed so abstract. I just wanted to know what had happened to my sister. Then at ten, amid the melodrama of the BBC's swanky-new news theme, Charlotte's face appeared on our TV. I felt sick, I wanted it to stop. But I was transfixed. It was the top headline.

'Murdered in cold blood – the British aid worker gunned down in war-torn Burundi', boomed the newsreader. So matter-of-fact. As if Charlotte was just another dead body in just another war. Didn't he know? A nice lady from VSO said nice things about Charlotte, but was careful to point out that she had ignored their travel advice. The Foreign Office said the same. 'We still don't know why Miss Wilson took the decision to travel to Burundi', noted the BBC reporter, as if to imply that Charlotte might have been on some kind of secret mission.

The story came back again at ten-thirty. The same melodramatic thudding, and beep-beep-beep of the Beeb's souped-up news theme. The same, washed-out, passport mugshot of my sister, one of the worst I'd ever seen. The same sick feeling in my stomach.

> Murdered in cold blood – the British aid worker gunned down in war-torn Burundi . . . An exceptional volunteer . . . We're going to kill them all and there's nothing you can do . . .
>
> And now onto other news.

I finally got hold of Emma. She sounded distinctly annoyed. 'Er – I can't come over and see you tonight. It's too late.' What a drag this must be for her. She remembered herself before the end of the conversation – 'Are you, er, OK?' – then went to bed.

It was midnight now. 30 December. Why did I keep watching? It was like seeing a film where you know the ending but wish things would go differently this time. That face, that photo. *We still don't know why Miss Wilson took the decision to travel to Burundi . . .*

A whole day had now passed that Charlotte had never seen, would never see. She was 27 years old and her race had been run. Already. Charlotte Wilson, 4 June 1973 – 28 December 2000.

By half past one, Charlotte's death had been relegated to the third item on the news. But I carried on watching. Anything but to lie awake, alone. Tiredness finally overwhelmed me around 3am. I staggered to the spare room, and a restful sleep.

For a few hours I was in a different world, a fuzzy, peaceful place where everything was OK. It was starting to get light when I woke up, and for a few seconds those peaceful feelings endured. Then I remembered, and I was back again in this new, cold, stupid, ugly world where Charlotte was dead.

Why had I so enjoyed tormenting my big sister? Because she was there, maybe. Because I was bored, because it was easy. Because I bore grudges. At the age of 12, Charlotte decided that she wanted to get a pet duck for her next birthday. Her friend Jenny down the road had one, and Charlotte wanted one too. Our mother wasn't convinced, but Charlotte wasn't compromising. 'I am going to get a duck', she would insist, repeatedly, in her 'I'm speaking in a *perfectly normal* tone of voice' tone of voice. And I, of course, would disagree with her. Sometimes I would bring the subject up just for the fun of it. She would always take the bait.

'Mum's not going to let you have a duck you know . . .'

'I am *going* to *get* a *duck*.'

'Nah, she won't let you – you'll see.'

'I am *GOING* to *GET* a *DUCK!*'

'Ha ha! What a stupid idea!'

'I am *GOING* to *GET* a *DUCK!*'

No you're no-ot! No you're nooooot!'

And so it would continue, until finally the inevitable scream of rage, frantic pursuit around the house and merciless violence.

I've since wondered if the whole duck thing might not have been an elaborate gambit. By asking so insistently for something completely absurd she could be sure that Mum would jump at the chance to settle for a more normal alternative. A week or so before her thirteenth birthday, Charlotte and our mother took the bus down to the local RSPCA centre. Most of the dogs in the kennels were barking excitedly, but one youngster, shaped like a Labrador with Alsatian colouring, stood quietly in her cage. Charlotte named the dog Lady (*Ha! What a stupid name* . . .), and brought her home the same day.

It was only much later that Charlotte told me the extent to which she was bullied in her first three years of secondary school. Catherine and I were still at junior school, so she was able to hide much of it from us. It's easy now to see where so much of her anger came from. Charlotte had stopped being posh and started being a 'boff', which was far worse. Anyone who got good grades was a boff. It was a condition aggravated by middle-class mannerisms and glasses. They picked on her accent, her studiousness, her glasses, her hair and her clothes with a viciousness that only teenagers can muster. And it was hard to make friends when everyone knew that they'd be ostracized for associating with her. The lowest point, she told me later, was one lunchtime when it seemed as if every kid in the school was pursuing her through the playground shouting abuse. But Charlotte stuck it out, and continued to get good grades. By the time I arrived at the school, she had a close circle of friends and was only being picked on occasionally.

I wondered if they'd called her 'Msungu', these killers? I wondered if she'd tried to confront them.

I thought again about what Charlotte's murderers had said: 'Tell the government we're going to kill them all and there's nothing you can do'. Surely they were wrong – surely there *were* things that could be done? The news reports had said that the rebels were fighting a war against Burundi's government. They'd decided to kill civilians in pursuit of a military objective. Surely that meant this was a war crime?

Charlotte's death had been a terrible blow, but that didn't mean we were incapable of fighting back. We might be a small family, but we were a resourceful bunch. Three years of philosophy had taught me how to put an argument together. Catherine was one of the most articulate people I knew, and my mother had been active in politics for nearly three decades. '*Dogged* persistence', she always told me, 'that's how you get things done.' And for as long as I could remember, she'd practised what she preached, persisting doggedly on everything from fair pay for school-dinner ladies to Third World debt and the rights of refugees. No case was too small, no issue too hopeless. A cause was never lost – it was just that you hadn't been persisting doggedly for long enough.

My mother's idealism had rubbed off on all of us to some degree – but perhaps most of all on Charlotte. While I'd rebelled by becoming cynical and worldly wise, Charlotte had gone the other way. She'd taken herself to Rwanda, one of the most forsaken places on the planet, and doggedly persisted in trying to do something to help. All I'd ever doggedly persisted in was the lining of my own bank account. I had thought that if I looked after myself then at least the injustices of the world wouldn't be bothering *me*. Well this was one injustice I wasn't going to be resigned to.

It was still early when I knocked on my mother's door, but she was already awake and sitting up in bed. She'd been thinking about some lines from a poem by Dylan Thomas. *Do not go gentle into that good night . . . Rage, rage against the dying of the light.* We both felt the same way. We could not just let Charlotte go.

My mother seemed quite chirpy at the thought of going out and getting the newspapers. We were in a different reality now. There were small, practical things to be done, and we could be cheerful about doing them – but underlying it all was this feeling of irredeemable awfulness. At the newsagent's I queued, smiled and gave my money like a normal person. But I wasn't a normal person any more. I was a 'grieving relative', while the rest of the world just carried on buying the milk and parking their cars.

Saturday's *Guardian* had a touching piece written by a journalist who had met Charlotte in Rwanda just a couple of months before. His description of her was instantly recognizable:

> A few weeks ago at an Indian restaurant in Kigali I sat next to Charlotte Wilson as she translated for me the agenda of a summit she had been attending with the Rwandan government.
>
> She was exasperated and mildly amused by the request that she attend. The meeting, to discuss the science curriculum in secondary schools, meant time away from teaching at her school in Shyogwe, about which she talked with bursting enthusiasm. She would rather have been with her students.
>
> At the same time she enjoyed recounting how the summons had come from the Ministry of Education, via her headteacher, with the clear instruction that it would be quite wrong not to attend. So she found her way to Kigali and turned up at a meeting with precious little idea of what they were supposed to be discussing or for how long she was expected to attend.
>
> Charlotte, like most Britons working in Rwanda for Voluntary Service Overseas, was passionate about what she did and also had no intention of carrying on schoolteaching when she returned to the UK. This was fantastic, she said, but her vocation was scientific research.

Other articles gave us more details about the attack. Two witnesses were quoted; Cadeau, the woman who'd been allowed to leave, and an unnamed man who'd managed to crawl into bushes by the side of the road after being shot. Cadeau had looked the leader of the group in the eye and called him 'brother'. Other passengers had also begged for their lives but been killed nonetheless. Was Charlotte one of them? Was Cadeau released because she was Hutu?

The bus that Charlotte was travelling on had been called 'Titanic Express', in honour of the film. *Bloody* Celine Dion. What were you thinking of, Charlotte?

Some details were reported that we knew to be wrong. One article said that Charlotte had been a primary schoolteacher. One said that she had been killed yesterday, when we knew it had been the day before. Some reports said that the attack took place 30 miles north-west of Bujumbura, others that it was just 18 miles away. And there was no mention of the fact that Charlotte had been travelling with her Burundian fiancé. Were newspapers always this inaccurate?

Another article had suggested that the killers were 'a freelance group motivated primarily by banditry'. Freelance murderers? I wondered if they'd have said this if the massacre hadn't happened in Africa. If the attackers were just bandits, why did they need to kill so many people? If they did it to stop the passengers from identifying them, why release one woman who had looked the leader of the group full in the face?

It was so confusing, so *frustrating*. Why couldn't someone just tell me what had happened to my sister? How could I ever accept what had happened if I didn't know what it was I was accepting? If I was to have any hope of coming to terms with this, then I needed to know the worst. Charlotte hadn't been spared it, after all. Had they tortured her? Had they raped her? Did she try to fight back? Did she beg for her life? Was she in pain? How long had it taken her to die?

Charlotte was dead and we knew so little about what had happened. We didn't even have a name for the killers beyond 'Hutu rebels'. Who were they, and what were they fighting for? Was Burundi about to be engulfed by the same violence that had torn Rwanda apart in 1994?

My mother's house was cold, but outside was colder. And this cold, normal world was starting to feel more dangerous. I didn't feel like going out any more. More friends and family called. I lost count of the number of times I heard the phrase 'I don't know what to say'. I told them it was OK not to know what to say. In normal life, even when something bad happens, friends can say things that help you to look on the bright side. There was no bright side, but I was grateful that they'd called. Charlotte's ex-boyfriend, Gordon, sounded breathless with shock. He'd contacted *The Sunday Times* because he was sick of seeing the washed-out mugshot of Charlotte, and wanted someone to print a story with a decent picture of her. I wondered how he must be feeling now. I knew that they'd tried to keep things going for the first six months of Charlotte's time in Rwanda, but I'd never asked who'd dumped who. I hoped that he wasn't blaming himself. Emma turned up with flowers and uncomfortable silences. I wanted to tell her to leave and not come back, but I couldn't bring myself to do so. Any kind of comfort now was better than being alone.

I woke up early again on Sunday morning. I was used to returning to the world with a sense of relief that whatever nightmare I'd been having was over. Now it was the other way round. Those few seconds of peace followed by that dark, disgusting remembrance.

I wondered if she'd been praying at the moment that they shot her. Charlotte was always more religious than me; as a child I believed in God and Heaven only until it occurred to me to doubt what I was told about the world. I'd given up church and the choir when my voice started breaking. I showed up a handful of times for the morning service, then never went back.

But Charlotte had kept on going. After finishing her undergraduate studies she became a regular parishioner at the Church of Saint Alban, in Holborn, where she was eventually confirmed. 'Maybe religion is a crutch', she once said to me. 'But is there anything wrong with that if it helps people?'

Sunday morning, still early. I made myself a cup of tea, and sat at the breakfast table, wondering where Charlotte was now. Over the years I'd made peace with my own mortality, and settled into a comfortable agnosticism. But I hadn't given anything like as much thought to the mortality of those around me. Now I found it very hard to accept that Charlotte might simply have ceased to exist. It was bad enough that she was dead. The thought that she might also be gone, completely, was intolerable. She seemed so familiar, still. I could imagine so clearly the sound of her voice, could almost hear it now. Could almost feel her baggy-jumpered arms around my shoulders.

I was staring at the strange, fibreoptic, Christmas decoration on the window sill, as it slowly changed colour. While it looked something like a space-age pot plant, it was beautiful in its own ridiculous way.

The kind of ridiculous beauty that Charlotte would have appreciated. It made me sad to think that she wouldn't be able to see it now. But if something of Charlotte had endured, maybe she *would* be able to see it. I felt that warm glow around my shoulders again.

And I wondered if this was just my mind playing tricks with me. This was a 'coping mechanism', wasn't it? This was just my subconscious telling me what I wanted to hear.

I looked across the table to the white, wooden chair where Charlotte had so often sat.

If she was here with me in the room now, that would be where she'd be sitting.

As a small child I used to live in fear of seeing my father's ghost, but now I'd have given anything to see Charlotte. I sipped at my black, bitter, lukewarm tea, and stared at the chair, willing her to appear there. If I could see her, even just for a few seconds, then at least I'd know she was OK. That was all I wanted, just to know that she was OK.

I told myself that this was ridiculous. If I was to hold on to any semblance of dignity then I had to stay rational. But what if rationality just wasn't enough? What if I needed this comfort blanket, this firebreak to irrationality?

Time seemed to be passing more slowly now. The warmth around my shoulders was enveloping me, and I felt a strange, sad, tired sense of calm. The more I stared, the more absurd it seemed that Charlotte could have just vanished into nothing at the moment her life ended. It was so cold. I was so tired. It was so early in the morning. The others weren't going to be up for hours, but I didn't feel like I was alone.

Gordon's photograph of Charlotte, barefoot and smiling in shorts on a beach, was on the front page of *The Sunday Times*, with the headline 'Murdered aid worker's vaccine legacy'. They had tracked down Charlotte's PhD supervisor, who'd said nice things about her and told them that her research might soon be helping to save thousands of lives in Africa. It sounded a bit too much like a fairy tale. With life expectancy as low as it was, I doubted that many African lives would be saved by a treatment for viral heart disease.

There was a knock on the door around three that afternoon. The tactful and sympathetic man standing outside in the cold was from the *Daily Mail*, and he was asking to speak to Mrs Wilson. He told my mother how sorry he was to intrude at such a difficult time, but he had a letter that he would like to give her. Would she be prepared to look at the letter, have a think about what it said and then give him her answer in around an hour? My mother agreed.

The letter from the man from the *Mail* offered his condolences, and asked if my mother would be willing to give an interview to his newspaper about Charlotte's life. When he returned an hour later, my mother invited him in, sat him down and calmly explained why she simply couldn't do it.

She told him that she was an English teacher, and for the last ten years she had been working with people who'd fled from some of the world's most troubled countries. Iranians and Iraqis, Congolese, Somalis, Bosnians and Kosovans, Turkish Kurds, Eritreans and Ethiopians – even a couple of Burundians had made it into her class-room. All had lost some members of their family – some had lost everyone. Several were still receiving treatment for the torture they had suffered. Those who were allowed to work at all had grinding, menial jobs. Large numbers faced the prospect of being forcibly returned to the war zones they had fled, amid government protest-ations that these countries were 'safe'. She had lost count of the number of times a student had mentioned in class that another loved one back home had been killed. And she had lost count of the number of newspaper articles she had seen portraying refugees as liars, cheats, frauds, 'bogus' people.

When the stories had first begun, in the mid-1990s, my mother had dismissed them. But then they'd continued, year after year, painting a picture that she just could not recognize of the desperate, traumatized people that she worked with every day. She and her colleagues had begun to wonder if there was something more complicated going on. It hadn't escaped their attention that so many of these stories were emanating from the *Daily Mail*, and its sister paper the *Evening Standard*. My mother had seen the effect of these stories on govern-ment policy, and she'd seen the effect of those increasingly harsh policies on her students. She would feel she was betraying them now if she had anything to do with the *Daily Mail*.

The man from the *Mail* took this so well that I felt quite sorry for him. More than anything, though, I felt proud of my mother. I knew something of the horrors she had heard from her students over the years, and the effect she herself had suffered from being so close to such suffering. I knew how angry she had been about the distortions and duplicity of newspapers like the *Daily Mail*. And yet, just three days after enduring one of the worst blows of her life, faced with a representative of an organization that she and most of her colleagues regarded as something close to 'hate media', she'd shown a calmness and dignity that I found quite extraordinary.

It was New Year's Eve, and that afternoon Catherine, my mother and I sat down and put together a letter to the *Guardian*, each writing a line at a time. The attack in which Charlotte died had to be investigated as a war crime, 'not dismissed as unsolvable simply because it occurred in an African country'. Carl, who'd studied journalism at university, helped us to edit and shape the letter. Catherine sent it through by email. None of us knew if anything would come of it, but it was good to be working together. We felt a little bit less like victims. This was only a small thing – but it was *something we could do*.

On the phone to my uncle again, I asked for his advice on starting a campaign for Charlotte's killers to be prosecuted as war criminals. He'd done a lot of media work through his involvement with tribal rights groups and his career as a writer, and I knew that he'd have some useful thoughts. But his answer wasn't quite what I'd been hoping to hear. We would have to be very cautious, he said. How much did we really know about Burundi, and the situation there? It might well be dangerous to assume that a Western idea like a war crimes trial could simply be juxtaposed onto a society so distant from our own. In clamouring for justice, how sure could we be that we might not be making the situation even worse?

I told Uncle James what I knew about Rwanda, the fact that its southern neighbour had a similar, colonial history, and the same kind of ethnic mix, the fact that the International Criminal Tribunal for Rwanda was widely thought to have been essential in ending violence there. But I also knew that I was blagging it, and my uncle's questions continued to nag at me. How sure could I be about this? I'd spent seven days in Rwanda and read a couple books. I could put what I knew about Burundi on the back of a small, brown envelope. In the end all I that had to go on was a gut feeling. Surely something like this transcended all cultural differences? Surely there could be no country in the world where it could be acceptable to let this go unpunished?

I woke up the next morning and realized that I was living in a year Charlotte had never seen. It was 2001. It was Monday. My sister died last year. My sister died four days ago. Time had moved on already, and I knew that I would move on too, whether I liked it or not. I could so clearly hear the sound of her voice in my head. But I knew that would fade too, just like my memories of my father. In a couple of years I would be older than Charlotte had been when she was killed. Whether it took one decade or two, there would come a time when I would look back and remember Charlotte as a part of my *past*. Who would I be in 20 years time? What would Charlotte, the Charlotte of December 2000, make of me then?

Through every stage of my life, Charlotte had been there. Sometimes we got on well, sometimes we annoyed the hell out of each other, but she'd always been there. Charlotte had introduced me to so many of the things I liked about life – London, good music, good films, good books, good restaurants. I knew that in the future there would be new places, new music, books and films that I would love – and I'd never be able to share them with her. It felt as if a part of me had been ripped out.

There were so many letters and cards that morning that the postman had to push them through the door in several batches. Hurriedly scrawled cards, long and thoughtful letters, from family, friends, colleagues and former colleagues. People who'd taught Charlotte at school and never forgotten her, people we didn't even know had our address, people we'd not heard from in years. Most had seen the news on Saturday and decided to write straightaway. When I counted the letters I burst into tears. There were more than 50, and all this for Charlotte. No one else I knew could have left such an enduring impression. No one else I knew had so many friends.

Among these letters one stood out. It was from Mia Naylor, who had introduced Charlotte to the Church of Saint Alban in Holborn.

There is something I want to share with you but I'm worried I will cause offence.

On the night of Thursday 28th December, I dreamt that I was sitting enjoying a drink with friends in Holborn. Suddenly I heard the sound of incessant, raking gunfire. I got up and went outside. It was hot, dusty and tropical. The sound of gunfire continued. Across the vivid blue sky arched a rainbow. It was obscured by a tremendous pall of dust and smoke, but it still glittered brightly.

On Friday morning I could not make sense of this. Yet, unlike most dreams, it did not fade away and has remained vividly in my mind. Nothing can bring Charlotte back. Whilst many knew her far better than I, in my heart she was my closest female friend . . . But the aforementioned vision tugs at the edges of my mind, and I can't help but in some curious way feel that it and Charlotte are connected. Somehow I feel that in spite of everything she is 'alright', blessed and safe.

I found myself desperately wanting to believe that Mia's message was proof of something spiritual – proof that Charlotte really was 'alright'. But for this reason, I also found it hard to trust my ability to think about it objectively. But might this not just be a combination of coincidence and wishful thinking? While it was bizarre that Mia had this dream a full day before Charlotte's death was reported, my sister *did* have a lot of friends, and people do have strange dreams all the time. Of course this dream had taken on an entirely new significance to Mia once she heard the news, but perhaps she had dreams like this more often than she was admitting to herself now. Perhaps this was merely *her* subconscious playing tricks with her, as mine had been with me.

Yet still I found it difficult to dismiss Mia's words entirely. Out of all my sister's friends, it was she, more than anyone, who had known and understood Charlotte's spiritual side. The fact that the message had come from her, in particular, seemed to make it even more of a coincidence.

Catherine and my mother were also very struck. We talked about what the letter could mean. The rainbow immediately reminded us of the biblical story of Noah. In the book of Genesis, after humanity had been decimated by a cataclysmic flood, God had sent the first rainbow, as his covenant that nothing so bad would ever happen again. Was this the message we were supposed to draw from Mia's letter? We agreed that it would be dangerous to interpret it in this way. If anything, Charlotte's death had shown us how fragile we all were, and how little we could take for granted. It was foolish to believe that nothing so bad would ever happen again. But there *was* another message we could draw – one that did make sense to us. Amid the violent noise, behind the clouds of dust and smoke, the rainbow continues to shine. Death cannot destroy the beauty in life.

I looked again at the last email I'd sent to Charlotte, on 11 December 2000. She'd asked me what I thought about her plans to extend with VSO for another year. I'd told her I thought she was taking part in something 'amazing', that she should do whatever she thought was right and 'follow her star'. It sounds clichéd to me now, but I meant it sincerely at the time. I was trying to tell her that I was proud of her, that she should trust her instincts and that she shouldn't feel guilty. I'd jokingly prefaced this exhortation 'Rikki's final thought' – it felt very strange to be reading those words again now. This was the last line of my last ever message to her.

When I read Charlotte's reply, the email she had sent a week before Christmas Eve, eleven days before the last day of her life, that too now seemed loaded with meaning.

I hope that we'll be able to spend more quality time together soon. After all we'll have decades to discuss things in the future . . . I am happier . . . than I have ever been in my life and having a fantastic time.

It seemed both cruel and consoling to know that Charlotte had been so happy in the last weeks of her life. But there was one line in that message that I now found very disturbing.

I'm definitely following my star even if it leads me to places that aren't part of the conventional road to happiness . . .

I was suddenly struck by the fear that my glib exhortation might have played some part in Charlotte's decision to get on the bus. What did she mean by the 'conventional road to happiness'? Was she 'following her star' by going to Burundi? I'd told her that she should do whatever she thought was right 'and have fun because you deserve it', and two weeks later she'd made the most catastrophic misjudgement of her life. Although I'd been talking about her plans to extend her time in Rwanda, she could easily have drawn a more general conclusion – particularly if she was already looking for an excuse. I'd thought I was being a good brother by expressing faith in her judgement, but her decision to take such an extreme risk seemed to be proof that this faith had been disastrously misplaced. I found myself haunted by the idea that my message might have tipped the balance. Maybe if I'd shown a little *less* respect for her ability to make sensible decisions, I could have made her think it through more carefully.

I loved Charlotte, but for much of my life I'd been convinced that she was dangerously lacking in self-awareness, and needed me to point things out to her. Part of this stemmed from my childish desire to prove that I knew best, but part of it was also based on a genuine worry that Charlotte had some kind of mental blindspot. My efforts to compensate for this had often been clumsy and insensitive, but on occasions helpful.

Now I was haunted by the idea that I might have been able to say something that *would* have stopped her from getting on that bus. I knew that this was dangerous thinking, and that there was little to be gained from it, but I didn't want to kid myself either. I found it impossible to be sure that there was nothing I could have done that would have made a difference.

I'd never replied to her last email. I'd never even got round to sending her a Christmas present. I'd told myself I'd do it in the new year, when I had a bit more time, and that Charlotte would understand, like she always did, and now it was too late.

The *Guardian* got back to us. They were going to print our letter in full. And Will Woodward, the journalist who'd met Charlotte in Rwanda, was asking for an interview. VSO rang with more news on Charlotte's last few days. She and Richard had spent Christmas with some of the other volunteers, in Kibuye, where we'd been with her during the summer. They'd taken the bus from Kigali to Bujumbura, hoping to spend New Year's Eve with Richard's family. Charlotte would have been meeting them for the first time. They'd been killed just 20 miles from their destination.

'I now seem to be going out with a 6 foot 6 Burundian ex-monk, also called Richard. Just hope it doesn't all end in tears', Charlotte had said.

It would have been too easy to blame Richard though, I felt sure that some people would have done so. Whatever else you could say about Charlotte, she always made her own choices. Nothing could have persuaded her to do something that she didn't want to do. Charlotte and Richard had both taken the same calculated risk, and both of them had paid a horrific price for doing so. I didn't want to be angry with either of them.

Will Woodward came to see us that evening. He stayed with us for several hours, listening and taking notes while Catherine, my mother and I talked about Charlotte. It felt like a kind of catharsis. Early the next morning my mother and I gave an interview to BBC Radio 4. I burbled something about how proud I was of Charlotte, the work she was doing in Rwanda and the fact that Britain was doing so much to help rebuild the country. My mother made her case rather more coherently: 'This was a political crime. If you're just stealing from people you don't then systematically shoot them all', she said, and made the stark point that 'the gun that killed Charlotte could have come from Britain or France'.

I wasn't unprepared for Wednesday morning's post. Charlotte wrote home so often that I'd wondered if this might happen. But it was eerie nonetheless, nearly a week after her death, to see an airmail envelope lying on the doormat bearing Charlotte's handwriting. The letter was dated 22 December – less than a week before she was killed.

Friday 22nd December 2000

Dear Mum,

Hiya! I was so sorry to miss you when I rang last week, but I was very touched to receive your email saying that anyone I choose would be nice. One of my old students came round today and I showed her his photo. Her comment was 'Il est un vrai noir'. Not quite sure what that's meant to mean!

I'm sorry that I'm late with this letter, I have been working virtually every minute I've been awake for the last week and a half, apart from a bit last weekend. Most of the 10th – 15th I spent invigilating and marking exams. On the Friday I went to Kigali to talk to the guy in charge of the Centre National de Développement de Programmes about a job next year.

In the evening was the Ambassador's Christmas party. Richard and I arrived a bit late and made a grand entrance down a big flight of steps. As soon as we arrived the VSOs started applauding because the news that we'd got engaged had spread on the grapevine. Virtually all the British expat community was in attendance. I had great fun because it was a carol concert in the Ambassador's Residence grounds. I belted away, alto main tune and descant as the mood took me. The next day I had to be in Gitarama early for the pasteurisation of some of my friends. Now the bishop's back all those people who had to wait to be ordained while he was away are able to be ordained. One choir member was made a deacon. Three choir members plus my friends Immaculée (one of the few Rwandan women I've met with balls and brains) and her husband François, all became pastors.

Afterwards there was a big ceremony at which I helped to serve the food. I went back to Kigali in the evening on Saturday to see Richard and we went to church at the English service in the Anglican cathedral at Nyami-rambo on Sunday morning. We saw the Ambassador there, which I was quite pleased about. We were introduced to his deputy, Paul, on the Friday. He didn't think it was likely that Richard would get a visa to come to Britain next summer because too many people before him had done a runner in similar situations. However, when we've been married for a year he'll probably get a residence visa, and as soon as he does he can start to work. I'm really disappointed about that, but whenever he gets to the UK we'll have some kind of ceremony, a marriage blessing or something. Of course, there's always the chance that he'll get the visa after all. We'll have to go to Kampala to get it – I'm quite looking forward to the trip.

I've worked out why the kids are always ill – they drink untreated non-boiled water! I was really shocked when I saw that. I was considering asking the préfet if it would be impossible to give them boiled water but I'm not sure that's within my mandate. One student came up to me today and said that he had mental problems, and he often thought he was going mad. With so many traumatised kids what can I do? There's no counselling service at school, but there must be something at the local hospital. I'll try and find out for him. I think every teacher should have training for coun-selling.

OK, well I want to get this posted! I'm out of Shyogwe for Christmas and it does me good to get out of this environment. I'll post this tomorrow. I'll be thinking of you on Monday and hope you have a fantastic Christmas.

Lots of love
Charlotte

Accompanying this letter were the first pictures we'd seen of her with Richard. So now we knew what he had looked like. They both looked so happy and relaxed together. The *Guardian* article appeared on Thursday, the cover story in one of the pull-out sections, with a photograph that I'd taken of Charlotte not long before she left.

We'd been using up the last few pictures on a black-and-white film. 'Look sophisticated!', I'd told her. Charlotte had thrown me her snootiest look, I'd taken the picture, and seconds later she'd been smiling and laughing again. But looking at her now, staring up at me from the pages of this newspaper, my sister seemed sombre, tragic even. Amid the laughter and lightness of that moment, neither of us could have had any idea that we were helping to write Charlotte's obituary. And yet, insane though it was, I found myself wondering whether some part of her had *known*.

— 4 —

Dear Mum, Richard and Catherine,

If you are reading this then something has happened and I am sorry to put you through this grief, especially you, Mum, because to lose a child must be one of the worst losses ever. I just want you to know that I love you all very much and that even though I chose to spend two years in a different continent, family, and especially you three, is the most important thing in my life. I am very proud to come from this family and think that I am very lucky that we are so close. There were a lot of tensions when we were growing up, but I think that they have been resolved now. Even Daddy's death, which I think probably traumatised me, had a positive outcome because it brought us closer together. I hope that my death can bring you still closer together and that some good may come of it.

I am sorry for getting myself killed, but apart from that I have no regrets and I have lived life to the full. One of the things that makes life worth living is my relationships with you all. I pray that you will be safe and successful in your lives to come. God willing, we will meet again. Until then, here is a poem

> Do not stand at my grave and weep;
> I am not there. I do not sleep.
> I am a thousand winds that blow.
> I am the diamond glints on snow.
> I am the sunlight on ripened grain.
> I am the gentle autumn rain.
> When you awaken in the morning's hush
> I am the swift uplifting rush
> Of quiet birds in circled flight.

I am the soft stars that shine at night.
Do not stand at my grave and cry;
I am not there. I did not die.

All my love, always and for ever
Charlotte

If it is possible and you wouldn't find it too distressing then I would like my
body to be dedicated to medical science, but I would like a memorial service
and a plaque in Barley churchyard. If not, I would like to be buried in
Barley. I would like my friends to sing Purcell's funeral sentences – please
include my friends esp. Amanda, Mine and Maria and Karen A because
they're almost as close as sisters to me.

I love you all

Charlotte had one more surprise for us, and it arrived with a box of her possessions, in an airmail envelope marked *To my family, to be opened in the event of my death.*

'I am sorry for getting myself killed but apart from that I have no regrets.' What an epitaph.

It was Charlotte's grand finale. I'd tried not to be angry with her but this really got to me. Apart from that one minor getting-herself-killed issue, Miss Wilson has no regrets. It's not enough to seek out the most dangerous country in the world and go out and get killed there, she also has to have the last word.

'I hope that my death can bring you still closer together and that some good may come of it.' How thoughtful of her. Most people like to bring their families closer together by showing up at Christmas, being a shoulder to cry on, helping out with house moves, etc. Charlotte does it by getting killed.

And that sappy poem – 'Do not stand by my grave and weep'. You don't want us to stand by your grave and weep? *Don't go and get killed then!*

Why, in February 2000, had she chosen to write this letter? Did 'living life to the full' mean taking life-threatening risks? Had she already decided that she was going to push herself to the limit, to go out of her way to put herself in dangerous situations? Was she excusing herself in advance? Was Rwanda not dangerous enough for her? Was this about thrill seeking or something more sinister? Did she have a death wish?

Our father's death *had* traumatized her, I knew that. And Charlotte had always been morbid. The girl had made a will at the age of 16. While I was growing up I'd lost count of the number of times that she talked about what we should do if she died. Even in her twenties Charlotte spoke of her grief over Daddy's death as a 'black cloud' that was always there, with the potential to overpower her in her darkest moments. Was it this 'black cloud' that had obscured her judgement so disastrously over Burundi? Might it be that our father's loss, so many years ago, had led in some way to Charlotte's death?

I didn't know what to believe any more. I was certainly sure that Charlotte's intensity came in large part from the trauma of losing her father. And without that intensity, perhaps she wouldn't have ended up working in Rwanda at all, wouldn't have met Richard, wouldn't have gone to Burundi, wouldn't have got killed. It reminded me of a children's verse that Charlotte had been fond of:

> For want of a nail the shoe was lost,
> For want of a shoe, the horse was lost
> For want of a horse the rider was lost
> For want of a rider the battle was lost . . .

But it was another thing entirely to think that she had actively gone looking for danger. Though she'd talked about travelling to the Congo, she'd not, as far as I knew, actually done it. When she decided to go to Burundi, it was to be with the man she loved on New Year's Eve, and to meet his family. While she must have known it was a risk, there were plenty of other explanations as to why she chose to take it. She and Richard were, by all accounts, in that first, heady phase of love; maybe they felt invincible. This particular type of bus, on this particular road, had never been attacked before. Dozens of other people chose to make the same journey every day. Maybe Charlotte thought that she'd had enough assurances. It was something she wanted to do, and when Charlotte wanted to do something, she was very good at kidding herself that everything would be OK.

As for the letter, the fact that she wrote it in February 2000 intrigued me. That month saw the twentieth anniversary of our father's death, and I guessed that this wasn't a coincidence. I knew that she worried about what might happen if trouble started again in Rwanda. Maybe she was just writing us the letter she wished her father could have written her? For all I knew, morbid soul that she was, she could have been keeping a letter like this for years – maybe this was just the latest version. Or maybe she never really expected anyone to read it. Maybe it was just a message into the ether, something she did to get things straight in her own mind, to help her deal with the dangers she felt in Rwanda.

I had to admit that it helped though. While it was disturbing to read Charlotte's apology for getting herself killed, it was also cathartic. At least she'd said sorry, and there was some comfort in knowing that she'd come to terms with her mortality before she died. I had wanted, more than anything, to have one more conversation with Charlotte, to have some proof of Mia's strange, hopeful conviction that she was 'alright', blessed and safe. Now here was this handwritten letter, making peace and saying goodbye. 'God willing, we will meet again', she had said.

The poem, too, had more appeal the second time I read it. It seemed to hint at an animistic view of nature that I'd always found more appealing than the dry Church of England Christianity I'd grown up with. If it was true that Charlotte, or some part of her, could have survived death, then it made much more sense to me that she would be in the world around us, not closeted away in some spiritual, never-never land. Right now, I seemed to see something of Charlotte in everything around me. Anything from a book to a bicycle could set off an association that led back to my sister, and the painful vacuum that she had left.

I stayed off work for as long as I could. There were still so many details to take care of. Charlotte's body was returned to the UK in a Burundian coffin. The Burundian death certificate had recorded Charlotte's death as an 'accident'. Was this just an error in translation or something more sinister?

Before we could bury Charlotte there had to be a post-mortem, and before that, her body needed to be identified. My mother calmly contacted Charlotte's dentist to let them know that Charlotte's records might be needed. I felt that if anyone was to do any identifying it should be me. Surely nothing could be worse than having to identify the body of one's own child? But my mother was insistent, and she had the power of veto. In the end we agreed to go together. I was dreading it, but I didn't want her to go alone. I asked Emma and my friend Greg to come with me. Greg had been my best friend since university, Emma was, still, my girlfriend. 'I'm dying to meet her', Charlotte had said, in her last email to me.

I wondered, awkwardly, if I was asking something that they wouldn't feel able to say no to.

My mother dithered as we waited to be picked up by our Police Liaison Officer, Jo Baxter. I'd been staying in this house for more than a week now, and it was starting to feel claustrophobic. I found myself getting irritated with her over the smallest things, which only made me feel guilty.

Jo calmly explained what we were going to see. Only Charlotte's face would be shown, and we would be looking at her from behind a glass screen. Charlotte's body had been in a better condition than they'd expected, but exposure to the air, after her sealed coffin was opened, had caused some 'discolouration'.

The mortuary was a grim-looking building, and it was a bitterly cold day. Inside, the air had a sickly scented, cheap air freshener smell that was almost overpowering. I felt the dim realization that this smell was there to hide the odour of death.

'I know that you may not be taking in much of what I'm saying.' It was the first time I had met Detective Superintendent Sands, who was heading the police investigation into Charlotte's death. They'd already determined that Charlotte had been shot in the back from a distance of two or three feet. She'd either have been kneeling or lying down. She would have died quickly. The only possible verdict was murder.

Next door was a small room. As I walked in I could see Charlotte's body through the long rectangular window at the far side. A white sheet covered all but her face. Her eyes were closed, her eyelids blackened, her lips slightly parted. She looked as if she was frozen in time, neither peaceful nor troubled. Just an incredible, terrible stillness. As though she had died mid-sentence, or mid-gasp. It could have been a plaster model. Her skin was mottled brown, black lines tracing the veins across her face, her dark hair pulled back from her forehead. Were there black tears in the corners of her eyes?

'Her hair looks thin – do you think she was eating properly?' my mother asked, and somewhere I could hear Charlotte laughing.

The others left the room. My uncle had asked me to say some words to Charlotte when I saw her body, so I stood there and croaked whatever came into my head, feeling like an idiot. I got the sense that this strange object was not Charlotte, merely the evidence of her death. When I emerged and sat again with the others I had a strong feeling that Charlotte was here, with us, not with that dead body.

Emma was stoical, but Greg seemed dazed and withdrawn. He'd met Charlotte countless times over the years. Had I not thought about how much this would affect him? Why had I brought him here? We were quiet in the car going back to my mother's house.

The autopsy ruled out sexual assault. Charlotte had been shot seven times in the back with an Eastern-European weapon. How much damage can seven bullets do? I wondered how long it had taken her to die. Did she lose consciousness instantly? What could she have been thinking as her life slipped away?

So they'd shot Charlotte in the back, not in the chest as we'd first heard. Something to do with 'exit wounds', I guessed, from the scant knowledge of autopsies I'd picked up once from a book about JFK.

As the days passed I felt an ever-greater need to know more about *who* had killed Charlotte, and why. Some reports were saying that the ambush had taken place less than a mile from a military base. The Hutu rebels had denied responsibility, we were told, and accused the Tutsi-dominated, government army of carrying out the attack to discredit them. Most worrying of all, the Burundian government had announced that their investigation into the attack had been closed, *and could not be reopened for eight years.*

Was it conceivable that Burundi's government would massacre 21 people in order to frame the Hutu rebels? It sounded too much like a conspiracy theory to me – but then why had the authorities said that Charlotte's death was an 'accident'? Why were they insisting that there could be no investigation?

The image of Charlotte's face stayed with me. That familiar yet strangely alien face, frozen in time, the rest of her body hidden under a white sheet. Sometimes it would appear in my mind sudden and unbidden, like a blow to the head.

Had they singled her out, or had they killed her with all the others as they lay together, face down on the ground? Was it true that she was the first to die? How long had she been lying there before they shot her? Why had they made everyone lie *face down*? I wondered if it was easier to murder someone when you don't have to look them in the eye.

Did they even know what they were doing? I thought about the number of people who'd been affected by her death, the hundreds of letters and phone calls that we'd had in the last fortnight. Charlotte had so many friends – from her last years of school to university in London, from the year she'd spent in Paris, the friends she made through her church and the choirs she sang in, the friends she'd made in Rwanda.

When I imagined the face of the man who'd killed Charlotte I thought of Sylvestre Gacumbitsi, the smug, swaggering Rwandan mayor who'd led the killing of hundreds of Tutsis in the town of Nyarabuye. Months after the 1994 genocide, Fergal Keane had tracked him down in the refugee camps of Tanzania, living under UN protection. Gacumbitsi had denied any wrongdoing, denied that the genocide even happened – but his expression seemed to contradict his words.

I pictured Charlotte's killer as he stood over her, some third-rate second-lieutenant, a Gacumbitsi-wannabe, just a little too fond of his job title. Paunchy, perhaps. Middle-aged, of course. As I watched him raise the gun I was there too, we all were. I wondered if Charlotte knew that we were with her.

'You *don't* know *what* you're *doing* . . .'

There was no way he could hear us but we shouted it anyway.

'You *don't* know *what* you're *doing* . . .'

We shouted it as he put his finger on the trigger, shouted it as each bullet left the gun.

'You *don't* know *what* you're *doing* . . . You *don't* know *what* you're *doing* . . .'

We shouted it as the bullets ripped into her back. We shouted it as her chest exploded, shouted it as she struggled to breathe with what was left of her lungs.

We shouted it as her life bled into the ground.

The flashbacks, if that's what they were, gave me renewed strength. Identifying Charlotte's body was the most harrowing thing I'd ever had to do. Nothing now could be as difficult as what I'd already faced. Although I was still torn apart by grief, I was becoming more and more sure that Charlotte was still around. And that sense of conviction gave me confidence. I had never felt less alone. When the tears came, as they often still did, so too did the warm, calming glow around my shoulders that I'd felt the day after we heard the news that Charlotte was dead. *I'm still here*, her voice would say, in the back of my mind. *I'm still here.*

I promised Charlotte I would do everything I could to see that her killers were tracked down and put on trial.

I wanted to feel angry now. Better to feel angry than introverted and helpless. Annoyed though I'd been with Charlotte for going to Burundi, she'd still be alive today if these people hadn't taken it upon themselves to murder a busload of innocent people. It was *they* I should be angry with. I knew that Charlotte would have fought relentlessly if anything had ever happened to me or Catherine. Now I felt as if some of her intense energy had been transferred to me. However small the odds, and however long it took, I had to channel every ounce of this grief into finding these bastards and confounding their smug assertion that 'there's nothing you can do'.

My comfortable lifestyle felt more empty and meaningless than ever now, and my navel-gazing relationship little more than an annoyance. How could either of these things be more important than proving that my sister's life was worth something? As much as anything, this seemed like a matter of psychological survival. The more I thought about it, the more certain I was that I wouldn't be able to live with myself if I didn't *try* – and try harder than I'd ever tried before. I knew it would be a desperate effort, and that the chances of success were doubtful, but it didn't feel like a choice. It would be too easy to pretend that there was nothing I could do – I'd barely even started trying. I might be ignorant now, but that was no excuse either. It just meant that I had to start making an effort to learn.

I wrote to the Foreign Office and asked to know everything they could tell me about the attack – did they think it was a war crime? What could they tell me about the Burundian rebels? What did they make of the claim that Burundi's army might have been responsible? I received a long reply a few days later. Despite the denials, they believed that Charlotte had been killed by the smaller of Burundi's two rebel groups, the Forces Nationales de Libération, commonly known simply as the FNL. The ambush had taken place in FNL territory, and the same group was believed to be responsible for dozens of similar attacks.

The next day, my mother and I met with Foreign Office officials at Admiralty House in London, close to Trafalgar Square. The meeting was chaired by Matthew Gould, the Deputy Head of the Consular Division, a youngish-looking guy who seemed quite sincere. The attack in which Charlotte died probably was a war crime, he said. It was highly unlikely that the Burundian government had been involved. We shouldn't read too much into the fact that the Burundians had closed the investigation. The judicial system was in a state of collapse, and attacks like this were rarely, if ever, investigated properly. The situation in Burundi made this an extremely difficult case, but everything that could be done would be done. The Foreign Office was on the point of delivering a Diplomatic Note to the Burundian authorities, demanding an explanation of Charlotte's death, posing a series of questions about the circumstances of the attack and offering the assistance of the Metropolitan Police. In the meantime, it would probably be best if we avoided saying anything further to the media.

It was an odd meeting, as though these civil servants were frightened of us, as if there was something they knew that we weren't being told. Or was it simply that they were expecting us at any minute to be overpowered by grief and start screaming at them? Afterwards, on the steps of Admiralty House, DS Sands told us, with some bravado, that he'd never failed to clear up a case. He wasn't planning on this being his first failure. He and Detective Sergeant Matthews would see us at the funeral.

Despite my reservations I was impressed. I knew that Diplomatic Notes were things that governments issued to each other when they meant serious business. Britain had declared war on the Germans in 1939 after they failed to give a satisfactory response to a Final Note demanding their withdrawal from Poland. With our influence in Africa, sending a message like this would have to make the Burundians sit up and listen. Even if it *was* the norm in a country like Burundi for this sort of attack to go unpunished, with the expertise of Scotland Yard all kinds of things would be possible. Surely the Burundians would see that it was worth trying at least?

I walked across Westminster Bridge with a sense of relief. I'd been half-expecting to be told that the Foreign Office wouldn't do anything to pursue the case because Charlotte had ignored their travel advice. But it seemed, for the moment at least, that they were taking this case seriously. Maybe they would have done anyway, but our efforts with the media certainly hadn't done any harm. I felt proud, and relieved. We'd come through the first couple of weeks and now the wheels were in motion. There were no guarantees but Sands was on the case. Maybe for a while we could just get on with the process of grieving.

Charlotte's funeral had been delayed because of the time it took for her body to be brought home, and then by the post-mortem. Now it was delayed again by my mother's indecision. She just couldn't decide on a date, it seemed. I wondered if underneath it all she simply might not be ready to draw a line under Charlotte's life. Or maybe she was just dreading the ceremony.

It didn't help that there were complications. Charlotte had been a regular at the Church of Saint Alban in Holborn, and had hoped to marry there, so it seemed right that this should be the venue for her funeral service. We'd initially talked about burying her in Enfield, a bus ride away from my mother's house. But in her letter, Charlotte had made it clear that she wanted to be buried in Barley, the small village in Hertfordshire where our father and grandfather were buried. She had also asked for her choir friends to sing at the ceremony. The funeral director patiently sat with us while my mother outlined what we wanted, stirring only slightly when she told him that the funeral was to take place at St Albans, and the burial in 'Baa-lee'. I hastily explained that this was Barley, Hertfordshire, not Bali, Indonesia. And Saint Alban's Church, Holborn, not St Albans, Hertfordshire.

Eventually we managed to settle on a date. The funeral service would be on a Thursday evening, 18 January, with the burial taking place the next morning.

Two days before the funeral my mobile phone was stolen. I was on my way back to Enfield, buried in a book on bereavement. The platform at Seven Sisters wasn't crowded at all, but as I got off the train, still engrossed, one of the other passengers went out of his way to barge past me. At first I thought he was just trying to pick a fight. Then I checked my pockets and realized that my mobile phone was gone. With it were the telephone numbers of several people who I'd promised to call with the final details for the funeral. The guy disappeared in the direction of the escalators, and I went after him. He wasn't any bigger than me. Well-dressed though, hardly the type who needs to steal in order to survive. He knew nothing about me but he'd taken it upon himself to make my life even more complicated at *this* time, the worst of all times. I could get another phone quite easily, but I was now cut off from the people I'd promised to keep posted. I'd lived in London for six years and this had never happened before. The *one* moment I'd let my guard down, wandering around in my grief-addled daze, and this nasty little scavenger had sniffed out my weakness and got me.

He wasn't that far away now. I could catch up with him quite easily. Should I confront him? Knock him to the ground and keep kicking him until I stopped feeling angry about Charlotte's death? Bit of Pavlovian conditioning for the next time he felt like messing with someone else's life?

I knew it was absurd. I'd not been in a fight since I was 17, and that, ironically, had been with Charlotte. What would I do if this scavenger was carrying a knife? My family really didn't need me to get myself stabbed. The little man quickened his pace; he was now running up the escalators. I followed him, but kept my distance. At the top of the escalators he took a left, through the barriers, out of the station, and was gone.

When I got to my mother's place, Charlotte's old dog, Lady, was gently dripping blood all over the house. Another dog had attacked her while she was being walked in the park – one of those big, army-camouflage dogs, bred to intimidate. She had a vicious-looking, open wound on her throat, although she seemed characteristically oblivious to it. This had never happened before either. What was going on with this nasty little world we were now living in?

Lady came back from the vet looking like the Dog of Frankenstein. Half of her throat was shaved, and a gruesome line of stitches made it look as though her floppy-eared head had been sewn back on.

To complete the effect, a small length of plastic tubing was protruding from the wound. The vet tastefully described this as a 'drain'. The dog looked a mess, but at least there was no permanent damage done, and she seemed as happy as ever. I could hear Charlotte laughing again.

— 5 —

It was a single bell, tolling insistently, and it seemed to reach right inside my head, simple, repetitive. It carried on, just a little too long, before it was joined in harmony by a slow, uninterrupted note from the organ. The music built softly as the bell chimed, calmly, incessantly. It was already dark outside. Charlotte's funeral had begun.

Charlotte was dead. It was beginning to make sense now. She had died exactly three weeks ago; I'd seen it on the news. We'd identified her body. I'd talked about it and thought about it endlessly. Although in my dreams it still hadn't happened, in my waking moments it was starting to seem real.

But then I caught sight of the long, wooden box, being carried slowly to the centre of the church, each step in time with the tolling of the bell. In my mind I was screaming for it to stop. Why was I standing here looking at my sister's coffin? Why were Mum and Catherine in tears? When I blinked I had a brief, vivid flash of another reality, a bridal couple kneeling together at the altar. This was the church where they should have been married.

Charlotte had known Father Howard personally, and he seemed tearful at times as he performed the rituals. His address was poignant and thoughtful. I could see why Charlotte had chosen this place. There were no tambourines or sappy, three-chord songs. The music was flawless. Charlotte's friends did her proud. The air was heady with incense.

I recognized faces from every stage of Charlotte's life, and didn't see a single empty pew. Most here were young. For many of Charlotte's friends, this was the first death of their generation. At my great-grandfather's funeral, ten years ago, there'd been only nine of us, including the Methodist minister and two gentlemanly souls who remembered him from the bowls club. The minister barely knew his name. Grandpa Fred had long outlived his brother, his wife, his only child and almost all of his friends. At least if you die young you can expect a decent funeral.

DS Sands and DS Matthews were waiting for us outside. 'These are the people who are going to sort it out', I told Catherine, bullishly. They seemed embarrassed – 'Try. Try to sort it out', said Matthews, sounding doubtful. We watched as the hearse carried away Charlotte's coffin. The hardest part was over, and I felt an enormous sense of relief. Charlotte had had the funeral she would have wanted. In the midst of this horror, we'd at least been able to do that for her.

It started to snow as we drove through the fields to Barley the next morning. As children we'd come here every Christmas. Charlotte had always insisted on taking a walk after lunch to put flowers on Daddy's grave. Now she was to be buried alongside him. Father Howard looked mediaeval as he intoned the funeral prayers, and all the time the snow kept falling.

'When our labours are done . . . our God for whom a thousand years are as the blink of an eye . . . we commit to the earth your servant Charlotte . . .'

It was a short ceremony. We got in the cars and drove back to Enfield.

Charlotte was dead, and over the next few weeks my own life began to unravel. I went back to work, but my thoughts went round in circles and I found it impossible to concentrate. Each reminder came as another sickening trauma, each day seemed harder than the one before. I had faced, and survived, a series of deeply traumatic shocks – but I'd not banked on this relentless stream of traumatic aftershocks. I knew that I was going under, and it terrified me. I gulped for air by talking endlessly to whoever would listen, going over and over the little that I knew about what had happened to Charlotte, trying to make some sense of it, trying to make it seem real.

I felt as if I had been catapulted into a world of extremes, both crueller and kinder than the one I'd lived in until a few weeks ago. We continued to draw comfort from the letters we received. They were the most moving letters I'd ever read – from the teacher who'd never forgotten the bright, forthright, teenage girl from his English class 14 years ago, the St John's Ambulance man for whom Charlotte had worked as a volunteer in Hammersmith. The college friend who'd lost touch after their undergrad days and always pictured Charlotte living happily with her then-boyfriend, Guy. Then there were the messages from complete strangers – a girl whose sister had been murdered in China less than a year before Charlotte, parents of other VSO volunteers, retired people who'd worked in Rwanda during the 1960s. People who'd read about what happened and decided to contact to us, for no other reason than to offer their good wishes and tell us how sorry they were. And yet at the same time as these small gestures of solidarity warmed my heart, they also shamed me. Would I ever have made the effort to write to a complete stranger and tell them how sorry I was about the loss that they had suffered?

Perhaps it was inevitable that some of the horror and disgust I felt in the aftermath of Charlotte's death should have been turned inward – or perhaps her death merely shocked me into realizing something I should have worked out many years before. I began to feel as if I had lived a very closeted life. At the same time as the cruelty and depravity of Charlotte's killers made me ashamed of my complacency about the world I lived in, the kindness of those who were showing us such compassion made me ashamed of my cynicism.

I'd seen little about Burundi in the international news since Charlotte's death, but an obscure website in Germany carried reports from the country almost every day. What I read there brought another small, sickening shock. The FNL had killed again, within days of killing Charlotte. On 9 January, the FNL had rampaged through one of the northern districts of Bujumbura, killing four civilians. Four more blackened, broken bodies, lips slightly parted, frozen in time. Four more tearful funerals, four more families grieving. Two months ago I could only have shrugged, unable to connect with the reality of it. Now it seemed sickeningly real. I thought again about the killer's words – *we're going to kill them all and there's nothing you can do*. I hated them more than ever. The fact that the group was continuing to attack civilians seemed to be the clearest possible proof that they were totally unrepentant. I had hoped that the international outrage over the 28 December attack might have made her killers think more carefully about doing the same thing again – and that this could, in some small sense, have brought good out of Charlotte's death. But that hope had been dashed. Somehow, this second attack seemed to make the Titanic Express – and by extension my sister's death, a little bit more *ordinary*. Charlotte's killing had changed nothing.

I dreamed that the news reports had got it wrong. Charlotte wasn't dead. She'd been seriously injured in the attack, but she'd *survived*. I was with her at the hospital. I was so relieved to see her that I cried. We still weren't sure if she was going to pull through – but at least I could *see* her. I told her how sorry I was that Richard had been killed, how sorry that she'd had to witness such a terrible thing, and my words seemed to comfort her. I asked her to tell me how it had happened. How many of them were there? Did they shoot the passengers together in a group, or one by one?

'There were three of them', she told me. 'Richard was the *second* person to die.'

But something wasn't right. It was as if my sister was speaking to me in riddles. As if there was something I'd forgotten – something important. I asked how long she had to wait before they shot her. I asked how long it was before she lost consciousness. And then I woke up, and then I remembered.

It was 27 January, and Charlotte had been dead one day short of a month. This was the first time I'd dreamed of her since we got the news. Richard had been the *second* person to die, Charlotte had told me. Had she been the first? I felt as if my sister had set me a test. I'd so badly wanted to know more about what had happened. I'd wondered if some part of her had survived death, and how I would know if it had. Now, in my dream, she had told me two very precise things about the attack that I could check. Charlotte, ever the scientist, had given me 'verifiable conditions'.

My comfortable agnosticism was teetering on the brink of collapse. It felt impossible to remain neutral any more. Mia's letter, the disturbing, prescient echoes there seemed to be in Charlotte's letters and emails, and now this dream, which felt like a direct challenge to me from my dead sister. *You want answers?* she seemed to be saying. *Go and find them.*

And yet at the same time I was terrified of becoming ridiculous. Emma was already treating me as if I had gone insane. She'd been trying, with increasing urgency and impatience, to persuade me to 'move on', but I found it impossible. The break-up, when it came, was messy and melodramatic, but it felt like a blessed relief.

A few days later, my friend Annarita, dealt a further blow to my teetering agnosticism. Though they'd never met, she too had dreamed that she'd seen Charlotte, walking in Kensington near the college campus, where I had spent so much time with my sister. 'She said that I should go and find you, that you were waiting for me. I was asking "Why don't you come too?" but she just kept smiling. Then when I woke up I realized why it was that she couldn't come with me.'

It was only many years later that Annarita told me that Charlotte had asked her not to 'go and find him', but to 'go and look after him'. And during these dark and difficult weeks, that was exactly what she did. As I became increasingly angry and obsessive, it was Annarita who called me every day to ask how things were going, patiently listening to my strange and surreal answers, reasoning with me where she could and humouring me when reason couldn't reach me.

Agnosticism was no longer a comfort. *Not knowing* now seemed like a kind of torture. I was haunted by the one dream I'd had in which Charlotte had spoken to me, and by the questions this dream seemed to raise. In trying to find answers to those questions, I wasn't simply looking for the truth about Charlotte's death, I was looking for a fundamental truth about life, the afterlife and my own mortality.

I waited in vain for more news from the police and the Foreign Office. The longer the silence continued, the angrier I became. How could I come to terms with what had happened if I didn't *know* what had happened? In desperation I turned to the Internet. I began to spend hours trawling through page after page of information about this distant country where Charlotte had died, looking for any scrap of information that might tell me more about how she had faced death, and what she had suffered. I forced myself to read and reread the news reports, trying to make sure that I'd understood everything, desperately looking for clues to substantiate the details Charlotte had told me in my dream. Was Richard the second person to die? How many of the ambushers had actually taken part in the killing of the passengers? But there were other questions too. As much as I needed to know what had happened during the attack, I felt an urgent need to understand *why* Charlotte had been killed and learn something more about the faceless killers who had taken her life.

In the evenings, I did little else but play games, creating and recreating orderly computer worlds amid the increasing chaos of my flat. During the day I spent hours frantically scouring the Internet. My colleagues pretended not to notice how little work I was doing. The more I was learning about this faraway country where Charlotte had been killed, the more it was drawing me in. Every new piece of information led to another website or article, each with some additional clue about the people who'd killed my sister and the motivations that had driven them to such brutality.

I discovered a report, from an organization called Human Rights Watch (HRW), entitled 'Neglecting justice in making peace'. I was amazed at the amount of information they had managed to find. I had pictured the FNL as a remote, faceless force, but this report, based on interviews with FNL deserters, gave a detailed account of the group's size, their methods, their command structure – and most vitally of all for me, the *names* of the people in charge.

The leader of the movement, Cossan Kabura, operates from outside the country. The local chief of operations is Agathon Rwasa. Albert Sibomana commands the Eagle (formerly Leopard) battalion which is divided into two companies, red and black, and which has operated most recently in the Isale region. Jean-Marie Hakizimana leads a second battalion deployed in the Mutambu-Kabezi area.

Reading these names was another small shock. I'd feared that the people responsible for Charlotte's death might forever remain anonymous and untraceable. But suddenly their names had been brought into sharp focus. Cossan Kabura, the man at the top. Agathon Rwasa, the Bujumbura chief of operations. And two battalion commanders – Albert Sibomana and Jean-Marie Hakizimana.

My anger was accompanied by a growing sense of defiance. Just sitting in my living room, taping away at my computer keyboard, in my increasingly untidy flat, I'd been able to learn something important about the people who had killed Charlotte. I no longer felt quite so powerless. *I knew their names.*

When I read these names again, I thought of other names – names I remembered hearing on the news as a teenager. Klaus Barbie, the Gestapo officer who'd been tracked down and prosecuted in France more than four decades after the end of the Second World War. John Demjanjuk, the former SS guard who stood trial in Israel in the late 1980s. Slobodan Milosevic, the Serbian leader indicted over war crimes in Kosovo was now a hunted man, unable to travel outside his home country. Milosevic died in captivity in March 2006.

The hope that we might one day see someone prosecuted for Charlotte's death suddenly seemed a little less desperate. If the Titanic Express massacre was a war crime, then couldn't some of these people be held accountable? If Agathon Rwasa was in overall charge of FNL operations around Bujumbura, then he must have command responsibility for the troops that killed Charlotte. Was it possible that one of these battalion commanders had actually taken part in the attack? According to this report, Sibomana's forces operated to the east of Bujumbura, and Hakizimana's to the south. All but one of the news reports had said that Charlotte's bus had been a few miles north-east of the city – Albert Sibomana's battalion was the likelier culprit. Although I had no way of knowing I had a strong feeling that this name had some connection with Charlotte's death. Could Sibomana have been the bragging killer who'd told one of the survivors to go and tell the authorities 'we're going to kill them all and there's nothing you can do'?

The atrocities listed in this single Human Rights Watch report alone seemed to be enough to put Agathon Rwasa and Albert Sibomana behind bars for a long time, whether or not we could link them to the Titanic Express attack. As I read through the report, I slowly began to realize that the massacre in which Charlotte died had been anything but a freak occurrence. It seemed as if ambushing buses, and killing the passengers, was one the FNL's main tactics. Hundreds of people had been killed in the last year alone. Human Rights Watch was accusing the FNL, and the larger rival group, Forces pour la défense de la démocratie (FDD), of conducting a 'war on civilians'.

When I'd read the first reports about the 28 December attack, I'd wondered if it might be part of some effort by deranged fanatics to trigger an ethnic bloodbath in Burundi. But looking at the dates in the news reports it was clear that the slaughter had already been going on for seven years by the time that Charlotte was killed. It had begun, in fact, six months before the Rwandan genocide. And in Burundi, it was a group of Tutsis who had started the violence by assassinating the country's first ever democratically elected Hutu President in October 1993.

One website showcased a documentary, 'Breaking the Codes' made by Bryan Rich an American film-maker, working with a Burundian journalist, Alexis Sinduhije. The aim of the film was 'to break the codes of silence and secrecy which surround ethnic violence, and to build a portrait of a war from the perspective of the perpetrators'. The website carried harrowing transcripts of young Burundians, both Hutu and Tutsi, who'd been sucked into Burundi's 'social and moral collapse' following the President's murder.

'Everything changed with the assassination of Ndadaye' said one young Tutsi from Bujumbura. 'Up country Hutus killed Tutsis and here in town we immediately woke up and thought they would kill us one by one'. A Hutu youth explained how he, in turn, had feared that the killing signalled the start of a genocide by the Tutsis against Hutus. The communities were polarized with shocking speed. Young people on both sides were encouraged to join armed militia to defend their communities – but this 'defence' more often than not involved attacking unarmed civilians.

'In time, any member of the other ethnic group was assumed to be a spy'. Longstanding friendships dissolved. One young Tutsi described how, after ambushing a bus carrying Hutus, he found, among the passengers, an old Hutu schoolfriend of his. 'Even you, Claude? Even you?' the friend asked. Claude spoke with wonder of the sound he heard, 'like a tyre deflating', as he pushed a knife into his old friend's stomach.

But while in Rwanda the atrocities had been very one-sided, in Burundi it seemed that the two sides had been more evenly matched. And while Rwanda's genocide had been far more intensive. Burundi's had carried on much longer. 'The death toll in Burundi continues to rise', an Amnesty International report had warned in 1996. 'Armed political groups are killing defenceless men, women and children without mercy and without fear of punishment. The lives and human rights of Burundi's people are being disregarded in a ferocious struggle for power.'

'When mass killing started, you never saw rich Hutu and Tutsi fighting each other', one young Tutsi, named only as Celestine, had told Breaking the Codes. 'The people fighting each other are poor Hutu and poor Tutsis. That is why I decided to tell the truth.' Burundi's politicians, he said, were the only people living in luxury in Burundi.

Naive as it may now sound, I found it shocking that the killings in Burundi had received so little international attention. Just the previous year, British forces had intervened in Sierra Leone to end the violence there. Even if there was no will for such an intervention in Burundi, I found it hard to understand why there was so little interest in setting up a mechanism that might at least deter the worst of the killings. When this Human Rights Watch report had been published, eight months before the attack in which Charlotte died, HRW had urged the creation of an international criminal tribunal for Burundi, but this call had been ignored. I found it impossible not to wonder if the Titanic Express attack might have been prevented if the international community had shown more interest in stopping the violence.

The HRW report had another disturbing detail. Documents seen by the group appeared to show that a formal cooperation agreement had been made between the FNL and elements of the militia who had carried out the Rwandan genocide, stating a 'common mission to liberate the "Bahutu" people'.

On 14 February, another five people were killed. This time it wasn't clear whether the attackers were members of the FNL or the FDD. If this continued, I knew that it wouldn't be long before this year's death toll began to exceed the 21 who had died in the Titanic Express massacre.

In addition to the psychological traumas that had followed Charlotte's death, I now felt a kind of moral trauma. I simply hadn't realized that this was the kind of world that I lived in. The latest estimates were that 200,000 people, 'mostly civilians', had been killed in Burundi since the war began. I tried to imagine what that number really meant. Two hundred thousand blackened, broken corpses, lips slightly parted, frozen in time – 200,000 dirty, bloody, terrifying killings. Burundi's dead could fill five Premiership stadiums – a lifeless, motionless man, woman, child or baby in every seat. I imagined Charlotte sitting there alongside them. This was on the same scale as Bosnia. Why had I known nothing about it?

In late February, DS Matthews called at my mother's house with an important piece of news. A survivor of the attack had come forward and spoken to a Reuters journalist who'd been doing some investigation on Matthews' behalf. The boy had confirmed that the killers were FNL rebels. They'd singled Charlotte out. 'You white people write bad things about us', they'd told her. Then she was shot. Charlotte had been the first person to die.

Matthews' news left me stunned. For some reason the knowledge that she had been singled out seemed to make it that little bit more personal. After all the effort she had made in Rwanda to be seen as something more than an anonymous body with an ethnic label, Charlotte had been killed just exactly because she was a *msungu*.

And yet at the same time this was an unexpected piece of progress. I'd feared that it would take years before anyone would have the courage to talk. Now it seemed as if we were ahead of the game. But I was desperate to know more. I asked Matthews if the boy had given any hint about when Richard had been killed. If Charlotte had been the first person to die, had he been killed next? I asked if he had any idea how many of the ambushers were directly involved in the killings.

But Matthews seemed taken aback that I was asking so many questions, and distinctly uncomfortable that I was writing down the answers he gave me.

It was time for us to be *realistic*, Matthews said. We were never going to find out much more about what happened that day. They do things differently in Africa. The Burundians weren't interested in carrying out any kind of investigation. The country didn't even have a functioning judicial system. Charlotte's killers were never going to be caught, or prosecuted.

We shouldn't expect any more survivors to come forward. What was in it for them anyway? Life is cheap over there, and these people are killing each other all the time. The most we should hope is that we might, one day, know the name of man who'd shot her – and probably only after he himself was dead. *Banditry* was rife in Burundi, and that had clearly been the motive for the attack.

Matthews looked blank when I asked him about the human rights reports, the pattern of other attacks on the same road, the FNL and their links with Rwanda's *genocidaires*. It was impossible to know what was really going on over there, or to explain it, Matthews insisted. 'We'll probably never know the real reason that they decided to kill Charlotte. You should stop looking for reasons', he told me. '*Sometimes there just isn't a reason.*'

My mother had been quiet during the meeting, almost dazed. For the last month we'd talked of little else but Charlotte's murder. Strong though she was, I could tell that this was hard for her. She was starting to seem very tired.It didn't seem to occur to her to question what Matthews was saying. But I was incensed. Why this sudden change of tone? As I thought and rethought what he had told us, I could smell again the sickly scented perfume from the morgue where we'd identified Charlotte's body.

They do things differently in Africa . . . These people are killing each other all the time . . .

Three weeks earlier, the Foreign Office had said that the massacre was 'probably' a war crime and Sands had proudly told us he'd never failed to clear up a murder. Now Matthews wanted to downgrade it to a case of 'banditry', and was telling us to give up all hope of ever getting justice. Why this sudden change of tone?

There was another unpleasant shock a few days later. The Foreign Office nervously admitted that the Diplomatic Note, with its offer of Metropolitan Police assistance, had never been delivered. This was due, they claimed, to problems in the Foreign Office email system. The mistake had gone unnoticed until I phoned them. The Foreign Office apologized for the delay, assured us they were looking into it but insisted that they were sure that it wouldn't have made any difference anyway.

It felt like another betrayal. Did they really think that it wouldn't matter if they hung around and did nothing for two months? The Foreign Office had made it clear that they would prefer us to stay away from the media, and we'd agreed to do so. Now that the story had disappeared from the headlines, Matthews was telling us that the British authorities were dropping their commitment to work for justice and decided to settle for nothing more than an explanation of what had happened. I began to wonder if this had been the intention from the outset.

I was so angry with the Foreign Office for their incompetence, with the police for their indifference, with Charlotte's smug, arrogant killers, angry with my stupid, dull job. Angry with my mother for not being more angry with the police, angry with myself for being angry with my mother. I spent hours scouring the Internet, and agonizing over whether or not to go to the media again. I wrote letters to my

MP, and badgered friends and family to do the same. I spent further hours composing angry emails to the Foreign Office, demanding to know if they still had any intention of pursuing Charlotte's case. The response was a resounding silence.

I don't doubt, now, that DS Matthews had been spelling things out to us as honestly as he could. Perhaps it's not surprising that he was so sceptical of the idea that anyone could have found so much information about an obscure Burundian rebel group from the comfort of their own living room. Certainly the Internet seemed to be an alien world to Matthews, as it still was to so many at the time. But I (even now) find it very hard to understand why the police tone had changed so much in those few weeks.

In late February, the FNL rebels got themselves back into the headlines, launching their biggest attack on Bujumbura for five years. After infiltrating the Hutu district of Kinama, FNL fighters attacked and overwhelmed six army posts simultaneously. Eyewitnesses reported hearing drums, whistles and religious songs as hundreds more troops poured down from the hills. The group's new-found belligerence had followed a change of leadership, according to their spokesman, Anicet Ntawuhiganayo.

Cossan Kabura, the FNL leader, whose name I'd found in the Human Rights Watch report just a couple of weeks ago, had been sacked for taking part in peace talks and replaced by another commander who'd been named in the report – Agathon Rwasa. The Kinama operation had been launched the next day. Ntawuhiganayo declared that they were now days away from sweeping into the city centre and winning the war. Aid agencies were evacuating non-essential staff.

I lost all remaining interest in my job. If the rebels were about to win, we could forget any hope of seeing Charlotte's killers prosecuted. For days I was engrossed, reading every scrap of news I could find about this battle going on thousands of miles away on the streets of Bujumbura. The Burundian army was fighting back hard, and inflicting heavy casualties. The FNL were besieged and on the defensive. They were continuing to hold out, but it was clear now that they had no chance of advancing any further. Dozens of FNL troops were reported dead. I wondered, with an odd sense of detachment, whether Charlotte's killers were among them.

If my mother was finding it difficult to talk about Charlotte's death, for Catherine it was literally unthinkable. For her, this had been an irredeemable loss. She would rather remember the life that Charlotte had lived than devote any thought to those who ended it. By focusing on the last terrible moments of Charlotte's life, she felt that we were merely compounding our own grief.

Catherine and I had always been close. Often I'd found it easier to get along with her than with my hot-tempered, older sister. But our reactions to Charlotte's death seemed now to be diametrically opposed. For Catherine, the question of who had killed our sister seemed almost irrelevant. All that mattered was that she had gone. And yet I found it impossible to get away from the fact that Charlotte was gone not through an accident or an illness, but because someone, somewhere, had chosen to take her from us. Worse still, the people whose job it was to do something about Charlotte's death seemed to want the whole matter to die quietly on a dusty road somewhere.

I was in a mess, and I knew it, and I didn't care. I would talk endlessly about Burundi to anyone who showed the slightest interest. At work, my colleagues would listen patiently, then gently move the subject back to our system testing. Outside of work, my little sister found it impossible to talk to me, my friendships were becoming one-dimensional and I'd seen my ex-girlfriend 'one-last-time' quite a few times now. Four weeks after returning to my job I realized that I'd barely turned out a day's worth of work. I took unpaid leave, asked to go part-time and started looking for a bereavement counsellor.

The condolence cards kept coming, along with contributions to the charity fund that we'd set up in Charlotte's memory. A note in the *Guardian* had led to a stream of donations from complete strangers. Within a few weeks we'd raised more than £2,000. Michael Palin agreed to be patron of the fund. VSO's head of fundraising, Dick Bird, agreed to be a trustee.

The violence in Bujumbura continued. There were more reports of civilian atrocities. One account suggested that the Rwandan government had been forced to intervene, covertly, to help keep the FNL at bay. The insurgents were eventually beaten back in mid-March, retreating to their strongholds in the hills above Bujumbura. After they had gone, 200 bodies were discovered in mass graves. There was barely a whisper about it on the news. The Foreign Office had finally delivered their Diplomatic Note just two days before the escalation of the war. The Burundians didn't even bother to answer.

With no commitments and no work for the time being, I was free to immerse myself in the safe, simple world of computer games. Life here was straightforward, like solving a puzzle. You follow a simple set of rules, over and over again, honing your skills and developing new tricks to help you to win. When you've won ten times you look for cleaner, neater, more elegant ways of winning. And when you win, you know you've won – they spell it out in big letters on the screen. Everything was so clear, so easy, and I knew what to do.

I knew that I was being self-indulgent, and wasting my time, but I had an excuse now. Charlotte was dead, my local bereavement service wasn't getting back to me and the wait seemed intolerable. For a couple of weeks I didn't think about work any more. I didn't think much about Burundi, the memorial fund, the Foreign Office or the FNL. I still thought about Charlotte, of course. But mostly I thought about games, and how to win them. I would play late into the night. When daylight woke me the next morning I would jump out of bed, walk to the dining room and turn on my computer. I would boil the kettle while the machine was warming up and eat breakfast at my desk. I washed clothes and dishes, went shopping and put out the rubbish from time to time. Everything else went to seed. The phone was an annoyance, so I stopped answering it. Now that I was at home all day, I realized how many door-to-door salesmen there were in the area. I stopped answering the door. I stopped shaving.

The bereavement centre made contact in the end, and I was allocated a counsellor. It was a huge relief. At last I could talk freely about Charlotte's death without feeling that I was forcing it on anyone. I left our first session on a high, feeling an immense sense of relief – and went home to play more computer games. My new reality seemed far more absorbing and comfortable than the drab, chilly outside world. Bad things still happened here, of course – but they didn't happen to me. In 'Age of Empires', massacring civilians was a winning tactic. I would watch enthralled as my computer-soldiers hacked to death the computer-enemy's farmers, priests, builders and miners. Of course this was just a game. The people I was killing, and their anguished cries, were nothing more than ones and zeroes arranged in a particular way. And yet I couldn't help wondering if the

FNL's commanders viewed their real-life activities with the same detachment.

> On 5 June, six people were reportedly killed in an ambush on the RN9 road, around 10km north of Bujumbura . . . On 3 August, three decapitated heads were placed on the RN9 following fighting between the FNL and armed forces . . . On 29 December, passengers on the Kigali–Bujumbura bus were forced off the bus at Mageyo some 15km from Bujumbura by members of an armed group, believed to be the FNL . . . Others killed included Charlotte Wilson, a British aid worker in Rwanda, Audace Ndayisaba, Richard Notereyimana, Aline Nzeyimana, Ibrahima, Innocent, Florence Hagatura and Nzeyimana. The FNL have denied responsibility for the attack . . .

Amnesty International released a new report in March. They'd got the date of the attack wrong, which annoyed me, but the misspelling of Richard's name was my fault – they'd used the erroneous version I'd given to the *Guardian* in January. The report listed yet more FNL atrocities, as well as abuses by another, larger rebel group, CNDD-FDD. But what stood out most was that, according to Amnesty, the Burundian government's Tutsi-dominated army had been killing at least as many people as the Hutu rebels:

> Between 25 and 28 June 2000 at least 44 unarmed civilians were extrajudicially executed – mostly apparently by bayonet . . . Between 17 and 19 August 2000 . . . at least 30 unarmed civilians were extrajudicially executed . . . children were among the dead and wounded . . . 65 civilians were killed . . .

The list seemed endless, a dizzying roster of deaths and death tolls in towns, cities and remote hill-top villages. There was the occasional name, or particularly gruesome detail:

> The bodies of two women and their children, still tied to their backs, were seen in Gasenyi district. All had been bayoneted to death. A 14-year-old girl, Francine, was amongst those killed . . .

And yet

> the few examples of human rights abuses given in this section of the report reflect only a minority of the abuses which have occurred . . .

I dropped a line to the police to let them know that Charlotte's murder had been mentioned in an Amnesty report. I had a call back from Jo Baxter; 'What's this about an amnesty?' I told her that it was an Amnesty International report, not an amnesty – perhaps the police should get in touch with them? She said that she'd pass the message on. I heard nothing more about it.

I couldn't stay away from my job for ever, and after a month of unpaid leave I tidied myself up and made a second attempt at returning to work. I would now be working four days a week, for a completely different team. I tried my best to concentrate on my job, and having a change of scene helped. But it still seemed impossible to look at my work in the same way. I settled into an uneasy, guilt-ridden routine.

— 6 —

Richard Ndereyimana came from a poor, though well-connected, family. His father died when he was two years old and his childhood was spent with his extended family in a small village in the south of Burundi.

Although a good student, problems of ethnicity hindered his education. Richard was of mixed race and, because of this, was forced to leave his secondary school and complete his education elsewhere, going on to study African Languages at the University of Bujumbura . . . It was here that he became particularly interested in the Burundian drums. He and his fellow students formed what proved to be a very successful troupe, which even had a world tour, although Richard himself thought it better to stay behind and concentrate on his studies. His hard work paid off though and in 1995 he graduated with distinction.

Afterwards, he worked as a teacher and also as a journalist . . . However, because of his political views and, again, because of racial issues, the situation in Burundi became increasingly dangerous for him. He was often threatened, sometimes physically, and when he arrived home to find an envelope with a bullet inside it, he decided that it was time to go.

He came to Rwanda in 1997 with the Dominican Brotherhood. Richard was always a strong believer and the Dominicans seemed to offer him many opportunities to help the poor and needy and perhaps provide some personal security as well. However, it soon became clear that such a life wasn't for him. He was criticised and regarded with suspicion by many in the Brotherhood for what was considered to be inappropriate behaviour, such as reading The Koran, swimming in public and talking to girls . . .

In 1999, Richard left the Dominicans and became a second-ary school teacher. His specialised subjects were Philosophy and French, though he also taught English and Political Education. While it is true to say that the authorities never liked him, his students certainly did not feel the same. For all his talents, and he had many, it was teaching that he was best at. He knew the problems his students faced and was always encouraging and sympathetic. One would often find students in his house, and Richard with them, patiently correcting their French or teasing them into English.

He was a man of great quality. He had an incredible physical presence and an unmistakable natural authority. On one occasion, when the Burundian President, Pierre Buyoya, came to give a speech at the university, Richard raised his hand and with a great deal of nerve, said: 'Your Excellency, you are the president of the people. You are like a teacher to us. Now isn't a teacher supposed to love his students and lead them by example? If that is the case, why don't you do the same?' Buyoya's reply was simple enough, 'Say that again and I'll arrest you myself'.

I was in his room the other day and I came across some quo-tations he'd copied down into a book. The first one read: 'One cannot kill ideas with bullets and bombs'. That's Richard for you – acutely aware of the injustices of this world, yet so passionate in his belief that one can transcend them.

Of course, he had been through so much before any of us met him, but he never let it get him down. He was a sociable man. Friends were important to him and he made them easily. Of all the people he met while I was with him, Charlotte was closest in spirit. It was like that from the beginning. And they did make a good couple, equally strong-willed and complex. When I first knew Richard, he told me that his heart was like a stone, that he had forgotten how to love. Of course, meeting Charlotte changed all that. For him, it was like first love. And small comfort that against the loss of him, I know that he was very happy, as though he'd suddenly found a new world. I think Charlotte felt the same.

In April, the staff of VSO Rwanda sent us a book of photos and letters, together with a piece written by Richard's friend Ben Pollitt, another VSO volunteer. At the front of the book was a picture of Charlotte and Richard, taken at Christmas 2000. She was grinning away from behind a pair of sunglasses. He looked smarter and more poised than he had done in the other pictures I'd seen. I found it eerie to think that this was just three days before they were killed.

Learning more about Richard's life made me all the more sad not to have known him – and also more intrigued. I wondered how his family were coping now, what they were thinking and feeling. It seemed extraordinary to think that this other family, thousands of miles away, was at this same moment going through the same traumatic grieving as we were. Was Richard their first violent loss or one of many? Did it get easier? I wondered if we would ever find them, and whether they would want to be in contact with us. I wondered if they felt the same need for justice as I did.

One cannot kill ideas with bullets and bombs. The fact of this message seemed itself to be the proof of it. Richard was dead, but his words lived on. The half-remembered quote that he had written in his notebook a few days before he was killed had been picked up by his friend Ben and relayed to us.

And there seemed to be another, deeper interpretation of these words – the assertion of a philosophy with its origins in Ancient Greece. One cannot kill ideas, because ideas are immortal – they exist independently of any human mind. Even if Charlotte's killers were able to deny and destroy all evidence of their involvement in war crimes, even if they managed to silence all those who accused them, and even if the rest of the world continued to turn a blind eye, the Titanic Express massacre was still a crime, and the FNL were still responsible for it. The truth about these 21 deaths was more than just a matter of opinion.

I looked again at the few lines that Richard had written to me in the last email I ever got from Charlotte. 'Sois fort dans ton travail', he'd said. 'Be strong in your work'. And as I looked at these words I began to feel the odd, irrational conviction that *the other Richard* was reaching out to me from some timeless place.

At the end of March my mother had been contacted via VSO by Rory Beaumont, an NGO worker based in London, who regularly visited

Burundi. He'd told my mother how moved he'd been by our letter to the *Guardian*, and that he was keen to do what he could to help. A Burundian human rights group, Ligue Iteka, was so concerned about the lack of an investigation that they'd decided to look into the massacre as a 'case study in impunity'. Human Rights Watch, who had a permanent office in Burundi, were also investigating. Rory had met one of their researchers earlier in the month, and she had asked him to let us know that they'd found and interviewed several more of the survivors.

The letter we'd written, just days after Charlotte's death had only been a small firework flare in the darkness, but someone had seen it. I was heartened to know that Rory Beaumont had gone out of his way to get in touch. I hadn't been aware that British NGO workers even operated in Burundi, let alone that there might be one who was willing to help us.

The police had doubted that any more witnesses would ever come forward, but now several more had been found. It felt like another small victory. We were one step closer to knowing the truth, and this in turn gave me renewed hope that we might one day see justice. The more we could learn from the Titanic Express survivors now, while memories were still fresh, the greater the chance would be, one day, of a successful prosecution.

We received another letter from the Foreign Office. The situation in Burundi was still grave, they told us – 'the army is struggling to keep control'. The Burundians still hadn't given any response to the Diplomatic Note – or the offer of help from our police. The British Embassy in Rwanda had sent their political officer into Burundi in March, to find out what progress had made. It had been too dangerous to go into Bujumbura, but he'd visited one of the northern provinces, where the governor had told him it was 'highly unlikely that anyone would be arrested'.

I felt deeply distrustful of the Burundian government's intransigence. Although the FNL still seemed to be the likeliest culprits for the Titanic Express massacre, the rebels' claim that government forces had carried out the attack no longer seemed quite so incredible. Each week, I was finding more accounts of gruesome massacres by President Buyoya's Tutsi-dominated army. Most disturbing of all, I'd seen a number of reports of government soldiers robbing and killing civilians, then pinning the blame on the rebels.

I wrote an email to Rory Beaumont, asking what he thought the rationale behind the Titanic Express attack had been, and about the FNL's claim that it was carried out by the Burundian army. Rory emailed back the same day.

There is I suppose a very slight chance that a rogue bunch of soldiers decided to rob the bus but I think that would have already become clear. No, all my instincts say it was a rebel group, to loot and frighten people in Buj and show rebel 'strength' at a critical time – there have been ongoing negotiations in Arusha as you probably know to make some peace deal for the country. The rebel fighters had not been allowed to take part and perhaps this was yet another ghastly way of making their presence felt . . .

It is widely believed that the fighting North of Buj is led by the FNL. I am 100% sure that it is, from my own sources. Therefore it is most likely that the attack was carried out by the FNL and not, say, FDD . . .

I suppose that the FNL denied the killing because there can be no possible excuse for it. No suggestion that the bus was carrying soldiers or arms for the army or anything of that sort. It is clearly an appalling murder of innocent civilians so not something you'd like to admit doing. Perhaps too the order did not come from the top. So while they may have intended to frighten people . . . maybe the public outrage in Buj and elsewhere silenced them . . .

It was the first time I'd had any clear suggestion of *why* the FNL might have carried out the attack – and it made me even angrier. Had Charlotte been killed just so that these people could show their 'strength'? Were these people big and tough enough to kill a busload of unarmed civilians but not to own up to it? I was reminded again of the Rwandan Mayor Sylvestre Gacumbitsi, and his nod-and-wink denial of any involvement in the 1994 genocide. What he'd really meant was 'you can't prove it'.

I found it harder and harder to concentrate on my work. Even as the Foreign Office and police continued to dampen our hopes, the leads that I was discovering seemed to be multiplying exponentially. On another obscure Burundi news website I found a sternly worded press release from Cossan Kabura, denying that he'd been ousted as FNL leader, and announcing 'disciplinary sanctions' against 'Mr. Rwasa Agathon together with Mr. Alain Mugabarabona and Mr. Anicet Ntawuhiganayo'. Kabura gave a series of contact telephone numbers at the top of his press release, along with an email address: Kabeberi@planet.nl. Was this a joke? It hadn't occurred to me that the man who'd been in overall charge of the group believed to have killed Charlotte, on the day that they killed her, might have an email address. But most intriguing of all, Kabura's mobile, telephone and fax numbers were prefixed with 0031 – the country code for the Netherlands.

It seemed almost too good to be true. What would an ousted FNL leader be doing in Holland? And if he really was there, shouldn't somebody be trying to arrest him? I was starting to feel like a child watching a pantomime. *He's in the Neth-er-lands!* I emailed the Foreign Office to tell them about Kabura, but got no reply.

Rereading Kabura's words, I found something vaguely comical about them. This man, who had once commanded one of Africa's fiercest rebel groups, been courted by Nelson Mandela and held press conferences in front of the international media, was now cooped up in some Eindhoven bedsit, trying to press-release his way back into control of the movement that had left him behind.

But laughable though he seemed, this was still the man who had led the FNL for nine years, during which time they'd killed many more than the 21 who died in the Titanic Express massacre. This was the man who in July 1999 had put out a statement ordering 'all foreigners' to leave Burundi, saying that his forces 'would not be responsible for any incident' that happened to them.

As the days passed, and I continued to hear nothing from the Foreign Office, my rage and frustration intensified even further. I began to wonder how long it would take to find someone in London who'd be willing, for a price, to go to the Netherlands and give us a more swift and irreversible form of restitution. I had an old friend who might have some connections. I hadn't seen him since he went down for assault a few years ago, but I was sure that he'd be sympathetic. The more I thought about this idea, the more I liked it. Sure, it would have been better to see Kabura face justice in a courtroom – but it didn't seem likely that we would be given that option. Kabura had no shortage of enemies, and there would be no particular reason to suspect me. If I was ever asked I could simply deny all knowledge, just as the FNL always did when they killed people; there was a nice symmetry to it. He'd never know what hit him, or why.

Or perhaps I'd *want* him to know what hit him. Perhaps I'd want him to know why. Maybe I could give them a photograph to wave in his face just before they did it. Just so he would know. 'This is for Charlotte', they could say. Then they'd make him lie face down on the ground and shoot him seven times in the back . . .

Was it *me* that just thought that? I was shocked by the sudden realization that I was musing over how I'd go about committing murder. But there was no getting away from it. I wanted Kabura dead, and if someone had told me that they'd killed him, I would have thanked them for it.

Yet would this really be justice? I remembered once, long ago, hearing the father of a murder victim on the radio, his voice strained, his pain all too obvious. He was angrily demanding the reintroduction of hanging, so that the sad loner who'd killed his daughter could be strangled to death on the end of a piece of rope. And it had seemed tragic to me. I couldn't help feeling that he was demeaning himself – that the murderer had also managed to kill a small part of this anguished, heartbroken father's humanity. I had wondered how I would feel if I were in his place, and I'd hoped that I would have been able to retain a little more dignity.

Strangely, while I found myself fixated with the notion of having Kabura 'taken out', Hollywood style, I still felt appalled by the idea of his being sentenced to death in a court and executed. But what was the difference?

At the end of April, I became enthralled with another news story. Under a new law which allowed the exercise of 'universal jurisdiction', four Rwandans had gone on trial in Belgium, charged with involvement in the 1994 genocide. Consolata Mukangango was accused of providing petrol to burn down a building where Tutsis were sheltering. Julienne Mukabutera had allegedly forced hundreds of others to leave the convent where they'd been hiding, knowing that they would all be massacred. Alphonse Higanaro, a former government minister, was charged with incitement. Only one of the defendants, Vincent Ntezimana, was accused of participating in the killings directly.

The trial raised eyebrows, not only because two of the defendants were Roman Catholic nuns, but also because it was the first time any country had exercised universal jurisdiction for such crimes. An Amnesty report urged other countries to follow Belgium's lead. I quickly became obsessed with the case. I'd had no idea that it was even possible for a national court to prosecute such crimes in this way, and I immediately set about thinking how we might use this to get justice for Charlotte. Could the Belgian system be a way around the Burundians' apparent lack of interest in prosecuting Charlotte's killers? Could we use it to go after Cossan Kabura?

We had another visit from DS Matthews soon after Easter. He seemed rather proud of himself. 'We've found some more eyewitnesses', he told us, meaning that Human Rights Watch had found some more eyewitnesses. But he did have some additional news. Another witness had come forward and spoken to the British Ambassador to Rwanda. The police were no longer sure whether Charlotte had been killed first or later, lying together with all the others. One witness said that he'd got a good look at the man who'd killed Charlotte – but they weren't sure if they could believe him, Matthews said, because 'he told one thing to Human Rights Watch and something else to the Ambassador'. Beyond this, Matthews refused to be drawn.

Maria Eismont, the Russian Reuters journalist who'd been helping the police gather information about the attack, had been in London recently, and Matthews had met up with her. She sounded like a flamboyant character, and he seemed to have been a little taken with her. Maria had made no effort to disguise her contempt for the FNL. A few weeks before Charlotte's death, she'd covered the group's failed attempt to shoot down a Belgian airliner with a surface-to-air missile. She'd been disgusted by their incompetence. 'How could they have missed a *fucking jumbo jet*?! In Chechnya, they'd have done the job properly.'

I told Matthews about the press release I'd found from Cossan Kabura, the ex-FNL leader who appeared to have been staying in the Netherlands. Surely this was worth looking into? Matthews didn't think so. 'We want the shooter', he kept insisting. He wasn't interested in leaders – just the man who'd fired the gun that killed Charlotte. He still seemed fixated on the idea that this was a case of 'banditry'.

The meeting left me feeling bewildered and frustrated. The more I read about the FNL, and Burundi, the less interested I was in 'shooters'. The FNL's foot soldiers were only pawns in the game. Hundreds had been killed in February's failed attack on Kinama, and dozens more since. For all I knew, the 'shooter' who'd killed my sister might already be dead. It was the ringleaders I wanted to see held to account – and how much higher could you go than Kabura, who'd led the entire organization on the day that the attack took place?

Matthews was giving very little away, and the Foreign Office seemed to have stopped replying to my emails entirely. In my angrier moments I wondered if he was being so secretive because there was something to hide. Why was it so important to him to stop me from asking my own questions about my sister's death? I felt as if it was now time to stop being nice about it, and attack the Foreign Office and police as publicly and vociferously as we could. But I was so angry now that I found it hard to trust my own judgement. My uncle cautioned me to 'keep my powder dry'. There was no point putting people's backs up if it wasn't going to achieve anything. Rather than trying to take them on in a straight fight I should do my best to find a way around them.

Rory Beaumont's office was only a few tube stops away from where I worked. I went to meet him the day before he was due to fly out to Bujumbura. A cheerful, animated soul, his office was reassuringly untidy, with piles of paper dotted around the room. On the wall, somewhat incongruously, was a picture of Major Pierre Buyoya, the Burundian President, in full dress uniform. Rory offered me his sympathies. Although he didn't yet have any more details on the attack, he'd been up and visited the spot where Charlotte had been killed. Of course there was no trace of the massacre now. It was a peaceful place, just a simple bend in the road, up in the hills of Bujumbura-Rurale.

Human Rights Watch would soon be passing on the eyewitness details to our police, Rory said. Having them on our side was a big asset. He'd worked with 'the redoubtable Alison Des Forges', now HRW's senior Africa researcher, shortly after the Rwandan genocide in 1994, going through the grim task of counting corpses.

Rwanda and Burundi were like fraternal twins, Rory told me, similar in blood but very different in character. While the general consensus was that Rwanda's problems were resolved, and Burundi was the dysfunctional trouble spot, Rory believed that Burundi was far healthier. The country's Byzantine coalition government was a long way short of perfect, but Rory believed that Rwanda's authoritarian dictatorship would be far more disastrous in the long term. Things were stable in Rwanda now, but for how long?

I asked Rory if he could find out anything more about Richard's family. I gave him a copy of the piece that Ben Pollitt had written about Richard Ndereyimana, and a letter for the family that my mother had written in French. I also asked him to pass on a note with my email address. Rory gave me a handful of news articles to read, and promised to do what he could.

My mind was racing as I took the tube back up to Warren Street. Rory seemed to know far more about Burundi and the wider region than anyone we'd spoken to in the Foreign Office, whose official line was that no one should travel there under any circumstances. And he hadn't just travelled there – he'd visited the spot where Charlotte had died. He shrugged when I'd asked him about the risks: 'If people like us didn't go, then no one outside Burundi would know what was happening there', he told me. I had mixed feelings about accepting Rory's help – how could I be sure that his doing us a favour might not lead him to take one risk too many? And yet I knew that if we were going to find a way around our information 'gatekeepers', we would need him.

I was astounded by Rory's optimism about Burundi – despite all the horrors that had gone on there, he actually seemed quite hopeful about the long-term prospects – but I was even more than surprised by what he had said about Rwanda. Wasn't this new government made up of the same people who'd liberated Rwanda from genocide in 1994? Surely they were heroes, not dictators?

According to the report Rory had given me, Rwanda's 'heroes' were using their occupation of the former Zaire – now renamed the Democratic Republic of Congo (DRC) – as an opportunity to enrich themselves. The second invasion of the Congo had begun in 1998, ostensibly with the aim of tracking down the remnants of the Rwandan Hutu-extremist militia who had fled there after the 1994 genocide. But the war had coincided with a massive upsurge in global demand for coltan, a mineral used in the production of mobile phones. The DRC was one of the few places in the world that it could be found, and the price was now five times as high as it had been at the start of the conflict. Both sides were making big money from coltan, and this money was fuelling the war. Alongside

Uganda and Rwanda, Burundian forces had also been involved, while Zimbabwe, Namibia and Angola had intervened on the side of the Congolese. The region had been flooded with guns and ammunition, and the conflict had devastated the Congolese infrastructure. According to the report, 1.7 *million* people had died as a result.

A report earlier in the month by a UN panel of experts had listed dozens of international companies, many of them European, believed to be profiting illegally from the war. It seemed as if Charlotte's death had taken place on the fringes of a much, much bigger conflict.

Until now I'd only been dimly aware of the anti-globalization movement, but suddenly it was coming into much sharper focus. If ever there was a globalization issue, surely this was it. Alongside coltan and diamonds, the Congo was a rich source of gold, copper, cobalt, tin and tropical timber. These too were being looted for profit by the various warring groups. Despite an international embargo, unscrupulous traders had been trafficking weapons into the Congo and buying up the goods coming out at bargain prices.

On 1 May, thousands of anti-globalization demonstrators marched through London, protesting about a range of issues from the greenhouse effect to the exploitation of developing countries by Western businesses. In the build-up to the protest, the British media had been largely hostile. Conservative critics characterized the demonstrators either as nihilistic 'rebels without a cause', or naive idealists who didn't understand how the world really worked. Veteran left-wingers sagely cautioned against the danger of protesting about too many things at once. Others claimed simply not to understand what the fuss was about.

News coverage the following day focused mainly on the fact that several dozen demonstrators had clashed with police towards the end of the protest, and then decided to attack the John Lewis department store. A more lengthy piece in *The Times* set out to debunk the anti-globalization 'myths', listing the many benefits globalization had brought to the world, decrying the dangers of 'over-regulation' and concluding that 'with a few mainly African exceptions' the benefits of free trade had been undeniable.

I couldn't help feeling that *The Times* might have been missing the point – the point being those 1.7 million Congolese 'African exceptions' for whom globalization had been anything but beneficial. These people hadn't died because of over-regulation – they'd died, in part, because the rules on war-zone profiteering were being disregarded.

What shocked me yet further was that the British media seemed to have taken a collective decision to ignore the Congo war almost completely. The one article I found that even mentioned it, on the pages of *Metro*, highlighted its effect on the gorilla population but said nothing about the millions of human beings who'd been killed.

A couple of weeks after the May Day protests, I got home to find an email from Rory Beaumont. He'd found Richard's family.

This is a small town. I asked our driver (an ex-university student) if by chance he knew Richard. He did. Not only that, he then says his brother-in-law is Richard's mother's nephew. (Work that one out!) So yesterday he took me to meet the family. At the house, in a distant and modest part of town, there were five family members plus a number of young children wandering in and out. Richard's mother is a lovely and venerable old lady who speaks no French, so we translated back and forth into Kirundi. Her name is Catherine. She told me that she prays for Charlotte and is sure that Richard and she are together in heaven.

Also there were Richard's two brothers, Jean-Bosco and Paul, and sister, Adrienne, all fluent French speakers. Pascal, the mother's nephew came too. He's a lawyer.

It was an emotional meeting. I think they were all very touched that your family wanted to contact them. I handed over the letter and also left a copy of the appreciation by Ben Pollitt, which I found really well done. This Richard sounds quite a character!

We sat and talked for 45 minutes or so (only because I had another appointment to keep). Jean-Bosco told me that he's been trying to contact your family and had asked some English chap he met to find you but hadn't heard back. He said he'll give me a message for you before I leave – he also asked for your email. (I'm sure he doesn't have email but he may try to get access.) Jean-Bosco is the elder brother and the person most likely to contact you, I think. I liked him. Actually I liked them all . . .

It seemed like another extraordinary coincidence. VSO had tried without success to track down Richard's family for us. What were the chances that Rory's driver would know them? I wondered, again, if the hand of providence might have played a part. Two days later the Russian, Reuters journalist Maria Eismont got in touch, promising to 'do all my best to help find out as much as possible'. She was true to her word. Arriving home the following week, I turned on my computer to find the email I'd been waiting for since Charlotte was killed.

Dear Mr Wilson, my name is Pierre Nzeyimana and I am a survivor of the TITANIC EXPRESS massacre 28/12/00. It is Miss MARIA EISMONT who gave me your email address.

As I stared at the words on the screen I felt a strange mixture of fascination and dread. Charlotte was dead, and this was an email from someone who had been with her when she died, someone who had lived through what she had experienced. More than anything, I'd wanted – needed – an explanation of what had gone on that day, something more than the jealously-guarded fragments of information that the police had been feeding us. But now it seemed I was so close to having it, was I really ready? What if there was something else, something the police had decided was just too horrible to tell us?

—— 7 ——

For our ambush, it was well lucid that it was a prepared stroke, because they were very numerous, very armed and they carried of the military uniforms all. I am going to tell you a little that is that happened for your dear soeur and his/her/its engaged Richard even though it is not easy for me, every time that I remember of our accident, I feel not well I believe that you understand me Mr Wilson, it was unhappy.

One had left Kigali without problem, one didn't fear anything. One passed the borders well without no danger, one also arrived in a dangerous place there one didn't fear anything and suddenly we are tomb in the ambush of the rebels.

They have fusilli our Bus of face, of side they were nearly everywhere in all the corners, our Bus skidded and bent on a mountain. They are approached of us, they terrorized us, they took all this us had, money, jewelries, telephones and our luggages also.

After them said us to get off the Bus and to lie down on the road and again it rained a lot. Then they said to your dear sister to give money since she didn't understand Kirundi, Richard said that she gave everything and that she remains him anything. One said Charlotte = EO that it is the blank spaces in a document that provide the weapons in Africa again it is necessary that she feels how that makes all badly that one said it in Kirundi, her, consisted of nothing.

Pierre's account made eerie reading, all the more so because he'd translated it into English using a computer program. What did they mean by '*the blank spaces in a document* that provide the weapons in Africa'? Was it some strange French idiom literally translated? Or had the translation program put the 'blank spaces in a document' there in place of some untranslatable word? It is the ____ that provide the weapons in Africa . . . it is necessary that she feels how that makes all badly.

I had a grim feeling that the missing words were 'white people'. I couldn't think of anything else that would make sense. We'd been haunted by the idea that Charlotte might have been killed with bullets manufactured in Britain, but this seemed even worse. Had Charlotte been killed, in part, as 'revenge' for the role played by international arms dealers in fuelling wars in Africa?

After the time flowed he believed that any moment he/it can have an intervention there, but no one was there to help us whereas it was not far from the military positions that that us =EO to astonish, =EO 100m had to have some soldiers nearly there of the ambush but no one came to save us.

Then they didn't especially remove also us our dresses the boys all. We were stretched out in the street and they pulled a lot of strokes of fires point-blank, there is what died there and of others that are survived, Richard and Charlotte died instantaneously. It is sad . . .

And that was it – no more nasty surprises. The attackers were all wearing uniforms. There were a lot of them. They'd ambushed the bus, and fired at it from all sides. They'd forced the passengers out, then made them wait while the stricken vehicle was looted. Because Charlotte was white, they'd singled her out and harangued her in Kirundi. The passengers had hoped against hope that the army would intervene to save them, but no help came. The rebels had forced the passengers to undress, stolen their clothes, forced them to lie on the ground and shot them. *Richard and Charlotte died instantaneously* – they had been killed together. Pierre was one of the lucky few who survived.

I have been touched by three bullets in the back, two passed without a lot of problem but there a that penetrated until the stomach in the gut. God thank you made one operation and that very past.

One evacuated us toward one hospital that is inside Burundi but the cadavers spent the night on the scene of the crime until the morning . . .

Although there were still many questions in my mind, I decided not to press Pierre to tell me anything more; he'd already said that it made him feel ill to have to remember. At last I had an outline of what had happened in the last moments of Charlotte's life, from someone who had been with her when she died. Pierre had felt the same terror as she did when the bus was raked with gunfire. Pierre had feared for his life, as she must have done, when the attackers dragged them out into the rain. Pierre been forced to wait, and wait, desperately hoping for some kind of intervention, while the killers looted the bus. Pierre had been made to lie face down on the ground. Pierre had been shot in the back. Pierre had experienced what Charlotte had experienced, right up until the last moment. She had died, he had survived. That was the only difference. What he and Charlotte and the others had been through was horrific, but it could have been worse. Pierre was OK.

And I suddenly had a feeling that Charlotte, and Richard, wherever they were, were OK too. I had thought about Charlotte's last moments every day for the last four months. But however much I was forced to relive her experience, however much it haunted me, for her it had only happened once. It was over now, past tense.

I wrote back to Pierre in my basic French, and he replied again the next day. He told me more about the injuries he'd sustained during the massacre, for which he'd had to seek treatment abroad.

'But what hurts me the most', he said, 'is that no investigation has been carried out.'

For some reason Pierre's words surprised me. So many people over the last few months had assured me, sagely, that Africans didn't think about justice in the same way that we do. Had I started to believe them?

I met up with Rory again on 23 May. He'd just got back from Burundi, bringing with him a letter from Richard's family and a tape of eyewitness interviews that Maria Eismont had made. He seemed embarrassed at my gratitude. 'It was really nothing', he insisted. 'I just asked the first person I met in Buj and he knew them!'

Cheerful though he was, Rory seemed more downbeat this time, perhaps even a little distant. There wasn't much news on the case, he said. It was looking, perhaps, as if it could have been a robbery gone wrong. The Burundians still seemed reluctant to do any kind of investigation. But he'd been in touch with Matthews, and he was going to pass on the tape that Maria had made. She'd done it at the request of the police, who had told her to tell the interviewees that this was a tape for Charlotte Wilson's family. We'd doubtless get a copy from Matthews pretty soon. I nodded and smiled – and doubted.

I was surprised by the change in Rory's manner, and I couldn't help wondering *what* Matthews had said to him. And what was on that tape? The truth about Charlotte's death had been there in front of me, but I couldn't have access to it – and I had a nasty feeling that we wouldn't be hearing it from Matthews any time in the near future.

I emailed Maria Eismont the next day to thank her for putting me in touch with Pierre. I was still at work when she replied a couple of hours later, with another gobsmacking detail.

I think we got the names of the guys who did the ambush but it will take time – we are searching now for their photos to show them to the witnesses and be sure they recognize them (but please don't tell that to anyone as if someone knows what we are doing, we are in deep shit).

My heart leapt. There were *names*. Not only that, but they were trying to track down *photographs?* I wrote back straightaway, trying not to sound too exuberant. Maria seemed a little cautious of me, and I didn't want to put her off.

Matthews was almost apoplectic when I told him I was in contact with one of the eyewitnesses. Although he stopped short of telling me to break off contact, it was clear from his tone that he would have pre-ferred this. On no account was I to tell Pierre that the British police were involved in the case, he insisted. And I had to be very careful, because if Pierre told me anything which contradicted the testimony he'd already given, a defence lawyer could use it to undermine his value as a witness. Matthews' reasons were plausible, but I got the feeling that his annoyance stemmed in part from the fact that it was now going to be harder to control the information we were getting.

Pierre and I began corresponding regularly. I would email him each morning, before I went to work, and by the time I came home again there would be a reply. Pierre told me he had a job in an Internet cafe, so he could use the computers and email for free. He lived in one of the quieter areas of Bujumbura. Nevertheless, every few days, he would mention hearing 'quelques fusils' overnight. Pierre told me he was terrified that the killers might come after him. During the attack, they had stolen his identification papers, which gave details of his address. The only safeguard he had was that they didn't know he'd survived.

Both rebel groups seemed to be stepping up their attacks. There was another big ambush on 25 May. No one was sure whether it was the FNL or the FDD who'd carried out the attack, but ten more people were dead. Ten more broken bodies, ten more funerals. Nearly half the number who'd died alongside Charlotte – and again, not a whisper on the international news.

The civil war was intensifying, according to a new report by a South African analyst, Jan van Eck. There'd at last been a lull in the Congo war – but this meant that thousands of FDD combatants, who had been fighting on the side of the Congolese government, were now moving back into Burundi. The attacks around Bujumbura were steadily increasing, and there were reports of a link-up between the two rival rebel groups. More worrying still, there were fears of a pan-regional, unholy alliance between the Burundian Hutu rebels and anti-Tutsi militia from Rwanda and the DRC.

Burundi is . . . considered to be the ideal location for continuing the war against Rwanda and Uganda . . . the temptation for them first to assist the Burundian rebels in toppling the 'Tutsi regime' in Bujumbura, before moving on to Rwanda, cannot be ignored.

Soon afterwards, the Burundian human rights group, Ligue Iteka, issued a warning that Burundi was 'on the brink of generalised war', on a scale comparable to Rwanda in 1994. They urged 'pressure on subregional countries where rebels train themselves, forge alliances and get arms and ammunition supplies'. The situation was looking increasingly desperate. On 31 May, a conflict-prevention NGO, the

International Crisis Group, held a news conference warning of 'impending genocide'. I felt a chill down my spine. What hope would there be for Pierre – and Richard's family – if these warnings were realized?

I wasn't surprised when Pierre asked me if I could help him leave Burundi, neither did I blame him – but I was at a loss as to how to react. Here was a real test of the Foreign Office's seriousness over getting justice for Charlotte. If Pierre was allowed to come to the UK, he would be far safer than he was now, and the police would be able to interview him in detail. And if he was willing to speak to the media it might also help us to increase pressure on the Burundian government for an investigation.

I emailed the Foreign Office to ask what would have to happen in order for Pierre to be able to come to the UK. There was no answer. But Maria Eismont's reply was encouraging:

Coincidentally I was talking to another friend of mine – an American guy from Human Rights Watch – about it a few hours ago . . . I know the witnesses are not very keen to talk to any government official. So we were discussing the matter and I was saying that the only way the witnesses would agree to testify is if they are brought to Europe under the law of something like 'witnesses protection' . . .

I wrote to the Foreign Office again. This time they did email me back, playing down the chances of Pierre being allowed to come, but suggesting I talk to the police. I phoned Matthews and left a message asking what he thought I should do. He called me on my mobile phone while I was on my way to work the following morning. He sounded livid. 'What you should *do*? You should do *nothing*, because he might be making things up to try and get asylum.'

Matthews' tone surprised me because both Maria and the Human Rights Watch researchers, Tony Tate, seemed to regard Pierre as a credible witness who'd been quite courageous in coming forward. Given that Matthews was getting all his information from them, I found it hard to understand how he had come to the conclusion that Pierre was so untrustworthy.

Despite sharing my annoyance with Matthews' attitude towards Pierre, my mother seemed increasingly overawed by him. For all her cynicism about politicians, she belonged to the post-war class of British people who'd been brought up with the sense that trusting the word of a police officer was practically a moral obligation.

Yet the things he was telling us seemed increasingly at odds with what I was being told by the people who actually worked in Burundi. I found myself getting more and more frustrated. I printed off the emails I'd got from Maria Eismont and the Human Rights Watch researcher and made my mother read them. I showed her the reports I'd found about Burundi, reports that actually named the FNL's leaders and listed the war crimes they'd committed – reports that cast serious doubts on Matthews' insistence that Charlotte's killers were mere 'bandits'.

'Maybe he knows something we don't?', my mother kept saying. But when I asked her what kind of information he could have that would trump the knowledge of the people who worked in Burundi, she was completely at a loss. In the end she solemnly informed me that a *feeling* had told her we should stop pushing Charlotte's case and allow whatever came our way to come our way.

I suddenly felt more isolated than ever. All my life my mother had told me that *dogged persistence* was the way to get things done – yet now, less than six months after Charlotte's death, she seemed to think that we should give up. In the days after Charlotte was killed I'd felt sure that whatever else happened, my mother and Catherine and I would keep on supporting each other. Now it seemed that we were increasingly at odds. Catherine and my mother both talked as if my desperate lobbying efforts were some kind of lifestyle choice – but it didn't *feel* like a choice to me.

At the same time as I felt angry and betrayed, I felt guilty. I knew that my mother was reacting like this because she'd just had enough. Enough of thinking about Charlotte's murder, and enough of me talking endlessly about it. Like Catherine, she was now almost completely unable to engage with it. She couldn't take it any more, and she wanted it to stop. My uncle seemed to be one of the few people I could talk to, and I began calling him more and more.

The situation in Congo seemed more bewildering each time I read about it. A US-based website, the 'Executive Intelligence Review' carried a conspiracy theory alleging that the Rwandan occupation of the DRC was part of a neo-colonial plot to create a British-controlled Tutsi Empire in the mineral-rich heart of Africa. And although this idea seemed outlandish in the extreme, there *were* consistent reports of British companies profiteering from the war.

An article in *The Financial Times* claimed that Avient Air, a British-run company, had been supplying weapons to Congolese forces, and that Britain had been criticized by the UN 'for failing to clamp down on mercenaries'.

The UN has warned that mercenary activity is increasing, but Tony Blair, the British Prime Minister, has blocked the Foreign Office's plans to publish proposals on regulation before the election . . .

Enrique Ballesteros, the UN special rapporteur on mercenaries, said the Foreign Office's failure to publish a consultation paper was 'a serious and deplorable backward step by the British government'. 'It is going to send a very negative signal to other European countries with interests in Africa who have been waiting for the British to introduce regulations before making any similar move themselves', he said.

Avient, an air cargo company in Harare run by Andrew Smith, is being investigated because of its role in the war in the Democratic Republic of Congo . . .

There is no suggestion that Mr Smith broke any laws, but his involvement in the war is embarrassing for London because the Foreign Office has insisted there can be no military solution to the conflict.

Britain is an important location for companies offering military or security services, but the UK has not introduced regulation, in contrast with South Africa and the US. Downing Street's insistence last year that a consultation paper on mercenary activity be delayed is a blow to the 'ethical' foreign policy of Robin Cook, foreign secretary . . .

Another website alleged that British and South African mercenaries had been actively involved on both sides in the war. Until now I'd not been aware that there was any such thing as a 'mercenary company';

let alone that my own country was an 'important location' for such enterprises. Dark conspiracy theories began forming in my mind. I began to wonder, idly, if there might be some connection between a British firm and the group that had killed Charlotte. Could this be the reason for the Foreign Office's awkwardness over the case?

I told my uncle that I was tempted again to try and shake things up by going to the media. At the very least, the fact that the Foreign Office had lost their Diplomatic Note and failed to notice for nearly a month should make an interesting news story. But my uncle cautioned me to 'keep your powder dry'.

I opted instead to try and get some media attention for our memorial fund. We'd raised more than £10,000 since the beginning of the year, far more than we'd ever expected. The original idea had been to set up a bursary fund to help poorer students at the school where Charlotte had been teaching, but so much money had come in we were beginning to look at ways of widening the scope. June 4 would be the day that would have been Charlotte's 28th birthday, so perhaps that would be a good time to try and get something in the news. Any renewed media interest in Charlotte would both be good for the memorial fund and help to remind the Foreign Office that the issue hadn't gone away.

When I woke up on 4 June 2001, the sunlight was streaming in through my window. I suddenly felt again that Charlotte was around. I looked over to the door. *If she was here, that's where she would be standing.*

An interview I'd given to the Press Association the previous day led to a news story on BBC Online, which linked to the website I'd set up in Charlotte's memory. Notwithstanding the odious headline 'Memorial fund for tragic Charlotte', it felt like another small victory. This website was read by thousands worldwide every day. Charlotte's case was back in the news. Later in the day I was interviewed by the London Live radio station, regional television news and Three Counties Radio. As I talked about my sister, and the reasons we'd set up the fund, I couldn't help feeling proud. Ten thousand pounds was a huge sum of money by Rwandan standards. Terrible though Charlotte's death had been, we'd been able to bring something good out of it.

Two days later, the *Washington Post* reported that the rebels were 'creeping closer' to Bujumbura. I found a UK government report that described Burundi as the 'African country closest to genocide'. But the Foreign Office still seemed reluctant to do anything to help Pierre. Matthews dropped by with the same information Maria had given me ten days earlier. But there was some more good news – our Ambassador had taken up the case with President Buyoya. Despite this progress, Matthews was still insistent that there was no chance that the killers would be prosecuted.

The following week, Amnesty International put out a new report on the conflict in the Congo claiming that Rwandan-backed forces had murdered, raped and tortured tens of thousands of civilians in the last three years amid efforts to clear the land for the mineral prospecting. The words of an unnamed Congolese church leader stuck in my mind.

The genocide that took place in Rwanda in 1994 is something horrible, but why should every Hutu feel guilty and why take revenge on us, the Congolese? Rwanda has succeeded in making the West guilty, so they send money and guns. Now, Rwanda can chase the militia, exploit the richness of our country, and us? We will just be sacrificed, it will be too late for us . . .

Amnesty's report came as another shock. In the weeks after Charlotte was killed, I'd clung to my sense of pride that my sister had been working for the 'good guys'. Even after hearing Rory Beaumont's thoughts on the Rwandan government, I had hoped that he was exaggerating. I'd wanted to believe that this was just a case of a few 'bad apples'. But the scale of the accusations in this Amnesty report made that very difficult to believe. If even half of Amnesty's claims were true, then the crimes of the Rwandan army in the Congo would seem to dwarf the atrocities of the FNL.

I began to hear from Maria more regularly, and she seemed to be becoming less cautious. I'd asked her about the reports of an impending rebel attack.

Don't take it too seriously . . . Something really outrageous must happen for the bloody rebels to take over the town. I don't believe in it as the only thing they showed themeselves capable of is stopping buses and executing unarmed civil-

101

ians. In case something happens I will keep you informed (and also will look after our mutual friend).

Maria's words reassured me – but the killings around Bujumbura were increasing in frequency, and Pierre still sounded worried. Then Maria went quiet for a few days. When she got back in touch she told me she'd been out of action with malaria:

Am doing OK now, though the bloody doctors (why are they always so unfriendly with their patients?) strictly prohibited to drink alcohol saying my liver is fucked up. I don't actually believe them but I feel quite miserable being unable to take my usual daily dose of alcohol.

Thanks a lot for helping out Pierre, I hope he will finally succeed to get a visa and go to Europe. He is still depressed from time to time and I try to spend more time with him . . . If you find someone to help Pierre with this – it would be great, and also he will have something to think about instead of returning to his nightmares.

I am in contact with people about those photos of those bastards who killed your sister. It is all going so slow!!! Sometimes it makes me depressed, but I realize here it is better to take time than to make an emotional move and get everyone and yourself in trouble. The only thing I promise – I won't leave Burundi before we find the fuckers, it became a personal affair of honour for me. Glad you are OK though you don't tell much about the European life (maybe because there is nothing special to tell about, I don't know).

I wrote Maria a long email, telling her more about my 'European life'. I told her about Charlotte, and her time in Rwanda, the effect of her death, and of my sense that I had to try to do something about it. I thanked her for her help with the case and asked her to be careful. But after I sent the email I wondered if I'd been doing the right thing. Maria hardly knew me – why was I pouring out my heart to her?

The truth was that I was lonely. In a strange way I felt that I could identify with Maria more easily than with most of my friends here in

London. The person they had befriended, and got to know over so many years, had been replaced by an angry, anguished man who did little but talk endlessly about a country no one else had ever heard of. This wasn't a normal twenty-something problem. There was no lightening up, no chilling out, no getting over it or going down the pub that would make it go away. Losing a sister wasn't like getting dumped or failing an exam, or having an unexpectedly high credit card bill. Charlotte's death had swept over me like a shadow, and much as my friends tried to understand, this was something completely outside their experience.

But Maria did seem to understand, or at least she understood my need to know that someone was doing something to investigate Charlotte's death – and she was prepared to be that person.

'Your e-mail was as long as it was nice', Maria wrote, in a long reply. She told me that she'd grown up in Moscow as the 'spolit child' of senior communist officials, but with the advent of Perestroika, her family had lost everything. At the age of 19, she'd become a war reporter:

I think I read too many adventure books and thought life is like that. I wanted strong emotions and also I think I wanted to show everyone, especially my parents, how cool and brave I could be. Not many war reporters, I think, will be honest enough to name this reason of their choice of profession, but I think it is the main one for almost all of them. I was nineteen years at that time.

Since then I am in journalism though I don't think I like this profession. The problem is I can't do anything else and I love travelling in remote wild places, where no other organizations are ready to pay me a ticket. I don't think I am ready to talk about my Chechnya experience – The main resume is – I thought I can save the world, but I found myself a shitty coward unable to resist the pressure from the government (that called me officially on the TV the enemy of Russian people) on the one hand, and permanent threat of death under the bombs in Grozny on the other hand . . .

When I saw the body of your sister on the road last December, I was very depressed. We are of the same age and I thought I could be easily on her place. I think the reaction of other members of your family is understandable – sometimes you want to pretend something never happened, as it is too painful to think about it. But I think you are doing the right thing in persuading police and authorities to continue investigations. Keep going. As we are saying in Russia, no water is streaming under the lying stone. And please, don't think I am doing something exceptional. If we don't care about what happens to the others, we are the next.

She had seen Charlotte's body. For some reason this took me by surprise. I tried to imagine what Maria must have been feeling. She had looked at Charlotte and seen someone like herself, someone who could have been her. I wondered how Charlotte would have felt if she had been aware of it. What could it be like to see a stranger looking down at your corpse?

Maria's message spurred me on. It seemed so strange that this was the person who had decided to help us. As a child in the early 1980s, I had lived in terror of the Russians and their nuclear bombs. And now one of *them*, a child of the Communist leaders I had so feared, was the one who was trying hardest to help us find answers.

As the month went on I became more and more obsessed with helping Pierre. Looking back I think that my desire to help him was at least as much about me as it was about him. If I could help get him out of this danger then this at least would be *something I could do*.

I wrote to the Foreign Office again, but there were still no answer. I looked up the visa section of the British High Commission in Kampala, and sent them an email. Within 20 minutes a man from the Foreign Office in London was on the phone to me. He carefully explained that in order to come to the UK, Pierre would have to go to Kampala and apply for a visa. But in considering any visa application, consular offices were obliged to reject anyone they thought likely to apply for asylum on reaching Britain. If the embassy in Kampala believed that Pierre wanted to seek asylum, they would have to reject his visa application. There was, in practice, no legitimate way for Pierre to come to the UK. The vast majority of visa applications from Burundians were rejected, exactly because the situation there was so bad. The rules didn't allow for any exceptions.

I felt angry and disheartened. The news seemed to be so full of stories about 'bogus refugees' – yet here was a person who undoubt-edly needed protection, and I was being told that there was no way to help him. I was being told, in fact, that there was no legitimate way for anyone in Pierre's position to come here. The system had been specifically designed to exclude people who genuinely needed help.

On 28 June, the Burundian army was quoted as saying that 'Bujumbura is surrounded'. A regional news service echoed the concerns that Jan Van Eck had raised about the FNL and FDD linking up with other groups to launch an all-out assault on the 'Tutsi Empire'. The following day, nine more people were killed in an FNL ambush. Pierre emailed me to say that the FNL had circulated a tract in Bujumbura announcing that they would be launching a massive assault on 1 July, with the intention of capturing the city. 'We're worried that it might be even bigger than Kinama', he told me.

I'd reached my lowest point. More than anything else, I felt a sense of defeat. The situation around Bujumbura had been escalating for weeks. Pierre had first asked me for help more than a month ago. I'd promised to do everything I could – and I'd achieved nothing. Burundi's government was now besieged in its own capital and it looked as if the rebels were preparing to finish them off. What would it be like in Bujumbura when the city fell to the FNL? Would Maria really be able to do anything for Pierre? And what of Richard Ndereyimana's family? I fired off an email to Maria but got no reply. There was no answer either from Rory Beaumont. I sent a series of increasingly desperate emails to anyone I could think of who might be able to do something to help. As the end of the day drew closer I began to feel empty and drained. All I could do now was pray to the God I wasn't sure I believed in.

I'd arranged to meet that night with some old schoolfriends in Hertfordshire. It was one of the strangest evenings of my life. I drove up from Enfield and walked through the streets of this market town where I'd spent so many nights as a teenager. The last time I was here, Charlotte had still been alive. It was good to see my friends Dodd and James again, and good to meet new people, but it took a supreme effort of will to separate my conversation from the obsessive thoughts that constantly ran through my head. I felt a sense of detachment that was becoming habitual. We sat and ate curry together, and I tried to act normal.

'What is it about you?!', the question shocked me – my normality act obviously wasn't very convincing. An affable couple of newly-wed friends of Dodd's had joined us at the curry house, and the more drunk the wife, Jo, became, the more probing questions she asked. She didn't know about Charlotte and I felt too tired to try to explain, so I made up a series of lies. If I seemed distracted, it was because I'd been having trouble with my temperamental girlfriend. What did I do in life? Hard to explain. Somehow the conversation got onto a friend of hers, an 'amazing guy' who had trained as a Church of England vicar but been unable to get a parish posting, even as a curate. She seemed to think that I might be able to do or say something that would help him.

I was tired, sober and there were drunk people saying bizarre things to me. I began to wonder if there might be some unknowable reason at work here, some purpose behind the fact that this random person I'd only just met was talking to me about this 'amazing', out-of-work clergyman who I'd never met. It was a desperate thought but once it appeared it wouldn't go away. Maybe this was someone whose *prayers* might help keep Pierre safe? When I got home I emailed Jo at the address she'd given me, telling her about Charlotte and explaining my logic as best I could. In the strange, desperate world I'd found myself in, it didn't seem like an odd thing to do.

I got back a short, nervous-sounding reply the next day from Jo, followed by a pleasant, puzzled-sounding mail from her clergyman friend. And almost immediately I began to feel embarrassed. Ever since Charlotte was killed I'd feared becoming ridiculous – now here I was freaking out total strangers with my quasi-mystical, crazy talk.

The FNL attacked Bujumbura in the early hours of 1 July, but quickly withdrew again to their strongholds in the hills. The huge onslaught that they had been trumpeting hadn't happened. When I finally spoke to Rory Beaumont, he seemed bemused that I'd been so worried. The FNL were a menace, but he was sure that they simply didn't have the firepower to take the capital by force. Things in Burundi were bad, but they weren't that bad. Maria emailed me a couple of days later, telling me to calm down. I felt ridiculous again. I'd convinced myself that Burundi was on the brink of the kind of hell Rwanda had seen in 1994. I'd got it wrong, and in the process I'd made a fool of myself.

I continued trying to help Pierre. While the situation was not as desperate as I'd thought, there was still a clear risk to his life, and an email from Richard Ndereyimana's brother Jean-Bosco did little to reassure me. 'People are dying like flies here', he told me. 'Every day those who can are fleeing.' It seemed clear now that the Foreign Office were determined to do nothing for Pierre, but having promised that I'd do everything I could, I felt that I had no choice but to keep trying. With help from my uncle I found an immigration lawyer, Wesley Gryk, who agreed to take a look at the case.

After visiting a friend one evening the following week, I had a call from my mother on my mobile phone. 'Richard, I've had the *police* round! I want you to *stop* emailing Pierre. I want you to stop contacting people about Burundi. You're making my life *hell!*'

The police had called my mother earlier in the day, and asked to see her urgently the same evening. Sands, Matthews and Baxter turned up at her house a few hours later and told her that I was jeopardizing their entire investigation. If the case came to court, they said, a clever defence lawyer could argue that Pierre had been given an 'inducement' by my efforts to help him get asylum in the UK, and this would destroy his credibility as a witness. My actions were so damaging, in fact, that they had decided to cut all communications with me, and instructed the Foreign Office to do the same. From now on, they wanted our family to talk about Charlotte's case *only* with them, and only through my mother.

My mother's phone call left me reeling. It was several weeks since I'd first told the police about wanting to help Pierre and while they'd clearly been trying to discourage me, they'd never mentioned anything before about 'inducement'. What they had told my mother, or at least the version of it that she relayed to me, didn't seem to make very much sense. How could I be 'inducing' Pierre into saying or doing anything? He'd already given a full account of what he'd seen. It wasn't as if I was dangling the prospect of asylum in front of him in order to get him to change his story – it was compelling enough as it was. How do you 'induce' bullet wounds?

Angry though I was with my mother, I felt far angrier with the police. My mother's fortitude over the last six months had been an inspiration to the whole family. If I was the one who happened to be on the receiving end when her rage over Charlotte's death finally burst out, well I could get over it. But these people were supposed to be professionals. They were supposed to be supporting my family, not trying to divide us from one another.

It was only several years afterwards that I learned that, alongside Charlotte's case, Sands had been heading the investigation into the high-profile, south London murder, in November 2000, of a ten-year-old Nigerian boy, Damilola Taylor. The case floundered and fell apart over fears that the star witness had changed her story because of financial inducements offered by the police. I still find it hard to understand what was going on that evening in July 2001, but I've often wondered if, at that time, the problems with the Damilola Taylor case might just have been becoming obvious, and that Sands could simply have been panicking.

It didn't take long for my mother to calm down and see the inconsistencies in what the police had been saying, and from that point on she became far more sceptical. If the intention had been to try to put pressure on me through my mother, it failed. The last thing my mother wanted was to have to be the single point of contact for Charlotte's case, and she too was angered by the feeling that the police had been trying to manipulate her. We agreed to carry on regardless.

We went to see the Foreign Office again in late July. At a pre-meeting meeting we met our MP Andy Love, a gruff Scot who reminded me of one of my primary schoolteachers. We agreed that our main goal was to press the case to allow Pierre to come to Britain as a refugee, on the basis that he was a valuable witness to Charlotte's death and, if all else failed, on exceptional humanitarian grounds.

The meeting played out like a rather clumsy game of tennis. The Foreign Office opened by claiming that there was no legal way for someone in Pierre's position to be allowed to come here. Wesley Gryk countered that every government can exercise discretion over these kinds of cases. There was no legal obstacle to his coming here if the government decided to allow him in. The Foreign Office then said that they might be able to look into it if the police agreed that it was a good idea. What did the police think? The police thought it was a bad idea. I pointed out that Human Rights Watch and Maria Eismont, the people who'd actually interviewed Pierre, believed that he was a credible witness and supported the idea of bringing him to the UK. Sands solemnly explained that our proposal, well-intentioned though it was, risked jeopardizing a valuable witness. I countered that he would have no value as a witness if he was dead. Sands said he had reason to believe that Pierre was a dishonest person, who'd not been entirely truthful in the interviews he'd given. I asked him what his reason for believing this was. Sands said that for security reasons he couldn't disclose his reason for believing it.

The Foreign Office agreed that if we made a representation about Pierre's case through Andy Love, they would present it to the Home Office, with whom the final decision would rest. It seemed clear now that this was a quixotic task, but if the government was dead set against doing anything to help an eyewitness to the murder of a British citizen, I wanted them to spell it out.

One further detail emerged from the meeting. Matthews quoted one of the eyewitnesses as saying that the attackers had separated Hutu from Tutsi. As we'd suspected, all the passengers they'd released had been Hutus.

I continued looking for ways to help Pierre. Would the Rwandans be willing to take him in? Seven of their people had been killed in the Titanic Express massacre, after all. And while Rwanda wasn't exactly luxurious, it was far safer these days than Burundi. I dropped a line to the Rwanda-UK Goodwill Organization, a small, friendly charity, run by Mike and Collette Hughes, a Rwandan-British couple, who had got in touch with us after Charlotte was killed, and whose meetings I had begun to attend. Collette phoned me back within a couple of hours. She'd been in touch with the deputy head of the Rwandan police, who said he'd be very keen to speak to Pierre, and could even meet him at the airport. The Rwandans would be happy to take him in. I emailed Pierre excitedly – but his response was cautious. Who was this guy? I told him, self-importantly, that this guy was the deputy head of the Rwandan police. This made him even more nervous. Pierre, I remembered, hadn't even yet dared go and talk to the police in Burundi. He was also worried, he told me, that he might not be able to support himself economically in Rwanda. It was a fair point, but it also suggested that he wasn't as desperate to leave as I'd first thought.

At the end of July, the DRC war finally began to make headlines. 'Huge death toll in Congo', ran the *Guardian* headline on the 31st, quoting estimates of up to two and half million dead. Four days later the newspaper published a piece by a London-based Congolese journalist, Antoine Lokongo, comparing the invasion of his country, with Iraq's invasion of Kuwait.

On August 2 1990, Iraq invaded Kuwait. On August 2 1998, a coalition of Rwanda, Uganda and Burundi invaded Congo. The difference between them is the international response. Western superpowers rushed to Kuwait's aid, driving out the invaders and punishing them relentlessly. By contrast, the invasion of Congo went almost unnoticed. The invaders remain to this day, plundering the country's wealth and murdering its hapless inhabitants . . .

Uganda, Rwanda and Burundi are . . . systematically looting Congo's riches, including gold, diamonds and coltan – the heat resistant mineral compound found in mobile phones and Playstations and defined by the Pentagon as 'highly strategic'. Is it possible that the superpowers' reluctance to act is motivated by the easier access to these riches afforded by the state of war?

Lokongo's suggestion shocked me. It was one thing to say that a few unscrupulous Western firms were profiting from the war, but it was going a step further to think that Western governments might be allowing the conflict to continue because it suited their strategic interests. Although I'd found similar claims on the website of the mysterious 'Executive Intelligence Review', this was the first time I'd seen them in a mainstream news source.

I found myself wondering again if there might be a grain of truth in the conspiracy theories. Perhaps the Foreign Office were being so evasive about Charlotte's death because they were worried that the case might draw unwelcome media attention to what Britain was up to in the region. Or maybe it was more specific than that. When I did some further digging on Avient, the British-run mercenary firm at the centre of *The Financial Times* story earlier in the year, I found an article on a Zimbabwe news site, Zim Today, alleging that the company had done more than just supply weapons to the Congolese army. Avient, it was claimed, had run bombing raids against Rwandan government positions and airlifted guns to the Interahamwe, who were fighting on the side of the Congolese dictator, Joseph Kabila. I'd seen consistent reports of links between the Rwandan Interahamwe and the Burundian Hutu rebels, including a suggestion that the Rwandan, had sold weapons to the FNL. If Zim Today's claims were true, then it seemed possible that Avient might have had a hand in supplying the gun that killed Charlotte.

I took unpaid leave again in the middle of August. I'd lost weight over the last couple of months, and developed an abcess on my chin that got nastier every time I shaved. The resulting beard aged me by ten years. I'd run out of contact lenses and started wearing my battered old glasses from my student days. My hair was a mess. Having tried for so long to be cool, I now had little interest in my appearance. I looked like someone who needed a holiday.

I spent the next two weeks in the small French village where my uncle and aunt had an old Norman cottage. For a fortnight I did little more than go for walks, play tennis in the sun, eat, sleep and drink coffee. Surrounded by family and away from my job, my computer and my phone, I began to unwind for the first time in eight months.

I returned to my four-day-a-week job, and my bereavement counselling, feeling more normal than I had done all year. I shaved off my beard and got a haircut, I started going to a yoga class, and joined the badminton club at work. I began, at last, to be useful in my job again.

Charlotte's case was no longer such an obsession, but it remained a preoccupation. One weekend in early September, at another meeting of the Rwanda-UK Goodwill Organization. I was surprised to see Graeme Loten, who until a couple of months earlier had been the British Ambassador to Rwanda. The country had left a lasting impression on him, he told me, and although he was soon to take up a new post, he hoped to maintain the personal links he had made during his time there.

I was eager to know what more Graeme Loten could tell me about Charlotte's case. The police had told me that he had raised the issue with President Buyoya shortly during his final visit to Burundi, and that he had personally interviewed a number of the eyewitnesses to Charlotte's death. I wanted to know what he had made of Pierre, who I guessed DS Matthews had been referring to when he said that one of the eyewitnesses had told 'one thing to Human Rights Watch and something else to the Ambassador'.

To my surprise, Loten told me that he had never met Pierre. The eyewitness he interviewed was a young Rwandan student named Eugene. More surprising still, Loten had been told by the Foreign Office in London that the police were casting doubt on Eugene's credibility. He had found this 'strange', he said, because he couldn't see what the police could have known about Eugene that he didn't.

Loten's comments sowed more doubts in my mind about what the police had been telling us. At the same time as they were undermining Pierre, it now seemed that they had been discrediting another witness they'd never met, and for reasons that were also very unclear. And if it hadn't been for this chance meeting with Graeme Loten, I would never have known.

Just after lunch one Tuesday afternoon, a colleague rang to ask if we'd heard that someone had flown an aeroplane into the World Trade Center in New York. At first I thought it was a joke. None of the Internet news websites were accessible, so I went down to check the TV in the office canteen. It wasn't a joke. The World Trade Center was on fire. And there had been two planes, not one. One of the towers had fallen. And now the other had fallen too. I watched, transfixed as the images were replayed again and again.

For days there was little else in the news, and the scant facts were padded out with rhetoric. Politicians talked about an 'attack on freedom'. A succession of pundits solemnly announced that 'the world has changed'. Others explained with equal solemnity that this was the inevitable result of American foreign policy in the Middle East. Conspiracy theorists blamed the Israelis. Someone sent me an email purporting to show the face of Satan in the smoke billowing out from the Twin Towers. One or two whispered that 'America had it coming'.

The Twin Towers attacks sickened me all the more because the logic of Al Qaeda seemed so similar to that of the FNL. Whatever these people *thought* they had been doing, whatever fantasy they were living out when, in the name of 'Holy War', they flew two planes into a building full of thousands of unarmed civilians, they had been deluding themselves, just as the FNL were when they murdered 21 people on 28 December in the name of 'Hutu Liberation'.

When I thought about Americans I thought about my gentle Aunt Paula, who I'd stayed with in Normandy just a couple of weeks ago, who had introduced me to Zen Buddhism when I was a teenager, and whose home-made card welcoming me to the world I still kept among my souvenirs, 26 years after it had been sent. And I thought about Carl, the good-hearted man who Catherine had decided to marry, who had always been so warm towards me, and who had been such a support to my family in the dark, chaotic days after we heard that Charlotte was dead.

Over the next few weeks, the death toll began to settle around 3,000. The mantra that 'the world has changed' kept being repeated, and more and more people seemed to believe it. The US President George Bush declared the beginning of a new kind of war – a war not only against the perpetrators of this particular terrorist attack, but against all those who pursued their goals through terrorism, and those who supported them. In early October, the British Prime Minister Tony Blair echoed this commitment but then went further:

> . . . out of the shadow of this evil, should emerge lasting good: destruction of the machinery of terrorism wherever it is found; hope amongst all nations of a new beginning where we seek to resolve differences in a calm and ordered way; greater understanding between nations and between faiths; and above all justice and prosperity for the poor and dispossessed, so that people everywhere can see the chance of a better future through the hard work and creative power of the free citizen, not the violence and savagery of the fanatic . . .
>
> It could, with our help, sort out the blight that is the continuing conflict in the Democratic Republic of Congo, where three million people have died through war or famine in the last decade . . .
>
> The state of Africa is a scar on the conscience of the world. But if the world as a community focused on it, we could heal it. And if we don't, it will become deeper and angrier.

It was the first time I'd heard a Western politician make any reference to the situation in the Congo, let alone express a willingness to 'sort out the blight', and I was surprised by the cynical response Blair's comments received. One of my colleagues flatly refused to believe that 3,000,000 people *really* had died in the Congo. Surely if it was true we'd have heard about it on the news? Media pundits poured scorn on the assertion that the state of Africa was a 'scar on the conscience of the world', and many accused Blair of neo-colonialism.

But it seemed to me that the critics were following the same logic as those who had obstructed international efforts to stop the genocide in Rwanda. If the current state of Africa *wasn't* a scar on the con-science of the world, then it seemed hard to see how the world could have any conscience at all. Notwithstanding the fact that he'd got the date of the Rwandan genocide wrong by a year, it was one of the few occasions in my life that I actually felt proud of my country's leader. 'Destruction of the machinery of terrorism wherever it is found' – it couldn't have been clearer. This had to mean that time was running out for the FNL.

A few days after Blair's speech, British and US forces invaded Afghanistan, where the Al Qaeda leadership, allied to the country's tyrannical government, was believed to be hiding. Within weeks the regime had been overthrown. In mid-October the police at last gave us transcripts of the eyewitness statements that Maria Eismont had recorded in May. My heart was thumping as I opened the brown, A4 envelope and read the first page.

— 8 —

Person one

First interview

The interviewee: The child in Kigali, I had seen her with Richard walking around the town . . . (inaudible) . . . I knew them, I had seen them in the town, no, I know Walter and the day of the journey, it was Thursday, I had made a booking two days previously and I had taken the last seat, on the left, yes she was in front of me with Richard also and we arrived without fear, we went down and once we got there, where we fell into the ambush, they fired on the bus, the driver wanted to drive on but because it was raining, he skidded, the bus skidded and turned on its side against the mountain. We were scared, we screamed, there were already two dead on the spot and they came and fired on the windscreens and they asked us to remove everything we had and to come out.

The interviewer: Everyone was on the bus?

The interviewee: Yes, I was on the bus, then straight after firing on the bus they said to us 'Bring everything that you have, everything, the mobiles, the jewellery, the money' and they said 'That's it, come out, it's finished', then we believed it was over, they had taken everything from us, maybe they wanted money and everything and we had confidence . . . before there were two persons who were allowed to go.

Interviewer: Two women.

Interviewee: Two women and one boy, there was also another who was a missionary and for me . . .

Interviewer: The girl who was not wounded, and the other one they pulled, she was not wounded.

Interviewee: She was not yet wounded, we got off, we were told to take off everything we had, our clothes were taken off, us the men, even her fob was taken off. She was wearing trousers and a shirt on top. She kept the trousers and she was told, bring everything you have, all the money and she did not understand 'Kirundi' Richard intervened and said 'Give everything you have' but she said 'I have given everything'. So after there was another Rwandan who was next to me, he was asked 'You "Muse" how many "Hutus" have you killed?'. He said 'No the Hutus, they were my friends' and he was shot on the spot, he was immediately by my side.

Interviewer: The one sitting next to you?

Interviewee: But by then we were already on the road, we were already lying on the road, we had already been taken off the bus.

Interviewer: Who was firing, it is the guy the Commander?

Interviewee: No everybody was shooting everyone was shooting, only there was one who was above, there was no one in command, each one was firing himself, the right to kill and . . . (inaudible) . . . and to the young lady who was asked 'Why did you come here?' She could not understand a thing and she was told in Kirundi 'It is you who supply the weapons, now you are going to feel what it is like'. They said it in Kirundi, we avoided looking them in the eyes because . . .

Interviewer: Who spoke?

Interviewee: It was one of them and then we were told 'Sleep everybody, you all lie down, she was shot on the spot, she was killed when they started firing on all of us, they were firing at close range, they were standing we were lying down. They were firing along on the other people who were there. Some were on top and myself I was hit by three bullets, one went into my stomach, two passed through. After they left we tried to lift ourselves, we tried to see if there was somebody else still alive but she was already dead.

Interviewer: It is . . . (inaudible) . . . who shot her or was it everybody who was shooting everybody?

Interviewee: No the shots that were fired, it was one person who was shooting everybody, he fired once, almost twice.

Interviewer: Kala Shimkor it was . . .

Interviewee: Yes I still have the bullet which was . . . I kept it, I did not bring it but it is from a Kalashnikov always.

Interviewer: And the other one, her 'fiancé' he was dead also?

Interviewee: Her fiancé was also dead.

Interviewer: But the guy who fired, in fact do you remember him, can you describe him?

Interviewee: No, we avoided staring in their faces because if you stare at them, they said that you would recognize them and they fired at you immediately. They already shot two people who said they were going to grass on them so we avoided looking at them, we looked on the side.

Interviewer: Yourself, you had the impression it was not led by anyone?

Interviewee: No, there was no-one giving orders, everybody was doing as they pleased and there was someone who saw we were still alive and he said 'There is somebody who is still alive, he must be shot', the other said 'No wait, because there was a lot of luggage, we have not finished taking all the luggage, we will come back' and we were lucky to be taken away before they returned, our friend 'Donkagara' was still there, he spent the night over there when they returned.

Interviewer: This one I remember, we came there the day after the attack, the next morning, we found a survivor, I think his name was Xavier, the driver of my colleague is French, he saw something, he heard something, he did not know who it was, he knew it was already the army but he was scared, it was him!

Interviewee: It was Xavier, yes they came back, they woke up the dead with bayonets to see if there were survivors, to wake them with bayonets to see if someone is going to wake up to finish them off but he was hidden at the foot of the mountains and they did not see him.

Interviewer: Goodbye!

Person two

Second interview

Interviewee: Yes thank you, it is true, I was with Charlotte on board the 'Titanic' when we left Kigali together in the same vehicle. We did not know each other unfortunately but all I know is that we have suffered. We have lived the same nightmare together. She was very young, but when I saw her, when I paid attention unfortunately she was dead. So I wish I had got to know all her friends but what is strange is that we left Kigali at 9 o'clock, the time of the attack was at about 3.00pm and then there were shots fired, the bus was hit, the driver lost control a little. We continued being fired upon, all I know is that they threatened us. We were told to get off, they were still firing at us. We got off and we were all sat with the officers lying down on the tarmac. She was next to me, but then there were threats. All I know about her, the threats were directed towards her, still in Kirundi. Unfortunately she did not understand, perhaps her friend had understood but he did not have the time to explain. Since she was a white woman, a European as they said, they threatened everybody, they said they write nonsense about them which is important on the radio and television, so I understood that these threats were specifically addressed at her and I believed it was going to be limited to this. They were demanding money, we had given everything. I think she had given everything she had, even the luggage. When they threatened us they finished the pillage with everything we had, the jewellery, the watches, the bags.

Interviewer: It has been said that they had undressed the people.

Interviewee: They undressed those who had training suits, we could see they needed clothes to protect themselves against . . . it was raining they no longer had their clothes, but during the attack . . . so they took the clothes off people . . . they started with the people who had tracksuits, those who had jeans, so the tough wearing clothes they took away.

Interviewer: And Charlotte did she give her clothing.

Interviewee: No she was dressed, she remained dressed, even I was going to take my trousers off but they were tight ?? so it was not really desirable but they took all the shoes away, they needed shoes, they were very keen on the men's shoes, but the ladies shoes, it was either to sell them or to give them away.

Interviewer: So they took everybody's shoes?

Interviewee: Everybody's.

Interviewer: Charlotte's also?

Interviewee: We were forced to remove jewellery, if she had it, she gave it. Myself I gave my watch, I gave my signet ring, I handed over everything that I had on me and this is what I got back, this, the driver gave it to me afterwards, it had fallen down when I gave the money, they did not understand . . . he brought it to me and he said 'Can you make a call?' I tried but there were no signals. Having taken everything, they even threatened . . . separating the detainees and I understood it was the end, death was going to follow. Apparently some did not want to kill but others wanted to kill, at this point they fired on everybody.

Interviewer: Did someone give the order to shoot?

Interviewee: They were firing indiscriminately but afterwards, I found out, I understood that some let the others escape saying . . . 'You must have fifty on me, I give you 1,000 francs', some were lucky they were allowed to go so as far as she was concerned, what I have seen is that when they started firing, some were asked questions, saying this and that, and if one answered the wrong thing you were shot or if you had hidden something. There were other girls who did not want to give some jewellery because they said 'It serves no purpose because you are going to kill me', so they were shot. There were young girls, mothers, children of three, of five, of six, they fired on everybody, there were old people. So as they were firing, when they had taken everything, this is why it took some time, thirty minutes, one hour, one hour and a half, they were still there, they had the time to take everything, they tried to set fire to the vehicle but because it was raining and the fuel tank was on the side of the bus which was lying down and it was diesel it was not easy to burn, had they succeeded in setting it on fire, we would all have been burnt to death, they were all armed to the teeth. One of them had a big . . . ? He was firing on the bus to try to set fire to it, so I thought maybe he did not want to waste his ammunition so they fired on everybody.

Interviewer: Did they start with Charlotte?

Interviewee: No! No they started with the others, it was even towards the end, there were many of them, each was firing on the people who were next to them, us, Charlotte was next to me, for example I realised that she had been killed at the same time as me, I fortunately was not dead but since I was immediately next to her, I was shot in the back, third and fourth, then I understood that it was finished. I had positioned myself on my side so that they would not fire on my chest, there was a lot of blood and I thought I was already dead, even towards the end I heard somebody challenging 'No, those who are still breathing we must finish them off!' and another one said 'No! Do this first, do that first!'. I was thinking they have seen me. I stopped breathing but with the cold and the fear I was shaking all the time. When they were firing, it was making me jump so I understood that they were firing on the people next to me. Then there was a big . . . ? . . . that they had just left, there were people who were breathing their last, others were calling 'Save me. Do this, detach my leg'. When I saw that I was still alive, it took me some time to sit up, I was covered in blood . . . death, there was the smell of the cartridges, of the guns. When I saw her, I saw that she was already dead, she had been shot, it was really sad. I said 'Why all this?' I could not get over it because there was myself, the driver and another one who was finishing at University his pharmacy studies. I tried to call out but there was no reply. We got back on the bus to protect ourselves from the rain. We tried . . . there were dead bodies inside the bus also. We decided to get back on board. Before leaving, the man who also had a child who was not dead yet, I told him off, I was telling him to lie down because he was standing. I told him 'They are still here, they are going to fire at us'. I told him off and he got frightened and he lay down. I tried to save the child, taking him with me but he was weak and beyond help, he only had one leg, only one arm, I could not carry him. I hid him in the . . . with a young lady who had lost an eye, she had received a bullet.

Interviewer: Was she saved later?

Interviewee: She was saved, because when . . . we were fired upon, we fled into the forest with the driver and this boy called Eugene. So I spent the night in the forest. Later at approximately 5.30pm there was a military bus which drove through there and they picked up the driver and this boy who was finishing his pharmacy studies. This lorry took those who were not dead yet, among those were this young lady and the little boy, because I understood that they were brother and sister, they were two sisters and the brother, one girl aged 16 died and the older sister lost an eye and her shoulder was hit. I even have photographs and then I asked them about the boy and I was told he was the younger brother. I asked about the mother and I was told that she had been killed. You understand that really it was atrocious, unfortunately Charlotte, and I tried to find out. . . . it is how I learnt that Richard was also on board. Now I was thinking I would like to know the family, have photographs because it is also my concern later if I can achieve it, to meet them because what is strange, when I left Kigali I was with my nephew, when he accompanied me, the first thing I said to him 'Listen! I am taking the "Titanic" but I hope I am not going to sink . . .' it gave him a fright but I did not know what was going to happen and there we are it is the first time it has ever happened and I am wondering 'What have I done which was so special to be spared?' and then I tell myself 'No my day had not come yet' so I prayed for all those people with whom I was really united when it happened.

Interviewer: The girl Charlotte, did she die instantly?

Interviewee: Yes she died instantly, because looking at the shots, the ones who were unlucky received the bullets either in the head or straight through the heart, you understand but there I understood that a person who dies from gunshot wounds I would not say it is an atrocious death, the atrocity, it is the people who commit the atrocity but I understood that if I had died, it would have been a painless death. The first thing is the fear, there is the fear one feels before being killed, but the gunshot wounds, I understood because they shot me in the back, even in my thigh it is as if one did not feel anything, it feels like something cold going through your flesh, it is like that, maybe it hurts, maybe one suffers when a bullet goes through the lungs, then I would suffer. But when it goes through, I understood this, seeing the faces, seeing the bodies, an atrocious death but I don't think they had the time to suffer. I tell myself that for her it was the first time, she did not even know what could happen, she did not even know the danger, but we died of fright because we already knew the road, although things had been going well for some time, there were not a lot of ambushes, but we were aware of the problems in the country, the ethnic problems on the border of Rwanda. We knew it could happen at any time. So we said she was taken by surprise, just the time to realize really what had happened, she was dead, she was dead and then I say it each time, unfortunately I say . . . the ones who died, may God protect them, but they had a good death, it was quick. One who suffered for instance, he was a driver 'Dego'. I tried to save him, he was sitting in the gutter, he could not even remove his shirt, then he said to me 'Can you help me?' as I was walking past. I retraced my steps. I tried to take his shirt off, this was on Thursday and he died on Sunday . . . the driver had his forearm shattered because he had his arm like this on his chest, they shot him in the chest and as they shot him in the heart, the shots tore his forearm apart. He is now in Kigali, they are going to take part of his thigh and do a skin graft. This one has really suffered. Most of the time I suffered, I suffer from this fear, no I am unable to follow this road.

Interviewer: You have not done this journey?

Interviewee: Not since. I fly as before, either I take a flight to 'A???' or I take a direct flight. But as I have seen what has taken place, I stayed until the morning and I came down with the dead and when I think about it I try very hard not to be traumatised. I understand now where the traumatism comes from, all these images rolling fast in your mind and one wonders why? During all this time there was no intervention, since 3.00pm, they stayed there until the morning, you have seen.

Interviewer: They left and they came back?

Interviewee: The assailants? No, they left but there were those who remained close by, that means the ones who never left, these are the ones who fired on us. But afterwards, this is the reason why I stayed in the forest because I saw others who were running down on the other side of the mountain towards us and I thought this time they are coming to burn all the vehicles and they are going to find us . . . (mobile rings) I really don't know what else I can say unless you want to ask me some questions.

Interviewer: There were the ones who stayed all the time.

Interviewee: Yes, when we escaped into the forest, the driver and this young man who is finishing his studies as a pharmacist, they were badly hit and they stayed by the road and myself I begged the driver because he was talking too much, he was saying; because the people have fired on us, it is likely that they are going to recognise us easily. I got out then and I saw other people coming, but they also had kidnapped certain people, but not people who were on our bus, they had kidnapped them before. Apparently they had stopped a minibus. They have also killed people and they have kidnapped them, this I heard afterwards. So when I saw them, I thought, listen they are going to come back because they were coming towards us and I thought NO! When they come back they are going to finish us off now, I thought I would rather go and hide in the valley and wait until the morning because then at least the soldiers . . . on the road will know the positions, that is why I went into hiding but when I hid I opened my mobile, it was gone 18.05 hours . . . I was scared . . . I hid somewhere but what is strange, later I realised that it was risky, there were other hiding places of these people, the assailants, there were shots also that evening at approximately 18.30 hours, 1900 hours. I think they shot a soldier, they came to hide but they remained above me but they did not see me, it was dark. I was among the trees, there I was really frightened, I thought they had seen me. I thought if they kill me nobody will find my body and nobody would ever know what happened to me, so as they were frightened, one went to the right and one went to the left, five metres away. They stayed over there . . . I stopped breathing, it is the longest night of my life, I prayed for rain to enable me to hide.

Interviewer: So that there would be some noise?

Interviewee: Yes, even the little rain there had been had stopped. I was thirsty, I even wanted to have a little water . . . so I thought if I stay until the morning, there is a danger they will see me and tear me to pieces. So I thought, what am I going to do, if I stay here it is even worse, so it is true it was midnight almost, I decided to leave very slowly like a small cat or leopard who sees a prey. I can assure you, I was very weak and I was crawling, I was trying to get on my feet but I was stumbling, to crawl on my stomach was painful. I was trampling here and there. I was afraid to get caught. I climbed up the mountain and I arrived near the road, thirty minutes, it was around four or five o' clock in the morning.

Interviewer: Have you tried to see whether somebody stayed with the bodies to kill them, to . . . ?

Interviewee: NO, from what I can gather they did not come back, the people who came back were peasants who were just nearby, they came to take what was left behind, shoes they had not taken but nobody came back to ill treat those . . . because looking at the traces of the bullets, one could believe that they were machetes but they were shots. Everybody is saying they took machetes, they beheaded people, there is a three year or six-year-old child they found but no! They were bullets which went through depending on the position in which one was lying. They did not use machetes or knives. So the people as I understand who??? came afterwards, they are little . . . villagers who passed to take things that had fallen on the ground. Even in the morning one could still see the passports . . . one could find a shoe when they had only taken one, nobody came back. After that there was a unit that only picked up the survivors. There were a lot of dead bodies, the others the units that you have seen in the morning, they were soldiers. Myself in the morning, there were certain people who were no longer there. Somebody had been. We had spent the night outdoors it was very cold.

Interviewer: The people were Burundis?

Interviewee: All the people who spoke were Burundis.

Interviewer: . . . (inaudible) . . . they only spoke Kirundi?

Interviewee: They threatened us in Kirundi. One of them when we were still on the bus he said (in French) 'Give the money!' He wanted to speak French 'Give the money! Give the money!' only these words. The other threats were really in Kirundi. They were young men.

Interviewer: The threats, it was 'you the Europeans you write bad things about us'?

Interviewee: Yes at that stage. I understood . . . against the other detainee . . . No you think you have won but we are still here, we are not giving up.

Interviewer: But nobody translated for Charlotte what they were saying?

Interviewee: No! Everybody was frightened, what they were doing then were praying, the people were praying. They said 'What! You are praying?' They threatened us and we all kept quiet. We already started to pray in the bus, there were some Muslims . . . you know the sound you hear at Church when you are outside, it was like that. They already threatened us in the bus but when we were lying on the floor . . . because I don't know whether somebody had hidden a watch, they started shooting, it was horrible, we prayed. I saw the person in charge say 'What is this?' . . . No, I mean, but I understood from talking to friends, Richard was saying to Charlotte, 'No. Don't be afraid they are going to release us, he tried to calm her down because in fact it was he who knew her and the woman who was next to her came to hide between my legs.

Interviewer: Why did they release these two women? They released some women!

Interviewee: Yes! This I don't know how it happened, it is luck, yes there is a woman who had a baby but the baby was held by another man, apparently a Hutu so when they wanted to spare him the man said 'No! What am I going to do with this child when his mother is here then. Go on, go together'. It was a psychiatrist, a woman, this woman, was saved. There was one who was dressed . . . a Muslim . . . 'OK, Go.' It is luck. There is another girl who I think was shot in the thigh. She works for Immigration in Kigali.

Interviewer: . . . take the property and go.

Interviewee: Yes at the beginning everybody was saying that they were going to take the property and go but some of them wanted to kill but I understood that among themselves, nobody wanted to oppose the others, each could do as he liked, except we could feel that there was somebody firing orders but in the meantime it was as if he was not in control of the situation. He was saying 'There is more luggage, come, no you come', there were many of them . . . I know that a girl was saved like this. She was on the lorry '???' you see but if you were alone with someone, he could let you go but for us who were all crammed together with . . . we, the survivors, they believed we were dead already, apart from the people who were saved, they could not imagine that among the bodies there was somebody who was still breathing. We had the courage to lift ourselves fifteen or twenty minutes later when we could no longer hear anything. To see the state we were in, we were like corpses.

Interviewer: Have you noticed anything? Did you look at the people who were shooting?

Interviewee: Yes we could see them but the ones who have seen a lot and who spoke a long time with them, it is the driver and the ticket collector because the assailants were making them work, they were saying 'No! Take this!' And the driver and the ticket collector, they did everything believing they were going to let us go, they were saying 'Hurry up!' They said 'Are there any hiding places where there are bags?' That's how they discovered the luggage compartment, where the bags were. There was a lot of baggage, they had the time to take everything. I was thinking OK! The longer it drags on, the more chance of an intervention maybe. Unfortunately there was no intervention. So they all finished, they even forced the driver and the ticket collector to lie down . . . the ticket collector was playing a very active role, he was already undressed because he had jeans, he was just in his underpants . . . even this boy from University he was lying on the tarmac, it was as if he had been forgotten and after he received a bullet in . . . but which hit twice, the bullet bounced on the tarmac and went into his throat. These people were taken into Burundi and were looked after over there. I think he was transferred a week later. I am the only living person who was taken to the hospital with the corpses. I even wanted to go to the military hospital but I said 'No! One must go and unload the dead.' I was completely . . . Because I had lost a lot of blood. I went to . . . and I was looked after there.

— 9 —

Gruelling though it was to have to read through the two eyewitness accounts, I felt as if I had drained a wound. I had the sense now that I knew, as much as I could ever know, what had happened in the last few chaotic moments of Charlotte's life. And now that I had pictured it, in all its horror, it had lost its power over me.

For months after Charlotte's death I'd felt the grief almost as a physical pain, as if I'd been stabbed in the solar plexus, just below my ribcage. All I'd wanted to do was to hide away. And yet something now felt different. The pain was gone, and I found myself wanting to live a normal life again. I could never go back to how I had been before Charlotte was killed, but perhaps now I could try to be someone other than the angry, anguished, self-absorbed loner I had been for the last ten months.

I was less cocky than I had been a year ago, less sure of myself and the world that I lived in – but perhaps also more curious, more sure of how much there was that I didn't yet understand. Charlotte's death had raised many questions that I still felt unable to answer with certainty. But slowly, tentatively, I was beginning to re-emerge into the light.

It was only a short time afterwards, at a party in Hammersmith, just a mile or so from where Charlotte used to live, that I met Heleen. We clicked straightaway. Alongside all the shocking and absurd things I'd been confronted with over the last year, the idea that this sweet, beautiful, Belgian girl might want to share her life with me didn't seem so outrageous.

I still thought about Charlotte every day, but her death was no longer the dominating feature of my life, and it was no longer such an effort to focus on other things. When I was with Heleen I felt like a normal person again.

We didn't spend a day apart for the next three weeks. I bounced into work each morning with an energy I'd not felt in years. At the back of my mind I still had a nagging feeling that fate had made a clerical error, but just like the man who's accidentally had somebody else's £100,000 transferred into his bank account, I was determined to make the most of it until the day the mistake was rectified.

Losing Charlotte was, by a long margin, the worst thing ever to happen to me. But I was beginning to think that meeting Heleen had been, by a similarly long margin, the very best. And both these things had happened in the space of a year. I found it impossible to understand, so I stopped trying to understand it.

Heleen left for Belgium just before Christmas Eve. On Christmas Day, in Bristol again, I tried my hardest not to talk about Burundi, or what had happened to Charlotte. In three days time it would be the first anniversary of her death, and the subject was just too painful. We drank a toast to 'absent friends' and made the best we could of it.

28 December 2001 was a Friday, and I'd taken the day off work. I felt strangely detached when I woke up that morning. It didn't seem so different from the day before. It was just a name and a number, after all. Today was the 365th day after Charlotte's death. Yesterday had been the 364th. Tomorrow would be the 366th. It just so happened that we measured time in a way that made this day seem significant.

But as the morning drew on, it started to feel less and less like just another day. In the afternoon I went alone to the Church of Saint Alban, where we'd held Charlotte's funeral. It was only the second time I'd been back there since the funeral. Then there had been hundreds of people here, and the air filled with incense, music, smoke from the candles. Now the building was empty and quiet. I walked over to where I had sat during the funeral. I looked across to where Charlotte's coffin had been laid, just in front of the altar. 'It's me', I said, in my head, wondering if she would hear me. I felt very alone.

I tried to imagine what the families of the other victims were doing today. I thought about the services being held, and prayers being said in Burundi and Rwanda. Catherine and I had planned to organize some kind of memorial event for today, but so many people were out of town for Christmas and the New Year that we'd postponed it. I felt ashamed that we'd not been able to do more.

What was I doing here, really? What would I say if anyone came and asked me that question? I walked over to the side of the church. Next to one of the pillars was a black, metal candlestand, with a box of thin, white, offertory candles. I dropped my money into the collection box, and counted out 21. I arranged the candles quickly into three tiers on the stand. I was getting jumpy now. I lit the candles as fast as I could, 2 first – for Charlotte and Richard, then the other 19, for the people who'd died with them. At the exit I looked back at my bonfire of candles, burning like a beacon in the dim, church light. Somewhere inside the building I thought I heard a door opening. I walked out into the end-of-year gloom.

It was 2002, the second year of my life in which Charlotte had never lived and a couple of weeks after the first anniversary of her death, we took her old dog to the vet to be put to sleep. The most gluttonous animal in north London was 17 years old. Lady had outlived all expectations, but when she was diagnosed with lymphatic cancer we knew that she didn't have long. It was clear that her time was up when she started refusing food. Lady protested loudly when the vet inserted the needle into her leg, and as I helped to hold her down, I couldn't help feeling that I was betraying this loyal, greedy, good-natured animal. It felt as if a part of my childhood was dying with her – as if another connection with Charlotte had been broken.

In early February the Foreign Secretary Jack Straw wrote to my mother to say that he'd raised Charlotte's case with President Buyoya. We'd heard little from the police – and nothing at all on the effort to find photographs of the men suspected of involvement in Charlotte's death, but at least the Foreign Office seemed to be taking the case more seriously.

Gradually, Burundi was beginning to creep back into my life, but there was a new dimension now. Britain and America were fighting a global war on terror. I wrote to Jack Straw, thanking him for raising Charlotte's case, and suggesting that Palipehutu-FNL should be proscribed as a terrorist group. I received no reply.

A few days later, the Foreign Office published its long-awaited proposals for dealing with the growth of British-run mercenary firms, or 'Private Military Companies' as it preferred to call them.

Today's world is a far cry from the 1960s, when private military activity usually meant mercenaries of the rather unsavoury kind involved in post-colonial or neo-colonial conflicts . . .

I read through Jack Straw's foreword with a growing sense of incredulity. Rather than clamping down on the illegal activities of such firms, the government had a novel solution – decriminalization. With a well-run system of licensing and regulation, Straw suggested, mercenaries might be a force for good in the world. The UN could even employ 'Private Military Companies' for peacekeeping operations. Furthermore:

> An outright ban on the provision of all military services would not necessarily contribute to global security. And it would deprive British defence exporters of contracts for services of considerable value.

The briefing paper seemed stronger on euphemistic management-speak than it was on detail, and I found it odd that it had so little to say about the distinctly neo-colonial conflict rampaging in the Congo. There was no mention at all of Avient, the British-run 'Private Military Company' accused of running bombing raids in the eastern Congo and airlifting guns to the FNL's Hutu-extremist allies, the Interahamwe.

At the end of the month Richard Ndereyimana's older brother Jean-Bosco arrived in the UK. We met in a small room, at the end of a long, badly lit corridor in a dingy and dilapidated 'hotel' on a Heathrow industrial estate. He looked painfully thin, but happy and, perhaps most of all, relieved. 'They are very nice here. They help me very much', he said before switching to his far more eloquent French.

Jean-Bosco had decided to leave Burundi because of *quelques problèmes*. He had escaped, and arrived here, he told us, through *la grace de Dieu* – the grace of God. Among the few possessions he'd been able to bring were photographs of his wife Carine, and their two small children – Simone and Rachel. He was hoping to be reunited with them soon. Only when he mentioned his brother, or the *problèmes* that had driven him to leave his family and flee, did a shadow pass across his face. I didn't ask what he had to do in order to get out.

Within four weeks Jean-Bosco had been granted 'exceptional leave to remain' on humanitarian grounds. My mother had never heard of a case going through so quickly. Perhaps *la grace de Dieu* had played a role here too. Jean-Bosco was sent to Nottingham under the government's refugee dispersal scheme, then Manchester.

Each time I spoke to Jean-Bosco his English had improved a little more. He'd been given his own flat, in a very nice place called Salford. Did I know it? It was on the thirteenth floor of a very tall tower. He could look out of his window and see the whole of Manchester. He'd found a job, packing chocolates in a factory. He was hoping to be reunited with his wife and children very soon.

Jean-Bosco told me more about the *problèmes* he had fled. At a government press conference a few days after the Titanic Express attack, he had spoken up and asked why the security on the road had been so lax, and what the authorities were doing to bring the perpetrators to justice. The death threats had begun soon afterwards – first the letters pushed under his door at night, then the phone calls. 'We're going to break your face, Jean-Bosco! Do you think you're the only one who's lost somebody?'

He still wasn't sure whether the threats had been made by the FNL, or by someone connected to the government, outraged that he'd had the audacity to criticize them. A family friend in the police had told him that the authorities knew where the killers were, but had no intention of arresting them. The friend had refused to say why.

The FNL's attacks were continuing unabated, and Jean-Bosco remained very worried for his family. The district where they lived was regularly attacked, and barely a night went by that they didn't hear gunfire. *Les assaillants* always came after dark, Jean-Bosco told me. Small groups of FNL combatants would sneak down from the hills, kill a handful of people and then retreat again before the army could intervene. They claimed to be fighting 'to avenge the death of Ndadaye', the elected president who had been assassinated in 1993. Anyone in Bujumbura was considered to be on the side of the government, and therefore a legitimate target. Things could have been very different if Ndadaye had lived, Jean-Bosco told me. For most of his life, Burundi had been a peaceful country, one of the richest and most fertile in Central Africa. Unemployment was low, and everyone had enough to eat. But the war triggered by Ndadaye's murder had destroyed the economy, and plunged thousands into extreme poverty.

The army could defeat the FNL if they were allowed to pursue them into their hilltop strongholds, but President Buyoya was insisting that they hold back, Jean-Bosco said. Buyoya was widely suspected of being behind Ndadaye's death. Some believed that he was deliberately prolonging the conflict because he feared being prosecuted if democracy was restored.

Eighteen months ago, this conspiracy theory would have seemed completely absurd to me, but after everything else I'd heard about Burundi, Rwanda and the Congo. I found it harder to dismiss. Whatever the truth, the very fact that these ideas had such currency seemed to say something about the suspicion with which Burundians viewed both their own government, and the rebels who claimed to be fighting in their name.

It was odd to think that the chain of events which led to Charlotte's death had begun nearly seven years earlier, and odder still to think that the murder of this one man could have triggered so many thousands of others. In October 1993, Charlotte had just been starting her third year of university; I'd been in my last year of school. Was it possible that Charlotte might have lived if Ndadaye hadn't been killed?

> For want of a nail the shoe was lost,
> For want of a shoe the horse was lost
> For want of a horse the rider was lost
> For want of a rider the battle was lost.

In May I got an email from a Burundian based in Canada, Kabonesho Kagongo, who'd been a close friend of Richard Ndereyimana's through both school and university. He was a member of a Burundian campaign group, Action Contre Genocide, and was keen to join forces over the Titanic Express. I still heard from Pierre from time to time, and although I never heard from Maria any more he often mentioned her in his emails. She seemed to have taken him under her wing.

Catherine and Carl got married in Boston the day before Catherine's 24th birthday. Apart from a short hop to Belgium earlier in the year, it was the first time I'd flown since visiting Charlotte in Rwanda. Catherine had asked me to make a speech at the reception remembering Charlotte and our father, but as the day approached I became more and more nervous. Though I'd spoken about Charlotte at the funeral, at our memorial concert earlier in the year and on the radio a good few times between, I suddenly felt as though the wind had gone out of my sails. She was dead, what more was there to say?

I spent hours mulling over my speech, but in the end I abandoned everything I'd written and went for a short, off-the-cuff two-minuter. I was nervous, which didn't help, and the tears and the nerves combined with unsightly effect. 'Charlotte would have been very . . .', I gulped, as the nerves cut in. I tried to recover by choking the word out again; *'very* . . . happy to be here today.' Ugh, why did I have to sound so mawkish? Now the whole room was thinking 'poor little grieving relative'. I wrapped it up quickly and sat down. Catherine came over and hugged me. Carl shook my hand, looking slightly relieved that I'd kept it so short. I'd wanted to do something to remember Charlotte. Catherine had asked me to make this speech. But for some reason it had just felt wrong.

I had a call again from Rory Beaumont soon after I got back. The Burundian journalist who'd worked on 'Breaking the Codes', Alexis Sinduhije, was coming to the UK, and was willing to meet with me. Alexis, who now ran an NGO-funded radio in Bujumbura, Radio Publique Africaine, was in Oxford, meeting his donors. He'd done some investigations on the Titanic Express massacre and had some information for me.

I met Alexis just outside the Oxford college where he was staying. He looked like someone who'd just flown out of a war zone, tough and business-like, yet slightly gaunt and very edgy. He chainsmoked throughout our conversation.

'Something has to change in Burundi – people are dying for *nothing*!', he told me. His radio station deliberately employed both ex-rebels and former government soldiers as journalists. The idea was to rebuild trust between different communities, but it also meant that he got the gossip from both sides, as many of the journalists still had friends in the various armed groups.

'You know, the FNL killed your sister because she shouted at them', he told me.

Surely this couldn't be right – why had I heard nothing about it before?

'Yes – they say that they were going to let her go, but when they started killing people she yelled 'You're mad! You're crazy!' at them, so they said 'OK, you can die too'.'

Surely Charlotte wouldn't be so reckless?

My problem was that I could easily believe that it was something she *would* do. More than that, I had *wanted* to believe that Charlotte might have given her killers a piece of her mind before they shot her. I'd wanted to think that she would have stood up for herself in the face of death, as she had always done in life. Yet what if her defiance was the reason she had been killed?

But the more I thought about it, the less it seemed to make sense. I'd read through two gruesomely detailed, eyewitness accounts of the Titanic Express massacre, and neither of them had said anything about Charlotte, or anyone else, confronting the killers. Was it possible that this was a story the FNL had made up in order to justify having killed a foreigner?

Alexis told me that he'd heard a rumour that Anicet Ntawuhiganayo, a senior FNL figure and their main spokesman, had been trying to sell on Charlotte's passport. He had been working to buy the passport from Ntawuhiganayo through an intermediary, but the FNL man had mysteriously disappeared. There were suggestions that he'd been killed, following a bust-up with the group's leader Agathon Rwasa.

More rumours about Ntawuhiganayo emerged a few days later. A rival Hutu faction had made an attempt on Rwasa's life, and Ntawuhiganayo was accused of being complicit. Some reports said that he'd been tortured to death, others that he'd been beheaded. The FNL leader was reported to be seriously injured.

In spite of myself, I couldn't help feeling pleased that the FNL were fighting among themselves, and that Ntawuhiganayo had come to such a sticky end. Whether or not he'd actually been present during the Titanic Express attack, whether or not he was the one who pulled the trigger and shot Charlotte, he was one of *them*. His was a name I'd seen in countless news reports. This was a man who'd filled endless column inches trying to justify what his group was doing without ever owning up to the atrocities they'd been committing. He was part of an organization whose main tactic was to kill innocent people, and if he'd not been involved in Charlotte's death, I was sure he'd been involved in others. Now his arrogance, his stupidity and the consequences of all those deaths had finally caught up with him.

For the first time I'd had a sense of what it *might* feel like to know that the account had been settled. To think that I might one day be able to stop being so angry.

To stop being so angry I remembered a time when I'd found it hard to understand other people's anger, found it hard to trust it. I used to tell myself that I needed to be a bit more aggressive, a bit more pushy. No such worries now. These days I'd embraced anger, and rage, and hatred. A man I knew almost nothing about had been killed, in a gruesome and disgusting way, in a country I'd never even visited – and here I was rejoicing about it. *Rejoicing* about his gruesome, disgusting death because he *might* have had something to do with Charlotte's gruesome, disgusting death. Rejoicing because he was FNL. Rejoicing because he was a Hutu-extremist. Because he was one of *them*. Meeting Heleen had created a space in my life in which Charlotte's death was not the dominant feature, but now that space seemed to be shrinking again. Was I slipping backwards?

'I'm not happy in London', Heleen told me, tearfully, one day in June. Before she met me she'd thought about joining the Belgian diplomatic corps, travelling the world, never staying in the same country for more than a couple of years. She had itchy feet. She wanted to go travelling. She'd been in London nearly two years now, and she'd had enough. Everything was so expensive. The trains were dirty and overcrowded. You couldn't take a walk without breathing in a head full of pollution. And she hated her job.

I wasn't faring much better. However much I liked my colleagues, and however much I was allowed to vary my work I was finding it more and more difficult again to avoid being distracted. It was nearly 18 months now since Charlotte had been killed, but my feelings about the job had barely changed at all.

It was the summer of 2002, and everyone seemed to be expecting that London would be the next target for Al Qaeda. Angry, stressed-out, commuter London seemed even more angry and stressed than usual. The beep-beep-beeping noises jarred our nerves more than ever these days. Yet the thought of leaving London to go abroad also terrified me. This had been my home for nearly eight years. I'd come here at the end of my teens, and lived here ever since. This was where all of my friends were, and I didn't see enough of them in any case. If I went abroad, how could I avoid creating even more of a distance? Yet it was clear that Heleen had her heart set on seeing Asia, and I'd seen too many long-distance relationships fail. I agreed to go with her, on the condition that we wouldn't just be tourists. We set about looking for volunteer work.

In August we at last heard back from the Home Office about Pierre. The Immigration Minister Beverley Hughes repeated the line that the Foreign Office had given us a year earlier, claiming that Pierre would have to go to Uganda to apply for a UK visa, and that such an application would almost certainly be refused if the embassy staff believed it likely he would apply for asylum, adding:

> No objective documentary evidence of the ambush has been provided nor has evidence been submitted to show that Mr. Nzeyimana has, or would, suffer a sustained pattern or campaign of persecution directed at him which has been, or would be, knowingly tolerated by the authorities or which the authorities were, or would be, unable or unwilling to offer him effective protection from. There is no evidence that a date has been set for a trial nor would there appear to be any certainty that a trial will indeed take place at any future date. The correspondence suggests that the ambush occurred some time prior to July 2001, since which time Mr. Nzeyimana has remained in Burundi; the passage of time would seem to mitigate against the credibility of Mr. Nzeyimana's fear of reprisals . . .

But the story didn't end there. I'd not heard from Pierre for some time when he sent me an email almost completely out of the blue: 'On 31st August 2002 I'M GOING TO MARRY MARIA!!!!' Bemused, I sent them both my congratulations. Maria had always talked fondly of Pierre, and I knew they were friends, but I'd never expected this.

The global war on terror was proceeding apace. Throughout the year the US government had been making louder and louder noises about the threat posed to the world by Iraq. But there was no sign, as yet, of any action against terrorism in Burundi. The Foreign Office told me that they were against the idea of proscribing the FNL as a 'terrorist organization' because it might damage the Burundian peace process.

I found this perverse. Kabonesho and Jean-Bosco both told me that the FNL raised funds from the Burundian diaspora in Europe. I'd seen numerous press releases from the Benelux section of Palipehutu-

FNL. There was even a Section Scandinavie et Grande Bretagne. Surely trying to cut off the FNL's funding would *help*, not hinder, the peace process?

A few days after my birthday, I was looking at BBC Online when I saw news of another big massacre in Burundi. The killings had occurred in early September, at Itaba, in the centre of the country. One website claimed that 1,000 people had been killed; the BBC said 173. But whatever the exact figure, the death toll clearly dwarfed the number who'd died with Charlotte on 28 December. At the lowest estimate, this attack had been six times more deadly.

But this time it was the Burundian army that was responsible. The army claimed that the civilians had been caught in the crossfire during fighting with the FDD. Local journalists cast doubt on this – many of the victims had been bayoneted or shot dead at point-blank range. Dozens of the dead were children. Almost all of the victims were Hutu. As more details emerged, the 'crossfire' claim looked less and less credible. The FDD had passed through Itaba, but they had left the area several hours before the Burundian army launched its attack. It began to look more and more as though Itaba had simply been a reprisal massacre, with the army deliberately targeting Hutu civilians in retaliation for losses inflicted on them by the FDD.

In character, this attack seemed no different to me to the one in which Charlotte had died. In both cases, simply belonging to the same ethnic group as the 'enemy' was enough to seal the victim's fate. The only real difference seemed to be that far more people had died at Itaba. And if the FNL had been sure of untouchability over the Titanic Express massacre, how much more untouchable must the Burundian government's own armed forces be? Except that there would, of course, be consequences. If the survivors of Itaba hadn't been Hutu extremists before they saw their loved ones hacked and shot to death by 'l'armée monoethnique Tutsi', there was a good chance that some of them would be now.

Since meeting Alexis Sinduhije in May, I'd heard very little from him. I'd passed on to the police his offer to put one of his journalists on the case full-time, if they could come up with some money to cover the salary. It was no great surprise when they visited my mother to tell her this 'wouldn't be possible'.

I forwarded Matthews a report I'd found by the International Crisis

Group, which spelled out specifically that the Titanic Express attack had been the work of FNL troops 'under the order of . . . Agathon Rwasa'. Might it be worth the police contacting the International Crisis Group to see if they had any new information? Even if it wasn't yet possible to identify the individual who'd fired the gun that killed Charlotte, surely there was scope for trying to go after those higher up the command chain?

Matthews gave me no answer. When we met him again at my mother's house in September, he told us there wasn't much more that he could do. In a way it was something of a relief. If the police were saying that they'd reached a dead end, then it would be harder for them to stop me from taking my own initiative. I was already working only four days a week. In a couple of months I'd be leaving my job, and would then be free for several weeks until we left for Asia at the end of the year. It would be interesting to see how much I could get done between now and then.

The pressure for military action against Iraq seemed to be growing by the week. In September, the British government produced a dossier, alleging that Iraq was trying to develop nuclear weapons. Most startling of all was the claim that the Iraqis had missiles capable of reaching Britain, and that they could deploy them at just 45-minute's notice. The US government, meanwhile, seemed convinced that the Iraqi government was linked to Al Qaeda and might even have helped organize the World Trade Center attacks.

But more and more people were questioning the basis of these claims, with some suggesting that the threat was being deliberately exaggerated. I found it hard to believe that our government would simply fabricate intelligence to help start a war – but then 18 months ago I could never have believed that the Rwandans could manipulate the threat posed by the Interahamwe to justify their resource-grab in the Congo. Although I suspected that the 45-minute claim was overblown, I couldn't help feeling uneasy. I'd never quite exorcised my childhood fear of the Russians and the bombs that *they* had targeted on London. It was definitely time to leave.

I kept up my search for information about the FNL's leader, Agathon Rwasa. Eventually, tucked away on yet another clumsily laid out pro-Hutu website, I found a long article in French that Rwasa himself had written. It was the first time I'd seen anything approaching a detailed outline of the FNL's world view. With the help of my French dictionary and the Babel Fish online translator, I slowly transcribed it into English.

> The major issue in the conflicts of the Great Lakes is that there is in this region a group of peoples who take themselves to be superior to others; supermen, they believe, who are prepared to impose and perpetuate their hegemony over the other peoples, if the need arises, by means of the sword and spear . . .

This was the accusation usually levelled at the Tutsis – what was interesting was that Rwasa wasn't merely talking about one ethnic group, but a 'group of peoples'. I'd read elsewhere about a kind of 'grand unifying theory' of Hutu extremism, which sought to define the Hutu–Tutsi conflicts in Rwanda and Burundi as part of a wider pan-African struggle between Bantu peoples and Hima or Nilotic ethnic groups. Bantu peoples would include the Hutus of Rwanda and Burundi, together with the majority populations in Tanzania, the DRC, Angola, Namibia and much of the rest of Southern Africa. The Hima would include the Tutsis of Rwanda, Burundi and the western DRC, along with much of East Africa – Uganda, Ethiopia, Somalia and Eritrea.

> These sly hegemonists find support from the arms-producing nations, nations who, for the purposes of selling and testing their weapons, want to export their politics and, through that, establish influence and strategic control over eastern and southern Africa. Also, these nations want to exploit the natural mineral resources of the region, exclusively and for a good price. That's why, even as they arm these dictators against the peoples of the region, they seek to beguile the oppressed by talking about, and supporting, peace processes which are, in reality, nonexistent.

When I read this I was immediately reminded of what Charlotte's killers had told her. 'It's the white people supplying the weapons in Africa.' Just as in colonial times, the Tutsis had been lackeys of the Belgians, so now the Hima were in league with the 'arms-producing nations'. The white people were 'arming the dictators' in order to gain control of Africa's natural resources, and Charlotte had to pay the price.

It was the first time I'd seen more than just a few short quotes from Agathon Rwasa, the first time I'd seen a really detailed explanation of what the FNL were fighting for. Rwasa went on to talk about the enemy's devilish plan to create a 'Tutsi–Hima Empire', which would dominate and control the resources of the DRC and the wider region. Chief among the malefactors was the Rwandan President, Paul Kagame, and the Ugandan leader, Yoweri Museveni.

It all sounded surprisingly similar to the conspiracy theories I'd seen on the website of the Executive Intelligence Review, where allegations of an international conspiracy to build a Tutsi Empire in Central Africa sat comfortably alongside more coded references to a 'Zionist conspiracy'. In a way, this seemed to make perfect sense. The idea of a powerful and shadowy Tutsi–Hima elite, ruthlessly manipulating the geopolitics of the region for their own wicked ends, was not so different from the 'Jewish Banking Conspiracies' which seemed to have inspired the authors of Executive Intelligence Review. Perhaps it shouldn't be a surprise that those who look at the world in terms of an epic racial struggle should mirror one another.

But Rwasa's wild claims did have an echo in reality. In October, the UN released its long-awaited, and snappily titled 'Final Report of the Panel of Experts on the Illegal Exploitation of Natural Resources and Other Forms of Wealth of the Democratic Republic of Congo'.

Rwanda's leaders have succeeded in persuading the international community that their military presence in the eastern Democratic Republic of Congo protects the country against hostile groups in the Democratic Republic of Congo, who, they claim, are actively mounting an invasion against them . . . The Panel has extensive evidence to the contrary . . .

A 30-year-old Interahamwe combatant living in the area of Bukavu described the situation in a taped interview with a United Nations officer in early 2002.

'We haven't fought much with the RPA [Rwandan Patriotic Army] in the last two years. We think they are tired of this war, like we are. In any case, they aren't here in the Congo to chase us, like they pretend. I have seen the gold and coltan mining they do here, we see how they rob the population. These are the reasons for their being here. The RPA come and shoot in the air and raid the villagers' houses but they don't attack us any more. If you are lucky, and you have a big brother in the RPA, he might be able to get you some food and ammunition.'

Eighty-five multinational companies were accused of violating the international guidelines on war profiteering. Most were Rwandan, Ugandan, Zimbabwean or from Belgium, the former colonial power in the Congo, but twelve were registered in Britain. One of the twelve was Avient Air, the British 'Private Military Company' which had been accused of supplying guns to the Interhamwe. The UN seemed to confirm one of the main allegations against Avient – that the company had been actively involved in bombing raids against Rwandan government forces. More interesting still, Avient were alleged to have links with a diamond-mining firm, Oryx, who were also accused of profiteering. And John Bredenkamp, a British-based Zimbabwean businessman with, according to the UN, 'a history of clandestine military procurement', was accused of breaching European Union sanctions by supplying British Aerospace equipment to the Zimbabwean forces fighting in the Congo.

The *Observer* reported that Bredenkamp, despite being a foreign national, had been given consular advice by Foreign Office staff in Zimbabwe, as he sought to dispute the allegations. Notwithstanding Tony Blair's pledge to 'sort out the blight' in the Congo, when a Liberal Democrat MP, Norman Lamb, had raised questions in Parliament about Avient Air and the nature of the Foreign Office's relationship with Bredenkamp, the response had been evasive.

I got more startling news from Pierre at the end of October. Maria was pregnant – and they would both soon be leaving Burundi to begin a new life in Moscow.

There were only a few weeks now before we were due to leave for Southeast Asia, and it seemed as if we'd reached another dead end with Charlotte's case. I had not had much luck getting the story into the media recently, so I decided to try something different. I wrote an article highlighting the inconsistency between the government's attitude to the FNL and their attitude to Al Qaeda, and it was published on one of the growing number of anti-war websites.

I forwarded the link to Kabonesho Kagongo, who passed it on to a journalist contact of his in Burundi. The next day, Burundi's Netpress news agency ran a story on the case, quoting some of my comments, and adding that the British government had issued an arrest warrant for Agathon Rwasa, in connection with Charlotte Wilson's death.

Kabonesho asked me if the report was true. I told him I didn't know anything about it, though of course it was possible that there were things going on that I hadn't been told. It occurred to me that there was a more straightforward possibility, however. Although my French wasn't that good, I'd noticed that I had been quoted quite liberally in the Netpress article. Kabonesho told me, with some amusement, that the report had kicked up something of a storm in Burundi. One of his contacts told him that a number of other politicians were starting to sound nervous – if Rwasa was likely to be arrested, should they be watching their backs too?

The next day, the Pan-African news agency reported the arrest warrant story, together with a defiant quote from Rwasa, angrily denying any involvement in the Titanic Express massacre, claiming that it was all a conspiracy to discredit him, and saying that he was ready to face any court. It was the first time I'd seen a statement from Rwasa specifically referring to the attack, and small though it was, this seemed like another step forward.

But I was now thoroughly confused about the report of an arrest warrant for Rwasa. I was doubtful about the truth of it, and even more uncertain about where the information had come from. But if Netpress had simply made it up, how come other news agencies had reported it too? Given our experiences over the last couple of years I was doubtful that I'd receive much clarification from the Foreign Office.

Yet there was also another issue. Whether or not the story about the arrest warrant was true, it seemed to have got Burundi's political elite worried, and brought the wider issues of justice and impunity back onto the agenda. If the Foreign Office wanted to issue a denial, then they could do – but in the meantime I didn't feel under any obligation to scotch the rumour myself. And there was also the question of the 'international community' in all of this. There was ample evidence of FNL atrocities, and little doubt that Rwasa was guilty of crimes punishable under 'universal jurisdiction' laws in a number of European countries – so if Britain *hadn't* issued an arrest warrant for Rwasa, maybe it was time that they did.

For the first time since I'd seen him in May, I had a call from Alexis

Sinduhije, asking if my mother and I would be willing to give an interview to his radio station, Radio Publique Africaine.

'Let's see if we can really point the finger', he said. 'We need to start putting some pressure on Rwasa.'

Alexis interviewed us in English, live on air, simultaneously translating our answers into Kirundi. As the interview progressed I felt more and more defiant. I knew there was a good chance that someone in the FNL would be listening, and I wanted them to know we hadn't gone away. It was nearly two years since they had killed Charlotte and the others, bragging that 'there's nothing you can do'. They'd thought that the crime would quickly be forgotten and it hadn't been yet. However much Rwasa was able to frighten and intimidate his Burundian victims, we were beyond his reach.

If the initial stories about Rwasa had shaken up the apple tree, the interview we gave to Radio Publique Africaine seemed to rattle it up even more. Kabonesho told me he'd picked up a rumour that Rwasa was now refusing to travel outside Burundi, for fear of being arrested. Jean-Bosco sounded upbeat when I spoke to him; his family in Bujumbura had heard our radio interview and were very encouraged by it. 'L'union fait la force' – 'In unity there is strength', he told me.

How to build on this momentum? Now that I had more time, I set about doing something I'd been wanting to do for quite a while – putting up a website focusing specifically on the FNL. I'd discovered that the domain name www.palipehutu-fnl.com was available. Unable to resist the temptation, put down my 35 dollars and reserved it. I was now 'domain squatting' the terror group that had killed my sister. Part of me hoped that they would try to sue me for copyright infringement.

I spent a couple of hours putting together a very rudimentary website, giving basic information about the FNL and Agathon Rwasa, with links to human rights reports about FNL atrocities.

Meanwhile, in Burundi, an apple had dropped out of the tree. Early one morning I had a phone call from Kabonesho.

'Good morning, Richard – I hope I didn't get you out of bed, did I?'

'I've had a message from a journalist friend of mine, in Bujumbura. He says that he has got hold of this FNL document . . . He thinks it's a report about the Titanic Express massacre.'

— 10 —

'It's handwritten. They've drawn up some kind of table . . . 28.12 –
presumably that's the date. . . 40 mils . . . on one line it says 'embush'
– then they've circled it and scrawled something else – 'Titanic – en
provenance du Rwanda'. But most of the page seems to be taken up
with a list of what they looted. There's a 'result' column, and on the
first line it says '21 tués' – nothing more than that. Twenty-one dead,
and they get just one line. Then it says 'butini' – booty, and it goes
into such microscopic detail . . . 'a bottle of Martini, shirts, trousers,
shoes . . . a television, a projector, part of a keyboard. Six pairs of
children's shoes. A bottle of vegetable oil. I can't believe that they're
given more space to a bottle of vegetable oil than they do to the
people they killed.'

Pascal, Kabonesho's friend in Bujumbura, had faxed through one of
the pages of the FNL report to my uncle, in Bristol. Now he was
talking it through with me over the phone.

The full report was too big to fax through in its entirety, Pascal told
me. The DHL office insisted on inspecting the contents of any
package sent through their service – and he was afraid that someone
in the office might be a rebel sympathizer. In Bujumbura you could
never be sure. In any case, the more people who knew that he had this
document, the more danger he would be in.

We were stuck. Pascal couldn't fax the document, he couldn't send
it by international courier. He didn't have access to a scanner. I was
going to have to ask for help from the Foreign Office. This time I
tried contacting the British Embassy directly. I'd picked up the name
of Tim Cooper, one of the staff in Rwanda who'd worked on Charlotte's case, in previous correspondence with the Foreign Office in
London, so early one morning I called the embassy. Cooper sounded
friendly enough, if a little surprised to hear from me. I told him

Pascal's name, and it turned out that Cooper had had contact with him before. He agreed to try and arrange a meeting to pick up the report next time he was in Bujumbura. 'And presumably you'd like us to forward you a copy?'

My uncle posted me the page that had been faxed to him, and I received it the next day. Every detail was meticulously noted on the FNL's little handwritten form, columns neatly drawn, titles underlined. Alongside the details of what they had stolen from Charlotte and the other passengers, the FNL had recorded the different kinds of guns they'd used – mostly Kalashnikovs, from what I could make out, and even the number of bullets expended: 647 – more than 30 for every passenger they'd killed.

The list of stolen items included Rwandan, Kenyan, Congolese and Burundian money, US dollars, Erikson, Motorola and Nokia mobile phones, shirts, trousers and, chillingly, children's clothes.

I started to hear from more and more Burundians. One email, from a man based in Germany, seemed especially moving:

Hi Mr Wilson,

I'm a burundi who leaves in Germany since 1997. A friend has send me your site you have created in memory of your sister who was killed in Burundi in December 2000 with Richard her boy friend. I didn't read all on your site, my first reaction is to write with attention to thanks. Richard was a friend at Burundi university, I was student in medecines faculty (2 years) and have moved from Burundi. There was a problem between Hutu and Tutsi's student. And I'm the product of both and I didn't have a place anywhere at moment. I took a long way to Germany, it took many time, finally I got it.

I didn't lost only Richard, there are 4 other friends from Rwanda . . . Not only friends, there was my sister, Mrs Mbyeyinzima Laetitia (Titi), we were like twins. I was 1 year old than her. She was pregnant, and waited of her Wedding in February.

You know, I lost so many members of family, oncles, cousins, ounts, friends . . . but as I have gotten the bady news, I have gone in Hospital for 2 weeks! Automatically, I got a crankest 'Morbus meniere'. It is very hard to me until now. But slowly it get me better.

I'm brimming with tears at now, I can't finish my mail, so . . . if I can do something for your target, which can be my, tell me. I'm ready, but you have to know something, I'm not a politician, but I'm adherent of peace and human rights.

I'm sorry of my bad English, I'm not english speaker . . . (only French and Germany).

God bless you,

Prosper

In his next email, Prosper sent me a picture of himself with his sister. I guessed that it must have been taken a few years before the attack, when Prosper was in his mid-twenties, and they both still lived in Burundi. Prosper looked like a gentleman, tall and thin, stylishly dressed, with a protective arm around his younger sister. Titi, a little smaller than her brother, had the same short hair and African clothing as the women I'd seen in Rwanda.

Another email came from a young girl in Rwanda. 'Monsieur Richard' had been her teacher. He'd never done any harm to anyone, and didn't deserve to die. She hoped that we would find justice 'un jour'.

But one email was very different in character. I got a sense of it just from the subject line: 'mensonge sur FNL' – 'lie against the FNL'.

Dear editor

I am a member of the FNL in Europe and I would like to talk to you about your web site. Please provide me with your telephone number so that I can contact you.

Charles Nzeyimana

It felt as if I'd crossed a line. For the last few months I'd been trying to provoke a reaction from the FNL, bouncing my rubber ball against Rwasa's door. Now the door had opened, and I was face to face with a representative of the group that had killed Charlotte. The real question was, now that the FNL had contacted me, what was I going to do about it?

Tim Cooper emailed me to say that he'd picked up the FNL report from Pascal, and dispatched it to London in a sealed diplomatic bag. 'It doesn't tell us much more than we already know – i.e. that the FNL were responsible', was his view. I told him that I was nonetheless looking forward to seeing a copy.

In early December my mother called me, sounding mightily amused. Agathon Rwasa was refusing to travel to South Africa for talks, fearing that the British government would arrest him over Charlotte Wilson's murder. The police had come and told her that I, personally, was jeopardizing the entire Burundian peace process through the efforts I'd been making to publicize the case.

It was a move that smacked of desperation. Through a combination of luck, good contacts and persistence I'd helped to uncover what appeared to be a crucial piece of documentary evidence relating to Charlotte's death – and the police wanted me to stop. It seemed clear now that the police and the Foreign Office were more worried about the risk of an international embarrassment than that of Charlotte's killers getting away with murder.

But if they were hoping for a similar response from my mother to the one they'd had when they told her I was jeopardizing their investigation by trying to help Pierre, they will have been disappointed. My mother calmly explained to them that she wasn't responsible for my actions, and that if they had something to say to me they should contact me directly. They never did.

Was 'peace' a euphemism for letting murderers off the hook? Kabonesho had warned us of rumours that the Buyoya government's negotiations with Rwasa would involve offering him an amnesty for his crimes. I'd always wondered if it might come to this. I knew that in South Africa dozens of Apartheid killers and torturers had been given a pardon in exchange for publicly confessing what they had done, and asking for forgiveness. I could imagine that some might want to make a case for a similar approach in Burundi. Was I sure that such a strategy was destined to fail? No – but I *was* sure that if the British authorities were in favour of it, they should at least be telling us straight, and put it in writing, rather than sending cryptic messages via the police. I emailed the Foreign Office asking them to clarify how, exactly, I was jeopardizing the peace process. I got no reply.

I wasn't the only one feeling increasingly doubtful about the British government's integrity. There was growing public scepticism over the claims being made about Iraq's Weapons of Mass Destruction. Reading through the Foreign Office dossier online, I was shocked at how vague it was. I couldn't escape the unsettling feeling that the WMD hypothesis was itself little more than a conspiracy theory. In media interviews, Tony Blair insisted that there was other more compelling evidence that he wasn't at liberty to reveal, and that the public would just have to trust him.

My gut instinct told me that he was lying and this came as something of a shock. Less than two years ago, in the aftermath of Charlotte's death, I'd been interviewed by BBC Radio 4 and talked about how proud I was, not only of my sister, but also of my country for being so closely involved in the reconstruction of Rwanda. Even when I learned that the Rwandan politicians we were supporting were not the 'good guys' that I'd wanted to think they were, and even amid the problems we'd had with the Foreign Office, I'd continued to believe in the government's essential good faith. But I realized now that I simply could not trust them any longer. And this realization raised a wider question – if the government might be prepared to lie in order to start a war with Iraq, how could I expect them to tell the truth over something so minor as Charlotte's case.

Charles Nzeyimana and I began to correspond regularly by email – me in my bad French, and he in his. I wasn't alone, he told me.

Many people believe the lies of the Buyoyistes . . . But no, I can guarantee you that we did not take up arms in order to kill innocent people, on the contrary, we took up arms to defend the civilian population being massacred day and night by the army of Buyoya. It is not us, these killings are organized by none other than the soldiers of Buyoya.

I wrote back saying that I'd seen plenty of NGO reports about massacres by the Burundian army – but that every report I'd seen on the attack in which my sister died suggested that the FNL was responsible. Most of the victims were Tutsi and the FNL are known for their hatred of Tutsis. Did he believe that these NGOs were also lying? I knew very well that Agathon Rwasa had blamed the Titanic Express massacre on the Burundian army – but was there any proof?

The Foreign Office had had the FNL report for a few days now. I wrote again to ask when I would be given a copy. Still no response. I was starting to get a feeling that this wasn't going to be straight-forward. I should at least have tried to get a written assurance from them before the document was handed over – but I was so desperate to see it that I hadn't stopped to think. Tim Cooper seemed like a decent enough man, but he couldn't dictate what his colleagues in London – or the Metropolitan Police, for that matter – would decide to do. What were the chances that Matthews would allow them to give me a copy of something as crucial as this FNL report?

Hello Richard,

Truly I understand very well and furthermore I share with you your pain. My family has been decimated by the Tutsi army, but I do not hate all the Tutsis. There are many Tutsi in our party and they work very hard because they too are for change and many are oppressed too. My sisters are married with Tutsi; I'm telling you that we are struggling not against the Tutsi, but against the system and for true justice for all, and against impunity.

Can you tell me which NGO goes where the population is really suffering? I can tell you sincerely that many NGOs are frightened to go there because of the lies propagated by the officials of the Tutsi army. And my question is this: Why are you using are name Palipehutu-FNL for your site? Many people are asking them-selves this question, especially the members of our party. Is it not true that you are working for the regime en place?

I assured Charles that I wasn't anything to do with the *regime en place*. Was this what the FNL leadership was telling its members, or was it simply Charles' own paranoia?

For all I knew Charles might be making up all the things he was telling me. For all I knew Charles Nzeyimana might not even be his real name. But whoever he really was, it sounded like he believed what he was saying. What came over most clearly was anger. Anger at the crimes and deceptions of the Buyoyiste elite, and at those elsewhere in the world who'd been deceived into believing the Buyoyiste lies, anger at me for adding insult to injury with what I'd been saying on the Internet about the FNL. Anger that the world had barely acknowledged the extent that his people had suffered; let alone tried to do anything about it. The NGOs always seemed willing to give aid to the inhabitants of Bujumbura, Charles told me – but where are our rations? For the villagers scraping out an existence in the hills around Burundi's capital, 'Nos rations sont les bombes qui tombent jour et nuit' – 'Our rations are the bombs which fall day and night'.

From the reports I'd read, I also knew that many more Hutus had died than Tutsis. Whether or not Charles was who he said he was, there doubtless were people out there whose families *had* been decimated in attacks by the Tutsi-dominated Burundian army – and these people were also, I didn't doubt, those most likely to support the FNL.

I told Charles I was sorry that he'd lost members of his family. I told him I believed that he believed the FNL were not involved in civilian atrocities, but that I had to be honest with him: the information I'd seen clearly pointed to his group's involvement. The reason I was using the FNL's name for my website was because I believed that they were responsible for my sister's death. I didn't mention that I'd seen detailed eyewitness testimonies describing the attackers as 'rebels' – and a document that appeared to be an FNL report of the attack. I told Charles I was curious to know how he found out about my website. He replied that he'd found it because he'd been hoping to set up a website giving information about Palipehutu-FNL, but discovered that the domain name he wanted had already been taken. The website I was running might 'cause some confusion'. Perhaps I could facilitate some kind of transfer?

I met up again with Rory Beaumont and showed him a copy of the page that Pascal had sent me. He studied it carefully. 'Well there's no way you can be sure, but it *looks* convincing. I mean, who would fake something like this – and why *now?* It just doesn't make sense. If you were going to fake it, why go into so much detail? And what would you get out of it anyway?'

He looked up. 'Have you shown this to DS Matthews? Talk to him – ask him about Interpol. They should get Interpol onto this. It's reached a different level now.'

Until this point I'd tried not to get too excited about the FNL report – but now that Rory had seen it, and given it his cautious, balance-of-probabilities endorsement, I started to feel euphoric. All my efforts over the past two years seemed to be coming to fruition. I'd worked hard to establish some credibility beyond being yet another 'grieving relative', and now at last I was just starting to get somewhere. If I carried on in this vein maybe I could get hold of more documents, find more contacts, gather more snippets of information. Maybe soon I'd have enough material to do what I'd wanted to do ever since Charlotte was killed – write something of my own, get something published about the case without having to rely on good-hearted journalists.

The surge of emails from Burundians around the world continued. One man based in the US suggested that we look into starting joint class action against the FNL, and this idea was taken up enthusiastically by others. I started doing more research on the scope for prosecuting Rwasa in the UK. I'd heard that torturers could be tried here regardless of where the crime took place. Britain was a signatory to the UN Convention Against Torture, which allowed for universal jurisdiction. Ironically, while we could prosecute torturers, there was nothing we could do against a mass-murderer who'd committed their crimes overseas. I mentioned this to Kabonesho when I was on the phone to him one morning.

'Well you know they tortured Richard, don't you?'

For a moment I was stunned. Surely this wasn't right? Pierre had told us that Charlotte and Richard 'died instantaneously'.

'Yes, I helped to identify his body, at the morgue. They had cut his nose. It's what they do to Tutsis, if they have time. They say that we have a big nose, so they cut it off – and then they say 'now you look like us'. They had the time to do it, because the rain drowned out the noise of their guns. The soldiers at the command post nearby didn't hear the shots.'

Kabonesho sounded quite calm as he explained all this to me, but I began to feel sick. I'd started to make peace with the idea that Charlotte, and the man she'd hoped to marry, were dead – but part of my consolation had been the belief that they hadn't suffered for long. However bad it had been for them, it could have been worse.

'They took out his eyes, too. Bosco and I both saw the body. I'm not sure if his mother knows. And I'm sorry to say that he wasn't the only one.'

I was in shock as I put down the phone. I began shaking with anger. Jean-Bosco had told me that he'd been unable to eat meat for a year after he saw his brother's body. Now I understood why. It had been far worse than I'd thought. Richard hadn't simply been killed, he'd been *butchered*.

It seemed unbearable that this gentle man, who my sister had loved, whose sparkling eyes smiled out from the few photos we had of him, could have met his end in this way. It was the detail about the eyes that sickened me the most. I tried to imagine how I would have felt. Did he cry out? Did he beg them to stop? Did Charlotte have to watch?

Why had none of the eyewitnesses mentioned this? I wanted to believe there was some explanation – some account of what had happened that could marry up what Kabonesho had seen with what Pierre had told us. I wanted to believe that Pierre had been telling us the truth – but now, at the back of my mind, I had doubts.

I felt angrier than I had done in a very long time. I couldn't get away from the image of Richard's body, lying in the morgue. That face I'd seen in the photographs, now so horribly disfigured. What could possibly have been going through Jean-Bosco's mind when he saw his brother's body? What must be going through his mind now? The image of Charlotte's dead, blackened face had haunted me for nearly a year after I'd helped to identify her – but this was ten times worse.

I was tired of my tactfully worded exchanges with Charles Nzeyimana. I was tired of being polite, and cautious, tired of feeling angry and powerless. All the FNL's talk of Hutu Liberation, all the grandstanding, all the Tutsi-banking-conspiracies, all the smug, nod-and-wink, implausible denials of responsibility for all the massacres they'd carried out, the sense of victimhood, Charles Nzeyimana and his righteous indignation; all the excuses, all the 'mitigating factors', all the apologetics seemed like empty noise to me now. Because behind all those words was the simple fact of a man's broken, bloodied body, riddled with bullets, his nose slashed off, his eyes gouged out, lying on a slab, in a morgue, while his brother and his best friend looked on. No amount of lying, or relativism, or rationalization could stop it from being horribly, disgustingly real.

I knew it was petty, but I didn't care. If annoying the FNL over the Internet was all I could do right now to get back at them, then at least it was better than nothing. I wrote to Charles saying that I wasn't willing to transfer the website over to him. I'd continue using it to publicize FNL crimes, because every credible bit of information I'd seen seemed to show that the FNL had carried out the Titanic Express attack.

I had another call from Alexis Sinduhije. 'Rwasa was very angry that I broadcast that interview with you and your mother – *very* angry', he told me, sounding amused.

'But there's another thing. We've got hold of this monthly report written by the FNL, from December 2000.'

Alexis went on to describe a document that sounded very much like the one Pascal had been given – but he mentioned one more detail.

'There's a cover page, probably a message to Rwasa – and it's signed by the commander of the FNL's RUK battalion. We're going to write a letter to him, and see if we can get him to write back – then we can try to match the signatures.'

My heart missed a beat. So the document actually named the FNL commander in charge of the unit that carried out the attack? This wasn't just a report – it was a signed confession. I asked Alexis the commander's name.

'Albert. Albert Sibomana.'

I recognized the name as soon as he said it. I'd read about this person before, in a Human Rights Watch report, more than a year ago:

> battalion commander Albert Sibomana directed the execution of Rwandans at several other posts near Kibuye in the commune of Isale . . . FNL fighters summoned a group of some twenty Rwandans and Burundians at 3 a.m., supposedly because Burundian army soldiers were approaching. They separated the Rwandans from the Burundians and ordered the Rwandans to hand over their weapons and to remove their military clothing. They put the Rwandans in a house and showered them with bullets. They left, believing all the victims to be dead, but several survived to recount the events.

When I first read this report I'd wondered if Albert Sibomana might have had something to do with the attack in which Charlotte died but until this moment it had been nothing more than a feeling. Now it seemed positively spooky.

Alexis offered to send me a copy of the FNL report and I gratefully accepted. Pascal had asked me not to tell anyone about his involvement, so although I was fairly sure he had the same document as Alexis, I had no way of checking. In any case, if Alexis could find a way of getting it to me, that would be a way around the problem with the Foreign Office.

By the time Charles Nzeyimana replied to my angry email, I was beginning to question the wisdom of what I'd done. I knew almost nothing about this man, except that he seemed very angry, he lived in the Netherlands and claimed to be a member of an organization that thought nothing of torturing people to death. For a couple of days I let the email sit in my inbox, unread. Before I looked at it I wanted to think about how I was going to react. I didn't want to make any more impulsive decisions. I would be off to Southeast Asia before long, but until recently my mother's address had been available on the Internet to anyone with a little bit of know-how. How would I feel if this ended up rebounding onto her?

Richard,

Just to confirm that if you continue to use our logo palipehutu-fnl.com you will be extradited to justice . . . I'm not so far away from you to pursue you to justice.

Charles Nzeyimana

I'd been an idiot. I'd wanted the FNL to know that Charlotte Wilson's family were on their case, and now they knew. I'd wanted to piss this guy off, and now I had. And what had I achieved? Nothing. I'd done it for no other reason than to make myself feel better. Maybe this was an idle threat and maybe it wasn't, but how much safer were we when the FNL knew nothing about us? The guy was obviously very angry and unpredictable. If he'd been in Holland long enough he'd have a Dutch passport. It wouldn't be that difficult for him to get himself over here. How could I be sure that he wouldn't decide one day to pack up a shotgun in the boot of his car, get on a cross-channel ferry and come looking for me? What if he turned up at my mother's house while I was in Asia next year?

Maybe I should threaten him back – show that I wasn't scared. Tell him that he was welcome to come over and try something – I and my friends would be waiting. I was still being an idiot. It was time to stop taking risks. I gave in, backed off, did what Charles had demanded. I took the website down, and gave up the domain name. I still couldn't be sure that he wouldn't try something – but by letting him win, I'd minimized the risk. Now I should 'lie low' in Asia for a while, calm down and shut up.

Jean-Bosco stayed with us for three days over Christmas, and only once did I catch a glimpse of the darkness behind his habitually cheerful demeanour. We were sitting in front of my computer, talking about ways of developing the Titanic Express campaign.

'Do you know what they did to my little brother?', Jean-Bosco asked me. 'I've never told this to anyone.'

I said that Kabonesho had told me something about it – but I didn't go into detail. It seemed as if Jean-Bosco wanted to talk now.

'There was a Minister from the government there, at the morgue – a Defence Minister. He knew Richard from university, but – but he didn't recognize his body – you understand? He had to ask me who it was. When I told him, he had to look away. Even the Defence Minister couldn't look. But I looked.'

He was angry now. His face had changed completely.

'I saw some of the other bodies. I wanted to see what they'd done to them. I lifted up the sheets and looked at them. They'd been tortured, too.'

'There were *children*. There was a Hutu woman there – she was one of the people the rebels had let go. She was hysterical. She was pointing at the body of one of the children. She told me – she told me . . .' There were tears in his eyes as he choked out the words: '"That-was-a-boy . . ." Do you understand? They had cut off his sex organs. I *saw* it.'

I tried to imagine what I had been doing at the moment Jean-Bosco first caught sight of his brother's corpse at the morgue, at the moment he saw the hideously mutilated body of the child, at the moment the Defence Minister turned away in disgust. It was the morning of 29 December 2000, and I still didn't know that Charlotte was dead. Burundi was two time zones ahead of us – was I still asleep? Was I just getting into work? Was I checking BBC Online, seeing a story that sent a shudder down my spine about a massacre in Burundi?

The Hutu woman had told Jean-Bosco that after the initial ambush the attackers had dragged the passengers from the bus one by one. As each one was taken out, they tortured them – 'ils les ont *torturé*'.

The attackers began dividing the male passengers according to their height, declaring that all those above a certain size would be killed. Richard and another passenger, Arthur Kabunda, were among the tallest.

'When they killed Arthur, Charlotte screamed out at them 'You're mad! You're crazy!' They shot her straightaway. Then Richard went mad. He jumped *comme un lion* onto the rebel who had shot Charlotte, and killed him with his own gun. Then he started firing at the other rebels, like this . . .' – Jean-Bosco gestured with an invisible gun of his own. 'The *rascapée* said that Richard killed *at least* two or three of them. That's why they tortured him so badly. They surrounded him and began stabbing him with knives – *stabbing and stabbing*. That's why there were those cuts all over his body. That's why they tortured him so badly.'

'When I think about those things that I saw – it makes me crazy, you know? Since that time, I have this *rage*.'

'*C'est naturel*; you're only human, after all.'

What could I say to someone who had seen such horrors? In my halting French, I offered Jean-Bosco the only thought I had that I felt might, somehow, mitigate the horror of his brother's and my sister's death.

'*Pour lui, maintenant c'est fini, maintenant c'est OK. Maintenant ils sont ensemble avec notre Dieu.*'

However often we had to relive what they had suffered, and however awful and disgusting it had been, for them it had only happened once. For them, it was finished now.

Yet no sooner had I taken in what Jean-Bosco was telling me than I started to have doubts. It seemed to be an elaborate variation on the rumour I'd heard from Alexis Sunduhije earlier in the year. Yet none of the eyewitnesses I'd been in touch with had ever mentioned anything about Richard, or anyone else, fighting back. Neither had any of the news reports. I could think of plenty of reasons why the woman Jean-Bosco had spoken to might have made the story up – but I couldn't imagine why, if it was true, Pierre and Xavier, another eye-witness to the massacre, would have left it out.

A few days into 2003, I wrote to Pierre again to ask if there was anything more that he could tell me about the Titanic Express attack. I told him I'd heard rumours that some of the victims might have been tortured with knives or machetes. I asked if he remembered any of his fellow passengers trying to do anything to fight back. His reply was categorical: 'One thing I remember very clearly is that no one con-fronted them. We were all too afraid'. As for the rumours of torture, he and a couple of others had been struck with batons as they emerged from the bus, but that was all. Sometimes, he told me, an injury from a bullet can look like a knife wound.

Whatever else had gone on during those last terrible few minutes, the story about Richard Ndereyimana fighting back heroically against the FNL now seemed even more difficult to believe. And yet the injuries that Jean-Bosco had seen on his brother's body couldn't simply be explained away. Was it really possible that they might have been caused by bullets? Could it be that Pierre was still holding some-thing back?

For now, these questions would remain unanswered. The last few weeks had been frantic, and I'd uncovered more information than I ever could have hoped, but now I had run out of time. In a couple of days Heleen and I would be flying to Southeast Asia to begin some-thing new.

— 11 —

Heleen and I had been held up at Heathrow by snow for four hours, as if the grey English weather was making one last attempt to stop us from leaving. But as our plane arched round for its final approach to Kuala Lumpur, the grim, cold, scared city we'd left behind seemed very far away. Our first glimpse of Asia was the dazzling blue and yellow coastline of the Malay Peninsula. We were a long way from the shadowy menace of Al Qaeda and their WMD. We were a long, long way from the FNL, and Charles Nzeyimana, from the London crowds, from the security alerts at Victoria Station, from the jumpy, jaded commuters barging past each other to grab themselves the last free copy of *Metro*. From 10,000 feet, this continent looked bright, vibrant, fresh and unsullied.

When I stepped off the plane, it took a few moments to realize that the warmth billowing in through the covered walkway wasn't from an overactive heating system. It was the first week of January, but it felt like midsummer. The cool, clean, air-conditioned bubble of Kuala Lumpur international airport was eerily quiet.

By the time we arrived in Bangkok, we'd been travelling for more than 24 hours, and the tiredness was starting to catch up with us. Heleen and I trudged irritably down the labyrinthine alleyways of the Khao San district, looking for the guest house that wasn't where the guidebook said it was. When we finally found it we did little but sleep for the next 24 hours.

A few days later, rested and refreshed, we caught a bus across town and moved into the top floor of the Bangkok office of Amnesty International Thailand, where we would be working as volunteers. My job was to edit the English-language section of the membership newsletter. Heleen's was to give research support to Srirak, the AI Thailand director. The 30-second walk down the stairs each morning was my shortest ever journey to work.

159

In our first week at the office, Srirak took me with him to one of Bangkok's new universities, where he was giving a presentation to potential new members. The idea of human rights was seen by many in Thailand as 'foreign', Srirak told me, and democracy itself was a comparatively recent development. Until the twentieth century, the country (still known as Siam) had been an absolute monarchy: 'If the King said you had to die, then you had to die!' But in the 1930s, a small group of French-educated radicals led a bloodless coup which brought in a constitutional monarchy and the promise of democracy. The new political class was not widely liked, however, and the country swung between democracy and dictatorship right up until the 1990s.

With easy access to the Internet, it wasn't difficult to keep up with the news from home. Our life in Bangkok seemed, at least to begin with, surprisingly similar to the one we'd led in London. We worked in an English-speaking office where the English-language *Bangkok Post* and *Nation* newspapers were delivered every morning. A few stops away on the pristine, new Skytrain, multiplex cinemas played the same US blockbusters as the Enfield multiplex. There seemed to be a Seven-Eleven on every street corner. With thousands of Western expats living in the city, English was so widely spoken that it was easy to go for days without speaking Thai.

But it wasn't long before I started to get the unsettling feeling that we were living in a bubble. In the evenings we would walk down our *soi*, past the small, open-air shacks where our new neighbours lived, catching snatches of incomprehensible laughter at equally incomprehensible TV programmes, or the sad strains of incomprehensible pop songs which sounded, for all the world, like Thai translations of Celine Dion.

At the end of January, a Cambodian mob attacked the Thai Embassy in Phnom Penh, and burned it to the ground. The crowd then rampaged around the city, beating up Thai expats and burning Thai-owned businesses and properties. Reaction among my colleagues was mostly bemused, until images emerged of the Cambodians stamping on a picture of the Thai monarch that had been looted from the embassy. 'Burning the flag, well that's OK I guess . . . but they *stepped on our King*!' Ampika the campaign coordinator was disgusted, and she wasn't the only one. In the centre of

Bangkok, patriotic Thais demonstrated outside the Cambodian Embassy and sang their national anthem. In the heart of government, Prime Minister Thaksin scrambled his F16 fighter jets and threatened to send in commandos.

When I asked why the Cambodians had burned down the Thai Embassy, the answer left me even more bewildered. They were angry because a famous Thai actress, Suwanan Kongying, had supposedly said that Cambodia's Angkor Wat temple complex belonged to Thailand. The actress denied ever saying such a thing. One news report claimed that she had made the comments in character, in a soap opera several years earlier, and that a Cambodian politician had seized on the comments to stir up anti-Thai sentiments in the run-up to elections. But how and why a comment in a soap opera could lead to hundreds of people going on the rampage was still a complete mystery to me.

The situation in Thailand became even more of a mystery at the beginning of February. Amid blood-curdling threats against the drug dealers 'destroying our country', the Thai government began a three-month War On Drugs. Within days, reports of extrajudicial killings were streaming in from the northern provinces. The Thai government insisted that the dead had all been drug suspects, killed either in self-defence by police who'd been trying to arrest them, or by 'rival drug gangs' who'd got to them first. The policy proved wildly popular in the local media, particularly the sections of it owned by the prime minister, and opinion polls showed strong support for the policy among the wider public. Reaction from human rights groups, fearing a backlash, was muted.

A few days later we took the hot, sleepy, overnight train to Nong Khai and the northern border with Laos. For much of the last month we'd been closeted in the office. This would be our first 'visa run', and our first venture outside of Bangkok. It would also be my first ever visit to a Communist country. I had mixed feelings as we crossed the Lao–Thai Friendship Bridge and entered Laos. When I was a child, just 20 years ago, the great, grand Marxist monolith had held half of Europe in its icy, atomic grip. Even at a young age I had been very aware of how quickly I, my family and all my friends could be killed if a nuclear war ever broke out. It was Charlotte who'd first explained to me that the ghostly chimes echoing late in the evening behind the BBC news on my mother's stereo were the call sign for Soviet radio. From then on that soft, sinister sound had become a regular, chilling reminder that *they* were still there, with their missiles trained on London. It still sent a shiver down my spine just to think of it.

Of course nowadays the old monolith seemed quite forlorn. The once-great beast had had its teeth drawn. Communism was now a caged curiosity to be gawped at by the people who once had feared it. The eighties children had grown up, bought Lonely Planet guide-books and 'gone backpacking round Southeast Asia'. I'd not just come here for a visa, I'd come to gawp as well – but there was still a little bit of me that had never stopped being scared. Perhaps that was part of the fascination.

The bombastic, red-braided Stalinist uniforms looked incongruous on the small, smiling border officials who wore them. But the Lao capital itself had a disappointing lack of Communism about it. I'd hoped to see reams of red flags and yellow stars, with platooons of khaki-clad troops marching up and down the grey, socialist streets. Instead, the centre of town looked rather more like a hot, dusty version of Harlow, Essex – and with fewer Trotskyists to boot. It was by far the smallest, quietest and most relaxed capital city I'd ever visited. There wasn't a yellow star to be seen anywhere, and the police seemed to spend most of their time slouching on street corners, smoking. Further out from the centre, Buddhism was in far more evidence than Communism, with a handful of gracefully decrepit temple complexes scattered along the Mekong River. What little Communism there was elsewhere seemed to be tucked away in the Lao National Museum just round the corner from our guest house. Alongside grainy photographs of the heroic Pathet Lao revolutionaries, a gallery of near-identical paintings depicted the injustices done to Laos by, in sequence, the Siamese feudalists, the French colonialists and the American capitalists. For ease of identification, the invading oppressors always wore blue, while the Lao patriots dressed in red.

Vientiane's other notable feature was the Patouxi Monument, a huge, grey, concrete arch just up the road from the Thai Embassy. The writing on the monument described it as a 'concrete monstrosity' using materials originally given by the US to the pre-revolutionary government, so that they could build an airport. Why the post-revolutionary government had decided instead to build an immense concrete arch instead wasn't at all obvious, unless it was just to stick one to the Americans.

There was a surreal, unassuming charm about Laos that was unlike anything I'd seen before. Although the country was clearly very poor, there was nothing like the extreme poverty of Rwanda, or the desperation that went with it. And the Lao people we met seemed both friendlier and more sincere than their richer Thai cousins. Perhaps this was a place, amid the warmth both of the weather and of the people, that I could start to put the horrors of the last two years behind me.

The day after we got back to Bangkok, I had an email from a friend in London, asking if I was OK. Laos was all over the international news. A bus had been ambushed north of Vientiane, near the mysteriously named Xaysomboune Special Zone, on one of the main routes through the country. The attackers had robbed the passengers and then started shooting them, apparently at random. Eleven people had died, including two Western tourists. Officials first blamed the ambush on 'Hmong rebels', before changing their minds and insisting that the assailants were just 'bandits'. It felt like an uncanny echo of the Titanic Express. We'd thought about having a few extra days in Laos, and taking a trip further north. If we had, we'd probably have travelled on that road. The Hmong rebels put out a statement denying responsibility and blaming the Lao government for the attack.

I'd had no idea there was a rebellion going on there. The country had seemed so peaceful. How wrong could I have been?

When I looked up 'Hmong rebels' on the Internet I found yet another conspiracy theory website. The Hmong 'freedom fighters', it claimed, were the last remnants of an army, who had fought a Secret War alongside US troops in the Indochina War. After the Communist victory in 1975, tens of thousands had fled or been killed in 're-education camps', with many eventually ending up in the United States. But thousands more had been left behind, trapped and surrounded with their families in the jungles of Xaysomboune Special Zone. Fearing that surrender would mean death, they had scraped out an existence in the forest for three decades. Over the last two years the Lao authorities had stepped up their efforts to finish them off. Now the Hmong were down to their last few hundred, desperately trying to scrape out an existence, constantly fighting off attacks, with the most meagre of weapons, not only from the Lao army, but also from the Vietnamese (who secretly controlled Laos, according to the website), who were attacking the Hmong with chemical weapons.

The website belonged to a small, US-based organization calling itself The Fact Finding Commission, and despite the grandiose title and hyperbolic rhetoric, I found the story behind it quite a touching one. The founder of the group was an American, Ed Szendry, who had been sent to fight in Laos during the Vietnam War. Szendry's life had been saved countless times by his Hmong comrades, and he had never forgotten the debt he owed them. Now he was campaigning for the US government to intervene and stop the abuses against the Secret War Veterans who had been left behind in 1975.

Although the spelling, in places, was awful, this conspiracy theory was nowhere near as vague and generalized as so many of the others I'd seen. The photographs of ragged and dishevelled fighters, some with missing eyes or arms, were convincing. And behind the hyperbole, the core claims were specific, giving dates, times and locations of alleged attacks on the Hmong by Lao and Vietnamese forces, with names, ages and photographs of many of the victims.

But there was something else. Although Szendry vigorously denied that the Hmong rebels had been behind the recent bus ambush, this site seemed to make some sense of why they might have done it. I couldn't help but be reminded of the FNL apologist Charles Nzeyimana, and his stories about the Hutus of Bujumbura-Rurale. How his family had been 'decimated by the monoethnic Tutsi army'. How, while development agencies brought food to the mainly Tutsi inhabitants of Bujumbura city, for the Hutus in the hills 'our only rations are the bombs which fall day and night'. I couldn't help but be reminded of Charles' anger at a world that neither knew what his people were enduring, nor cared enough to try to find out. And while I knew that this anger had made him prone to exaggeration, I also knew from the reports I'd read that the essence of what he was saying was true.

What mystified me about the claims Szendry was making was that

I could find no information anywhere to corroborate them. Although our Laos guidebook gave a detailed account of the US-backed Secret War, it also told us that the conflict had ended with the victory of Communism in 1975. The few vague references I found in the news to 'Hmong rebels' came nowhere close to the claims this website was making. And although there were some detailed Amnesty reports on Laos, there was no mention at all of the hundreds of ragtag, Hmong fighters supposedly holed up there with their families in Xaysomboune Special Zone.

Yet it was difficult to believe that anyone would knowingly invent something like this. Szendry certainly didn't come over as someone trying to hide behind obfuscation. His claims were, in principle, verifiable. These photos had to have come from somewhere. If they *weren't* real then someone had gone to a great deal of trouble to fabricate them.

February's bus massacre soon drifted out of the news. The tourists who'd killed hadn't been specifically targeted – they were just very unlucky. They had been cycling past the bus when it was attacked, and got caught in the crossfire. The media seemed to have concluded that it was part of some kind of business dispute. But what did that mean? Who was disputing what with whom, and why did they have to shoot up a busload of innocent people? Why had the authorities initially blamed 'Hmong rebels' and then denied that they existed?

I found myself completely intrigued, and a little torn. Whichever way I looked at it, this story seemed like an untold tragedy. I felt that I ought at least try to find out more about Ed Szendry – and, if his claims were true, try and do something – even if that was only to pass on the message to someone within Amnesty. The problem was that without going into Xaysomboune Special Zone to find out for myself, I had no way whatsoever of checking them out. And given what had happened there just a few days ago, I wasn't going to be doing that in a hurry.

It was now nearly three months since the Foreign Office had been given the FNL report. I wrote again, asking when we would get to see it, repeating my earlier questions about the police claim that I was jeopardizing the Burundian peace process and querying them on the issue of an amnesty for Charlotte's killers. The reply I received was a cool one. They didn't want to hand over a copy of the report yet, because it was *still* being translated. They gave no reply as to how my talking to the media could endanger the Burundian peace process – instead the Foreign Office now claimed that my doing so could jeopardize the security of their staff in Rwanda. The question of an amnesty was a matter for the Burundian authorities. 'We cannot interfere.'

And yet I now knew that this wasn't true. From the articles I'd been editing and rewriting for Amnesty Thailand, I knew that international law actually forbade amnesties for war crimes, crimes against humanity and genocide – and 'national sovereignty' was no barrier to prosecution. All countries had a legal obligation, even if they chose to ignore it, to oppose such measures. As a permanent member of the UN Security Council, supposedly the guardian of international law, Britain had not just the right but also the responsibility to ensure that the rules were upheld. When I wrote back to the Foreign Office pointing this out, and asking for clarification of what they'd meant by 'we cannot interfere', I got a satisfyingly nervous-sounding holding reply.

Guardian or not, however, it seemed that my country was itself about to break international law in fairly devastating fashion. On 20 March 2003, British forces joined the long-awaited, US-led invasion of Iraq, with the stated aim of eliminating a global threat posed by the country's Weapons of Mass Destruction. The British and American governments claimed that a UN Resolution had authorized the invasion. Other members of the Council, and many international lawyers, disagreed. But whatever the true reasons for the war, it seemed clear that America was going to go ahead with it, and that Britain was going to go along with America, regardless of what the UN or international law had to say about it.

'Why you country wanna invade Iraq?' Now when I told Thai people I was British, alongside their warm praise for David Beckham and Manchester United football club, I began to be asked more pointed questions. The honest answer was that I just didn't know. While I no longer found it difficult to accept that my government was capable of pursuing a narrow, national interest at the expense of innocent, Iraqi lives, it seemed hard to understand how the war would benefit Britain even in that very selfish sense.

As I helped to prepare our press release to the Thai media, relaying Amnesty International's statement urging all sides in the Iraq War to respect international, humanitarian law, I couldn't help thinking how lame it sounded. Was it even meaningful to talk about the *existence* of 'international law' when the rules were so routinely flouted and ignored? Did any state ever respect international law except when it suited them to do so?

A few days later I heard from Kabonesho again. Our friends had finally found a way to get the FNL report out of Burundi. When he emailed me a few days later he seemed jumpy. He'd seen the report. He didn't want to talk about it on the phone. Over MSN messenger, Kabonesho confirmed that the FNL battalion commander who'd signed off the report was the same Albert Sibomana who'd been named in the Human Rights Watch report from early 2000. But there was something else. The report contained some phrases of the Rwandan language, Kinyarwanda. The person who'd written it was either Rwandan, or had spent a lot of time there. Could this be one of the ex-FAR – the former members of the 'Forces Armées Rwandaises', who'd fled to Burundi and joined the FNL after taking part in the 1994 Rwandan genocide?

At the end of the month, Heleen and I travelled back into Laos. The media seemed to have dismissed February's attack as an isolated incident. We were joined by Chris Dodd, an old friend of mine who'd flown out to spend a few weeks in Southeast Asia.

This time we'd decided to spend a little longer in the country. From Vientiane, we headed up the Mekong by boat towards Luang Prabang. The town of Paklai was quieter and more remote than anywhere I'd been since I visited Rwanda three years before. As we walked through the main street a giggling huddle of children pointed at us, excitedly chanting 'Farang! Farang! Farang!' – the Asian equivalent of 'Msungu!' We slept in a guest house where the insects and lizards competed with each other for space on the ceiling.

We travelled across country the next day, on a succession of local buses which were little more than covered trucks. Our spirits cooled with the weather as we climbed higher into the hills. Laos was looking more and more like Rwanda, and very much as I imagined Burundi to be. I was jumpy, thinking again about the Hmong rebels who'd been accused of the bus ambush in February. Passing through a remote logging village, we stopped to drop off and pick up passengers. Just a few yards away, a man was watching us, with what looked like a home-made rifle slung over his shoulder. I held my breath nervously until we moved on.

The sleepy, hill-top city of Luang Prabang was a different world again from Vientiane, and without a 'concrete monstrosity' in sight. Luang Prabang's opulent, red and gold temples were immaculately maintained – the centre of town had been dubbed a UNESCO World Heritage Site. The Hmong were a significant minority here, and the streets thronged with pretty girls selling local handicrafts; hats, shirts and cushion covers with remarkably chic brown, grey and black spiral designs.

The girls spoke to each other in a language that sounded more Chinese than Lao, and there was a kind of feistiness about them, which, after spending nearly three months in demure and deferential Bangkok, I found quite refreshing. As I watched them bartering jovially with Dodd over the price of a blanket or a hat, it was hard to reconcile this image with the pictures I'd seen of battered and des-perate Secret War Veterans allegedly holed up in Xaysomboune Special Zone. These women might be poor, but they were anything but powerless.

The next day, admiring the view from Luang Prabang's Golden Mount, we were approached by Dou Xong, a friendly, young, Hmong tourist guide, who offered to take us trekking in the hills above the city. 'I can show you *real* poverty', he promised. His eyes widened. 'I will take you to the poorest village in the *world*'. Although he seemed quite sincere, I was hesitant. Was this what the people who went trekking with Dou Xong wanted – to see the *real* poverty freak-show? But Heleen and Dodd were less tortured by liberal ethics. This was no commercially organized hill tribe trek, imposed by outsiders. We were interested in seeing the hills, and learning something about Hmong culture, not being poverty-tourists. And Dou Xong was, at least as far as we could tell, doing this of his own volition.

As we waited for Dou Xong in the centre of town early the next morning, a long line of orange-clad Buddhist monks walked past in single file, ceremonial begging bowls in hand. I'd read in our guide-book that the Hmong followed an animistic religion, believing that spirits lived in and controlled the natural world around them. It reminded me of the poem that Charlotte had quoted in the letter she had written to us, almost exactly three years ago, 'to be opened in the event of my death'.

> I am a thousand winds that blow.
> I am the diamond glints on snow.
> I am the sunlight on ripened grain.
> I am the gentle autumn rain.
> When you awaken in the morning's hush
> I am the swift uplifting rush
> Of quiet birds in circled flight.
> I am the soft stars that shine at night.
> Do not stand at my grave and cry;
> I am not there. I did not die.

I wondered where Charlotte was now. For a long time after her death I'd felt that she was around me, animated in nature very much in the sense suggested by the poem that she had quoted. I'd long found such beliefs both alien and mysterious and yet also oddly familiar. It sometimes seemed as if animism, or at least some form of it, was hiding behind many of the traditions in my own culture. It was only after 14 years of living in Hertfordshire that I discovered that the name of the River Lea, which had been such an enduring feature of my childhood, went back thousands of years, deriving from the name of a Celtic river god, Ligea. In the spring of 1994, largely unaware of the genocide raging thousands of miles away in Rwanda, I had spent hours in local libraries reading the history of the old waterway. More than a thousand years before, Danish 'pagans' had sailed up this river and fought a battle against one of the most celebrated kings of English history, Alfred the Great. No one knew exactly where the fighting had taken place, less still what kind of people had fought it, what their names were and what they believed. But in digging through history to try and understand these things, I wasn't just looking for a good grade in my A-level exams. I was trying to find a sense of my own identity.

And I knew that this was an obsession Charlotte also had. Perhaps that was where I'd got it from. All through my teenage years, my sister had spent her summers literally digging through the past, as an amateur archaeologist. In the process she'd become more and more interested in Britain's Celtic history, and the traditions that went with it – the Druidic animism of ancient Britain and its enduring legacy in Celtic Christianity. It was through her archaeology that she had made friends with Mia Naylor, who had first introduced her to the Church of Saint Alban, in London, where she had been confirmed into Christianity, where she had hoped to marry and where, during her beautiful funeral ceremony, I had been a different mystical side of Christianity that I had never seen before. It seemed no coincidence that the message my sister had written to be read in the event of her death should hint so strongly at these ancient traditions. The fact that so many of the events that made sense of this letter had occurred *after* it was written further underlined my feeling that in writing it, Charlotte might have touched on some timeless truth.

I knew that animism, and the shamanistic traditions that accompanied it, were thought by scholars to have once been common to the whole of humanity. Such practices were still strong throughout Africa, and in Thailand, even though the country was overwhelmingly Buddhist, spirit worship was, for many, a part of everyday life. Many trees in Bangkok were draped with coloured ribbons as a sign of respect to the spirits believed to dwell within them, and many Thai households had a lucky 'spirit house' prominently placed in the front yard.

Many of the superstitions that surrounded me as I grew up seemed remarkably similar to the animist traditions often looked on as 'primitive' by Westerners. The more I thought about it, the more I started to wonder if we might all be repressed animists, unwilling to accept the superstitious thread that ran through our society but unable to let go of it either. And in denying it, I couldn't help but feel that we were denying something that linked our culture not only to the ancient past but also to other cultures around the world, like that of the Hmong.

Dou Xong arrived, chirpy as ever, despite the early hour. We bought food and water for our trip, and then made our way to the river. Dou Xong had a friend in Luang Prabang with a boat, and he took us to the beginning of the trail. For the first few hours we passed only Lao villages, with their distinctive, traditional stilt-houses. The

Hmong were largely confined to the more remote areas; the windy tops of hills, where no one else wanted to live. Dou Xong's family were 'dry' rice farmers, he told us. Every year they would burn down a section of forest to create fertile land in which to grow their crops. By the end of the year the land would become unusable, and they would have to burn more forest. The government had told them that they must stop growing rice in this way, because the woodland destruction was causing erosion and blocking up rivers. The problem was that they had no other means of supporting themselves. They were told that they should grow mangoes instead – but without a proper road to carry the perishable fruit into town, they couldn't make enough money to survive.

It was still early in the day, but the heat was already intense. I was surprised that Dou Xong talked so freely about the government, but didn't press him. I asked how his English had got to be so good; he told me that it had been his favourite subject at school, but that he'd also learned a lot from his 'Western friends', like us. He'd been educated at a government school in Luang Prabang, and he'd wanted to go to university, but it was hard for Hmong people to get the chance.

Many Lao looked down on the Hmong, Dou Xong said: 'They say that we smell, and they have a bad name for us'. The Lao were more mean-spirited than the Hmong; 'We will always offer to share our rice with them, but they don't share their rice with us'.

It was close to midday now, and the heat was raging. There was still a long way to go, and the half-bottle of tepid water I had left was hardly thirst quenching. At the top of the arch marking the entrance to the first Hmong village we passed was a strange, star-shaped symbol made out of straw. This sign meant that there was some kind of problem in the community: perhaps someone was ill. It might be that the village was closed off to outsiders, Dou Xong said. He called out to one of the villagers, who shouted back that the place was out of bounds. It wasn't clear what the nature of the problem was. We would have to take the long way round.

Every village had a *txi nee*, Dou Xong said, a shaman who knew the rituals of the Hmong religion. When someone got ill, they would send for him and he would decide what needed to be done in order to heal them. 'He might say that you need to sacrifice a kitchen', Dou Xong explained. It took me a few moments to realize that he meant 'chicken'. If we were lucky, Dou Xong said, we might see a kitchen-sacrificing ceremony when we reached his village.

It was early afternoon by the time we arrived in the next village, where Dou Xong's brother lived, and I was more thirsty than I could ever remember being. We drank boiled water and ate our lunch sheltering from the sun inside Dou Xong's brother's wooden house. As we ate, we were surrounded by a crowd of Hmong children, who seemed intrigued by us, if a little frightened. One or two seemed a little put out when we didn't answer their questions. These kids were so small that they didn't yet know that not everyone in the world spoke Hmong. After a while I began to wonder whether the youngsters were watching us so intently because we were strangers, or because they were hungry. Conditions here were worse than anything I'd seen in Rwanda. I wondered if this was what it was like in Bujumbura-Rurale.

The children kept looking at us, and we kept smiling back, awkwardly. Should I offer them the rest of my sandwich, or would that be demeaning? Not knowing what else to do, I performed my one and only party trick, tearing out a page from my notebook and folding it into an origami bird. This proved such an instant success that I was soon frantically tearing pages and handing out origami birds, while the children walked up and down on the mud floor, flapping the birds' wings and making cooing noises. One of the kids ran back and rattled off a question in Hmong. 'He's asking where you learned to do this', Dou Xong explained.

As we were leaving the village, a grim-faced man held up his half-naked baby for us to see. The child had a grotesquely enlarged scrotum. Did he think that we were doctors? Did he think that we would know what to do because we were *farangs*? Did he want money so that he could take the child to hospital? Should I offer something? I was gripped by the same sense of helplessness that I'd felt in the bus park in Rwanda. I could think of nothing else to do but nod in acknowledgement, and walk on.

As we got back onto the trail, Chris asked Dou Xong about the road from Luang Prabang to Vang Vien. Did he think it was safe now? 'Yes, it's very safe, especially for tourists. Now, every tourist bus is given a military escort.' I asked about the rumours of political trouble in the area – but Dou Xong had heard nothing about it.

We began to meet more people as we made our way higher into the hills. Descending apace in the distance I could make out the black-clad figure of a woman. Dou Xong recognized her as one of his sisters-in-law. As she came nearer we could see that this woman, moving at twice the speed we were going and carrying a heavy load of rice on her back, was heavily pregnant. Dou Xong assured us it was 'not far now', but the hours kept passing. Our ever-jovial guide, who had to make this journey every time he went to or from Luang Prabang, showed no signs of tiring, but the heat, and the uphill climb, was having its effect on the rest of us. It was taking all my strength now just to keep going.

It began to cool a little in the late afternoon, as the sun began to slip behind the hills. I thought again about Charlotte. I liked the idea that she, or some small part of her, might be here with us now, amid the buzzing of the cicadas.

I asked Dou Xong what Hmong people believed about the after-life. He told me that when someone in his village died, everyone would gather together beside the body, and carry out a special ritual to guide the person's spirit to paradise. If they didn't do this, then the lost spirit would wander off into the forest, and might come back at a later date to cause problems in the village. Every Hmong family had a *zu gah*, Dou Xong said, a special spirit who would watch over and protect them wherever they went. He would show me his family's *zu gah* when we arrived at his village. It was hanging up on the wall of his parent's house, although only his father, as head of the household, was allowed to touch it. 'The *zu gah* is a small piece of paper, like this', Dou Xong motioned the shape of a small square. 'We make a new *zu gah* every year, and have a big party. We sacrifice kitchens, to thank the old *zu gah* for helping us, then we burn it and make a new one.' I asked Dou Xong what happened to the *zu gah* after they were burned. Did the Hmong believe that the spirit itself had been destroyed, or merely the vessel that contained it? Was a new spirit created, or merely a new vessel for the old spirit? Good though his English was, Dou Xong couldn't quite get what I was asking. Now we were both confused. Actually, his father knew these things much better, Dou Xong told me. If I was interested, we could ask him about it when we got to the village.

'You know that there are Hmong peoples all over the world', Dou Xong told me. 'Many went to America, after . . . after 1975.'

'But if you ask any Hmong people, anywhere you go, who is the leader of the Hmong, they will always tell you the same thing.'

I asked, and got the answer I was expecting.

'Mist-er Vang Pao', Dou Xong said, his eyes wide. I'd heard the name before. Vang Pao had been the leader of the US-backed Hmong army who'd fought against the Communist forces of the Pathet Lao, hoping to win an independent homeland for his people.

It was getting dark by the time we arrived in Dou Xong's village. Dou Xong's parents were small, shy and welcoming. Their house was close to the edge of the settlement, which was much larger than the one we'd visited earlier in the day. The children seemed happier and better fed. Plump pigs, chickens, exuberant dogs and the occasional pink buffalo wandered along the mud track that ran through the village. One of the houses had a generator, and outside sat a noisy television and a sizeable crowd of neighbours sat watching it, laughing loudly every so often.

It got darker still as we took a walk around the village towards the highest point on the hill. A slight, black-clad figure tagged along amiably, chatting occasionally to Dou Xong. From his voice we could tell that he was an old man. This part of the village was flat, dusty and strewn with boulders. Over the ridge, on the horizon, we could see the lights of Luang Prabang. We sat on a boulder each, and the old man began talking.

'He says that the village has been here since 1951! Can you believe?' said Dou Xong. 'He says that before 1975, they used to call this place 'the airport'.' I asked why they'd given it that name. 'Helicopters used to come, from Luang Prabang, and the Plain of Jars, to bring rice for the villagers. In those days many people were hungry here.'

I asked Dou Xong to ask the old man who had sent the helicopters.

'Mist-er Vang Pao.'

The old man had done military service in Vang Pao's army. He had seen him once, a long time ago, when they were both still young. Mr

Vang Pao doesn't look so young any more, the old man told us, laughing. He is old, like me. He lives in America, with the other Hmong who had to leave after 1975.

The government had tried to kill Mr Vang Pao many times – with knives, with bullets, with electricity, but nothing worked. Finally, they took him up in an aeroplane and threw him out – but Mr Vang Pao fell down to earth unharmed, and carried on fighting. In the end the government said that he must leave Laos and go to America. Many Hmong followed him, but the old man had to stay because his cousins didn't want to go. Nowadays, the helicopters don't come any more. Life hadn't been so easy after 1975.

Heleen, Dodd and I slept alongside each other on a raised table in Dou Xong's family home. At four in the morning an oil lamp was lit – the family was already preparing to go out and work in the fields, but we were still exhausted from our 15-mile, uphill trek the day before.

We slept in until long after it had got light. If we wanted to set out before the worst of the heat set in, we would have to leave quickly. As we were preparing to go, Dou Xong showed me the *zu gah* which hung on the wall in one corner of his home, the religious object which connected his family to the spirit that watched over and protected them. But looking at it, I couldn't help but feel disappointed. Whatever the truth about this object and the animistic cosmology it represented, whatever Dou Xong saw when he looked at it, and whatever it meant to him, all I could see now was a small piece of paper hanging on the wall with a grubby feather attached to it.

I knew that I should have known better. What could I have seen here that *wouldn't* have been a disappointment? And what did I think I was going to learn in a day? I was appalled by the thought that I might be just another naive Westerner, in love with the idea that traditional cultures had some pre-packaged 'ancient wisdom to go', that I could just pick up and take home with me. Dou Xong wasn't an anthropologist or a shaman – he was no more an expert on Hmong cosmology than I was on Christian monotheism. While he could tell me a lot of interesting anecdotes, it was absurd for me to have hoped that he'd have any kind of profound, life-changing answers.

The trek back down to Luang Prabang was easier than the journey up, but we were still exhausted by the time we arrived. We paid Dou Xong for his time, bought him a late lunch and promised to tell our friends to look for him if they ever came to Luang Prabang.

Dodd decided to take Dou Xong's advice and head down to Vang Vien by bus. Heleen and I still weren't convinced that the road was safe, and wanted to stay in Luang Prabang for a couple more days. Taking a shower that evening, I felt a hard, painful lump in my right armpit. When I looked more closely, I discovered a beetle-like creature clamped onto my skin, sucking away at one of my veins. It was some kind of tic. I gritted my teeth as Heleen twisted it off. I awoke the next day feeling slightly sick. Our guidebook listed a whole selection of diseases that were spread by tics, and reading about them did nothing to alleviate the nausea. By midday I was sick and feverish and barely able to move. Heleen asked the guest house if they knew where we could find an English-speaking doctor. After a couple more hours, an elegant Lao woman in her mid-forties knocked on the door. It was the guest house owner, who spoke excellent English and told us she had trained as a doctor in Cuba. If I'd been up in the hills then it was probably scrub typhus, she said, and gave me a handful of green antibiotics. I should take these pills and get myself back to Thailand.

Within half an hour of taking the medicine I was halfway recovered, and by the next day I almost felt normal again. I felt like something of a fraud as I boarded the plane back to Bangkok, leaving Heleen behind. She would go down to Vientiane, as we'd both originally planned, to get a three-month visa from the Thai Embassy. It seemed surreal to be stepping into this fastidiously clean aeroplane plane so soon after sleeping in a village that didn't even have mains electricity. Even more surreal was the fact that our polite and deferential air-hostesses, and several of my fellow passengers, were all wearing enormous, white, surgical masks.

At Bangkok airport, mobs of white-clad, thermometer-wielding nurses patrolled the immigration counters, watching out for sickly-looking passengers. In the week and a half since we'd been away, SARS had made it into the big league, and Thailand was on a major alert.

I made my way nervously through immigration without being arrested as a SARS-suspect, and got a taxi straight to Bumrungrad hospital. While I was waiting to be seen, I was asked to fill in a form asking if I'd had a raised temperature in the last week. I ticked 'yes' and my fate was sealed. From then on, every member of staff I saw sported a white, surgical mask. The doctor who treated me wore one so big that I could hardly even see his face. He assured me that I didn't have malaria, gave me some more pills and sent me home. Some of the passengers on the bus were wearing surgical masks too.

That evening, I looked up 'Mister Vang Pao' on the Internet. He was indeed alive and well and living in the United States, and he looked every bit the American politician. I wondered what relationship he really had with the impoverished people who, nearly three decades after he had left them, still hailed him as their leader.

I had another look at the 'Fact Finding Commission' website. Mister Vang Pao had also, it seemed, been supporting their Secret War Veterans campaign. Yet the Hmong people I'd actually met seemed to know nothing about the hundreds of their fellow tribesmen supposedly holed up and fighting for survival in the jungles of Xaysomboune Special Zone. Dou Xong had seemed sure that February's attack was nothing more than a business dispute. And while the Hmong I'd met had been very poor, I'd seen no evidence at all that their government was committing a genocide against them. Could this website just be an elaborate hoax – a smear campaign orchestrated by disgruntled exiles?

I had an email from Heleen the next afternoon. Her camera and most of her money had been stolen with her bag in Vientiane. After dropping off her passport at the Thai Embassy, she'd decided to hire a bike and take a tour of the town. Lulled by the innocence of the place, she'd left her bag exposed in the bicycle's front basket. Five minutes after she set off, two locals had sped past on a motorbike, snatching the bag as they went by. She had just about enough money to make it back to Bangkok.

As I lay alone in bed that evening I felt empty and foolish. I'd been hoping to find something in Laos, something that would help me make sense of the world and my experience of it. But all I'd found was confusion, and a nasty case of scrub typhus. It was some time now since I'd felt that Charlotte was around me, some time since I'd seen her in my dreams. Was she becoming less familiar? I'd lived nearly four months now in a culture where most people believed that the dead returned to earth in a new body – an idea that seemed strange and alien to me – but of course the ideas I'd been brought up with were equally strange and alien to them. When I'd explained the concept of Easter to one of my Thai colleagues, she'd laughed in disbelief. So this guy died – and then came back in the *same* body?

Soon afterwards I read one of the saddest news reports I'd seen all year. A Thai woman called Jamlong Taengnian had become convinced, after her son was killed in a motorbike accident, that the monitor lizard she found crawling under his picture at the funeral had been the reincarnation of her child. She'd taken the creature home and looked after it, feeding it on milk and yoghurt, her son's favourite food. The lizard had become something of a local celebrity, with hundreds of Thais coming to see the miracle for themselves, in the hope that this would bring them good luck. But then, two years after the accident that took Jamlong's son from her, the lizard she had adopted in his place also died. She'd been inconsolable, and insisted on holding a public funeral for the creature. 'I am so sad. I feel as if I have lost my son a second time', she told reporters.

I found myself becoming obsessed with this story, and read everything I could find about it. While the local media reported it simply as a sad story about a devout Buddhist mother, it had soon been picked up internationally and became a worldwide, strange but true feature. The tale of the crazy Thai lady who mistook her son for a lizard.

'Mummy misses her widdle weptile', sneered one of the many bloggers who commented on it. Another carried a cartoon of two lizards talking to each other about reincarnation. I couldn't help feeling that this lizard was just something Jamlong had seized on because she wasn't yet ready to accept that her child was gone – that this article of religious faith was, as Charlotte might have said, her 'crutch'. And I couldn't help wondering if it had really been good for her. Now that the lizard was gone, it seemed that she'd been bereaved twice over.

And yet was I any less ridiculous than Jamlong Taengnian? Why was it any more absurd for her to believe that her son had been reincarnated as a lizard than for me to think that my sister's spirit might somehow have been united with the natural world, or that she might be in some other plane of reality, waiting to see us all again when we joined her in death? How sure was I now that the moment my sister had breathed her last breath, in the mud and the rain two and a half years ago, wasn't also her last moment of existence? I waited for Charlotte's reply, and heard nothing but the echo of my own mind.

— 12 —

REPUBLIC OF BURUNDI   TNG, January 12 2001

PALIPEHUTU-FNL
JUSTICE-PEACE-DEVELOPMENT
UBUGABO BURIHABWA

COMDT Bn RUK

Subject: Monthly report for December 2000   E.M.G.

As indicated above, we hereby send you the monthly report for
December 2000. The S4/Treasury Report will follow shortly as
we do not yet have all the necessary information. We would
appreciate it if you could send us the framework for the annual
report if possible.

May the Almighty be our protector!

The Comdt Bn RUK

Bn/C SIBOMANA Albert

Just before Easter, I finally received my copy of the FNL report. It
was written entirely by hand and ran to more than 30 pages, with the
first being a covering note, written in French. Tantalizingly, the recip-
ients were not addressed by name, but the author himself had left his
signature clear and proud at the bottom of the page. SIBOMANA
Albert.

Only one of the pages in the report referred to the Titanic Express attack. There were dozens of smaller ambushes, some fatal, some not. Most of the events listed involved just a handful of 'mil', which I supposed must be the abbreviation for *militaires*. On 8 December, eight *militaires* had carried out an ambush on Route Nationale One, capturing 96 cases of Fanta – no fatalities reported. On 18 December, in another ambush on the same road, four *militaires* had fired off 60 rounds, killing one person, and looted 168 bars of soap, a towel (sold for 20,007 Burundian francs), a diploma, 29 pens and 3 pairs of shoes. But by far the longest list of booty had come from the attack on 28 December. It looked as if the Titanic Express attack had been the highlight of Albert Sibomana's month.

There were pages and pages of names. Jean-Pierres, Jean-Pauls, Simons, Onesimés and Pasteurs. Ndayizeyes, Nsengyumvas, Habya-rimanas, Nkurunzizas, Ndoricimpas, Sibomanas. I guessed that this must be a list of FNL personnel. Beside many of the names was a code, a short collection of signs. A Greek Psi (ψ), followed by a vertical line. Two musical quavers joined together. Or a backwards, upside-down, lower case h followed by a triangle, followed by a small cross perching above a circle.

A section headed '*Materiel*' seemed to be a collection of weapons. RPGs – rocket propelled grenades. KVs of various different types – Kalashnikovs, I guessed. And FALs – this stumped me at first – but a little research revealed that this was the *Fusil Automatique Léger*, a Belgian-made automatic rifle. While most of the document was made up of lists of one sort or another, there were also some narrative sections written in full sentences. One of these was headed 'Observa-tion' – but, tantalizingly, it was written in Kirundi rather than French.

'Fresh bus attack in Laos', ran the BBC headline on 21 April. Unknown attackers had ambushed another bus between Luang Prabang and Vang Vien, killing ten of the passengers; nine Lao and one Chinese. Dodd had passed through the area just a couple of days before. The Western tourists might be getting an armed escort, but clearly the local people still had to take their chances. Another business dispute? This time the media didn't seem so ready to believe that this was just 'bandits'.

Then eight days later, *Time Asia* ran its scoop of the year.

There were hundreds of them, perhaps a thousand. They wept and knelt before me on the ground, crying, 'Please help us, the communists are coming.' I had hiked four days to reach this forsaken place deep in the jungles of Xaysomboune, northern Laos. The Hmong rebels prostrate before me were convinced they would all soon die. They knew they were a forgotten tribe, crushed by a military campaign that is denied by the communist leaders of their small, sheltered nation.

With Ed Szendry's help, journalist Andrew Perrin and photographer Philip Blenkinsop had tracked down the Secret War Veterans in Xaysomboune Special Zone. Before my eyes, I had seen an obscure conspiracy theory transform itself, through the magic of mainstream media, into an established fact. It was an extraordinary process to watch, and it made me question my own assumptions about conspiracy theories in general, and the people who made them. Although I'd been sceptical of Szendry's story – in part, because of the amateurish nature of his website and his hyperbolic writing – my main worry had been that it lacked any independent corroboration. I'd assumed that if his claims *were* true, someone, somewhere would have taken them seriously long before now. And I'd been wrong.

How many other conspiracy theories had I dismissed on the same grounds? It was only because I'd taken such a close interest in this particular case that I knew how long Szendry had been screaming into the ether before the world finally responded. It disturbed me to know that he'd been right all along – and that apparently no one had taken him seriously – even those whose *raison d'être* was to bring this kind of abuse to the world's attention.

I'd arrived in Asia hoping to find peace and tranquillity, but all I'd found was more of the same. In Laos, hundreds of desperate Hmong were holed up in the jungle fighting for their survival. In neighbouring Burma, with its vicious military junta, the situation was equally bad for the Karen and Shan tribal peoples. All I knew about Cambodia was that mobs of hate-filled xenophobes were prepared to attack Thai expats and burn down their embassy simply because of some comments supposedly made by a character in a soap opera. In Vietnam, it was very difficult to know *what* was going on because information was so tightly controlled by the government. And here in

Thailand, hundreds of 'drug suspects', a disproportionate number of them members of ethnic minorities, had been killed in the streets by the police in the last few months, while the Thai media applauded enthusiastically.

Meanwhile in Iraq, US and British bombing had already claimed hundreds of civilian lives in 'collateral damage'. There was, as yet, no trace of the Weapons of Mass Destruction.

I'd grown up believing that human nature was essentially good, that violence was the exception rather than the rule, that politicians told the truth when it really mattered and that the steady spread of democracy and rational governance was inevitable. But much of what I'd seen over the last two years seemed to point in quite the opposite direction. Human nature was, it now seemed to me, at its heart dark, dishonest and violent. And I'd seen enough of that darkness in myself to know that I was no different. While most of us, most of the time, were not actively running around trying to hack each other to pieces with machetes, it really didn't take much to set us off. The institutions holding back the darkness were far more fragile than I could ever have believed. Even in Western democracies, politicians seemed prepared to put those institutions in jeopardy for short-term, political or economic advantage. And wherever those institutions failed, it seemed, the resulting violence was cold and vicious. The fair and prosperous peace of the comfortable life that I had lived until now wasn't just an exception to the rule – it was an extraordinary, miraculous exception to the rule.

And yet, whatever the prognosis for humanity as a whole, in Burundi there were signs of hope. On 30 April, the near-universally despised Tutsi President Buyoya finally handed over power peacefully, in keeping with the agreement that he'd signed 18 months earlier. His Vice President, Domitien Ndayizeye, a Hutu from the Front pour démocratie au Burundi (Frodebu) Party, took over the role. The group that had won Burundi's last democratic election was now leading the government for the first time since 1993, and plans were being made for fresh elections in the next 18 months.

I'd heard mixed messages about Frodebu. Jean-Bosco and Kabonesho seemed to think that they were little better than the FNL. Rory Beaumont had been rather more positive – and the fact that they'd actually won an election had to count for something.

In June I had an email from Antoine Kaburahe, a Burundian journalist, who'd known Richard Ndereyimana at university. He told me
he wanted to do an article about Richard and Charlotte for a new
Burundian website, www.in-afrique.com. Following my altercation
with Charles Nzeyimana I was still nervous about Burundians who
contacted me out of the blue, but my Burundian contacts assured me
that Antoine was a good guy. You should talk to him, I was told. I
explained to Antoine that I would be 'out of the country' for some
time, but that I'd be happy to answer his questions over email.

Antoine's article cast Charlotte and Richard as the 'two lovers' of
the Titanic Express, whose lives had been tragically cut short by 'an
iceberg of hate', and finished with some of the comments I'd sent him
about justice and impunity. I had mixed feelings about the tone of the
piece – I didn't recognize the Charlotte he imagined 'whispering
sweet nothings' into Richard's ear as they made their way through the
hills above Bujumbura, but it was a clever idea, and it provoked a
lively discussion on the 'In Afrique' website.

Most of the comments were sympathetic, but a few were strikingly
different. 'C'est la guerre', said one contributor, dismissively. The
'two lovers' knew the risk they were taking. Richard Wilson should
cry for his sister and move on. Why focus on these two people, he
asked, when thousands more had died in attacks by government
soldiers, or starved to death in the 'regroupment camps'? An FDD
website described Antoine's article as propaganda for the 'Extrême-
droite Burundaise'.

Until now I'd heard largely from a self-selecting group of Burundians who'd contacted me because of some direct connection with the
political situation. But not even the FNL people who'd contacted me
to make threats had said that I was wrong to look for justice – they just
told me I was looking for justice in the wrong place. It seemed to take
a particular kind of logic to be *morally* outraged about a brother
wanting to see his sister's killers prosecuted. I was also intrigued,
because it felt as if I was getting closer to the Burundian exiles trying
to give an intellectual justification for the FNL's crimes – the people
who raised money for the FNL in Europe, and rattled off one press
release after another from the Benelux section of Palipehutu-FNL.

I found it interesting to read what other Burundians had written in
reply. 'Quelle cynicisme!', said one, accusing the critics of 'la banali-

sation de la mort'- trivializing death. Antoine saw the comments after I did, and sent me an apologetic email, promising to take them off the site. By the time I told him that I'd have preferred them to stay, they'd already been removed.

In early July, the FNL launched another massive assault on Bujumbura, the largest since the Kinama attack two years previously. But it soon became clear that the attack was destined to fail, as the 2001 attack had done. Within the first few days, the BBC reported that dozens of FNL fighters had been killed. I couldn't help feeling smug about it.

I felt less smug when Antoine emailed me the pictures of the FNL fighters whose bodies now littered the streets of Bujumbura. They were children. Armed with hoes and magic amulets which, they were told, would protect them from bullets, the children had been sent by the FNL to liberate Bujumbura from the Tutsi oppressors. The amulets hadn't worked.

In one photograph there was a boy who looked to be around 14 years old. He wore plastic bags on his feet instead of shoes, tied on with string. His hand still clutched at the small iron hoe attached to his belt. His eyes were open as he lay there, looking out at me from my computer screen. And although a piece of his head was missing, there was a curious look of hope in his eyes.

I guessed that this boy had died instantly. Hit by shrapnel, perhaps – knocked out cold, without the time even to feel frightened before unconsciousness swept over him, bringing death in its wake. What life had this boy lived? What had those eyes seen? How would I feel if I found out that the man who killed my sister wasn't a man at all? How would I feel if I found out that Charlotte's killer had been a child soldier?

A few days later, my mother emailed to say that she'd been invited to meet the Burundi's new President, Domitien Ndayizeye, who was going to be visiting London to drum up donor support for Burundi's transition to democracy. At last we were getting somewhere.

The summer of 2003 was one of the warmest on record in London, and my mother met the President on one of the hottest days of the year. Ndayizeye was short, fat and charming: 'Je me suis dis que je *dois* la voir' – 'I said to myself that I *must* see her', he told her, offering his condolences. He was only slightly taken aback when she replied in fluent French.

When she asked him about the issue of an amnesty, Ndayizeye promised that war crimes and crimes against humanity would be excluded from any such deal. 'I just can't understand why they do these things', he said. 'And to think that I used to be one of them, too.' He agreed that the Titanic Express attack was a crime against humanity, but explained that finding those responsible would be no easy task. He'd love to be able to lay his hands on Rwasa, but 'these people don't leave addresses'.

My mother was impressed with Ndayizeye, who was clearly a consummate politician, but she found it strange that he was here hobnobbing with the UK Foreign Office while his capital was under attack. And though he seemed like a decent sort of chap, it was a shock to hear the president of the country where her daughter had died saying to her face that he used to be on the same side as her killers.

'I know this is very silly', she told me later, 'but on the train home I was looking round at everyone, thinking: *would you be a Hutu or a Tutsi?*'

The meeting with President Ndayizeye had, of course, been little more than a PR exercise, but PR still has its uses. My mother wrote another letter to the *Guardian*, giving a glowing review of her meeting with Ndayizeye – and explaining how pleased we were that the Burundian government had acknowledged that the attack in which Charlotte died was a 'crime against humanity'. It wasn't much, but it at least it was another firework flare in the darkness.

— 13 —

On 14 September 2003 I became older than my big sister. Charlotte had been 27 since 4 June 2000. She'd stayed 27 on 4 June 2001, 4 June 2002, 4 June this year. I was now 28. How strange it would be to meet her now – my younger, older sister. Doubtless I had a few more lines on my face than when she last saw me, just a few weeks after *her* 27th birthday. From time to time Heleen would find a strand of grey in my hair.

It was more than three years since I'd last seen Charlotte alive, and already she seemed a little distant. In my mind's eye I imagined myself in a boat, drifting steadily away from the shore. I could still make out that it was Charlotte waving to me on the horizon, but her face was beginning to seem indistinct. At least I had the photographs – what did people do in the days before photographs? But I also knew that the more I relied on these pictures the more *these* would become my memories of Charlotte. Charlotte smiling for the camera in the last photo ever taken of her, Christmas 2000, forever frozen in a frame, static, two-dimensional, predictable. The Charlotte I'd known had been none of these things. If I tried too hard to keep my sister's memory fresh I would do the exact opposite. I'd end up thinking of Charlotte as nothing but a series of grinning freeze-frames staring out from a photo album.

So much had changed in my life since the last time we saw each other. The brother that Charlotte knew had never been so jumpy and uptight. I'd been in *sabaai-sabaai* Thailand, supposedly the most laid-back country in the world, for much of the last year, and yet I was still so angry. It was only when I enrolled in one of the free meditation classes offered to *farangs* in Bangkok that I realized how long it was since I'd *not* felt angry. An hour and a half of sitting still and breathing deeply and I felt like a different person. If still not entirely at peace with the world, then at least I'd reached some kind of ceasefire truce. I'd been carrying this anger for so long that I'd stopped noticing it was there. Or was it just that I'd given up trying to control it?

I was grumpy and jumpy as we travelled from Hanoi to Ho Chi Minh in October. If Laos had been the *sabaai-sabaai* version of Communism, Vietnam was 'in yer face'. There were tannoys on every street corner, issuing public announcements at 6am every morning, urging the People to arise and help build a happy, prosperous, socialist future. Red and yellow banners in the street proclaimed that 'Ho Chi Minh lives forever in our hearts'. And whereas in Laos the people we'd met seemed happy to speak openly, in Vietnam it was hard to talk to anyone but touts and tour guides. In this long, narrow country it was difficult ever to get far from the tourist trail that snaked down from Hanoi to Ho Chi Minh, and everyone we spoke to seemed to want to sell us something.

Cambodia was just as hard sell as Vietnam, but at least it was less buttoned-up – and perhaps I was becoming a bit more thick-skinned. Drugs were so prevalent here that you could order magic mushrooms as a pizza topping. On our first evening in Phnom Penh, the waiter asked politely if we'd like something to smoke with our meal. The city was only marginally less rubble-strewn than Kigali, but there was even more of a Wild West feel about the place.

'You wan' go shooting range?!', we were asked, within an hour of arriving. Cambodia's 'shooting range' was notorious among backpackers. For a handful of US dollars, you could fire off a Kalashnikov rifle to your heart's content. Rumour had it that for a few dollars more, you could blow up an old bus with a rocket-propelled grenade. Looked at from one point of view, it seemed like an ingenious way of dealing with the huge stockpiles of ammunition left over from the Khmer Rouge era. Looked at from another, playing shooty-bang-bang in Cambodia was one of the sickest ideas I'd ever heard.

According to backpacking lore, if you offered the right kind of money, the bus would be substituted for a live cow. And if you went for that, there was only one more place left to go. The bright-eyed, young English teacher we spoke to on the way into Phnom Penh swore that a friend of a friend had been offered the chance to shoot a live human being. As the fragments of frazzled beef were being wiped off the walls, a sickly Cambodian man had emerged from the shadows.

He was terminally ill, he said, and his family desperately needed money. The friend of a friend could shoot him dead for $100. The friend of a friend had declined. Whether or not the story was literally true, it did seem to epitomize *some* truth about this desperate place, and its relationship with the tourists who came to consume it.

Cambodia seemed to be the most angry and unhappy country I'd ever been to. The young man who drove our bus into Phnom Penh had explained, in broken English, that Cambodia had once been an empire, owning most of Thailand and some parts of Vietnam. But now, he said, all this had been taken away. To add insult to injury, the Thais were teaching their children in school that Cambodia's Angkor Wat temple complex belonged to *them*. I had my doubts about this, but I didn't try to argue. I remembered what had happened to the Thai Embassy in February.

While in Vietnam politics had been a forbidden topic of conversation, many Cambodians we met were eager to tell us how bad their government was. Prime Minister Hun Sen had just won another term in the elections, but no one seemed to have a good word to say about him. An international analyst I'd spoken to in Bangkok had told me, with a certain amount of bitterness himself, that most Cambodians seemed to expect Hun Sen to hang onto power regardless of the result of the elections. The only real question was how many people he would kill in order to retain his grip on government. Many Cambodians were voting for him simply to ensure that their part of town didn't get targeted by Hun Sen's thuggish security services.

A Buddhist monk we spoke to at one of the main Phnom Penh temples told me that a popular opposition singer had been shot in the face just a day before we arrived. Everyone knew that the government was behind it, he said. Hun Sen was a killer, leading a government of killers.

I felt quite alarmed – I hadn't realized that the situation here was quite so unstable, particularly now that the elections had passed. What could it possibly be like to have to live with this day after day? And yet, this bright, young monk seemed to have a tremendous optimism about him. Things were going to change one day, he told me. And he said it with such conviction that despite the chaos around us I found it possible to believe him. He had come to the monastery to get an education, he told me. For most Cambodians this was the only way to get beyond high school. There were some good people in the opposition, and he was planning to join them. Cambodia could be a peaceful and prosperous country with the right government, he said.

Yet even this idealistic young man seemed troubled by the same demons as so many of his compatriots. As we were talking, a group of laymen walked past – and his tone changed abruptly. They were from the Thai Embassy, he told me. 'Did you see the way they looked at me? They think I can't understand them because they're speaking in Thai, but I do understand. I know what they are saying. They think we are . . .' he searched for the right word, 'ants!', he said, holding up his finger and thumb.

At the Killing Fields memorial at Choeng Ek, half an hour's drive out of Phnom Penh, we tagged along with a friendly, portly, apopleptic, Norwegian who'd hired his own private guide and invited us to join him. The price we paid for his generosity was a heavily accented lecture on the meaning of socialism. 'Did you know', he asked, 'that there are shtill some people in Norway who call themshelves socialishts?' We nodded gravely. 'Just look at *thish*!', he said, pointing triumphantly at the tower of 8,000 human skulls that formed the centrepiece of the memorial.

'*Thish* is what socialishm means!'

The skulls were arranged in rows on glass shelves inside a 20-metre-tall mausoleum. They were organized and labelled according to age, sex and ethnic origin. Most were Asian. I knew from the guide-book that the handful of European skulls were mostly those of Western journalists who'd been sent to Cambodia and never returned. If you looked closely you could see neat bullet holes in some of the skulls. Others had larger holes hacked into them. Some had no marks at all. Perhaps these were the people who'd had their throats slit with palm leaves. I couldn't quite believe that these bones had once been human beings.

The UN wanted to put some of the Khmer Rouge leaders on trial, the guide told us, but many in Cambodia were afraid that this would plunge the country back into war. Under a peace deal signed in the mid-nineties, many of the Khmer Rouge commanders had been bought off with big houses and government jobs. These people were still very powerful and if the UN came after them, no one knew what they would do.

All over the site, human bones were emerging from the mud, together with the ragged clothes of the victims, colours and patterns still visible. The dead were rising, and there were so many bones coming out of the ground that it was hard to avoid walking over them. Our guide explained that the killers had been in such a hurry that they hadn't even bothered to bury their victims properly. Now, with the rain and subsidence and decomposition, pieces of the corpses were returning from the earth. Or was it that the Khmer Rouge victims were refusing to remain buried while their killers were still at large?

We stayed at the site after the Norwegian had finished his tour. It was a grim, perhaps even a ghostly, place, and Heleen seemed uneasy. But I didn't yet feel ready to leave. As we walked round again we were pursued by a crowd of small, ragged, Cambodian kids. 'Shaaaare one doll-ar, go 'way . . . Shaaaare one doll-ar, go 'way' they intoned, sombrely.

A notice next to one of the trees explained that this was where the Khmer Rouge used to kill children, by swinging them round and bashing out their brains on the tree trunk. I wondered if the Cambodians believed, as the Thais did, that the trees had spirits.

Choeng Ek was more than just a grim place – it felt like an accursed place. Was it my own anger that I had been feeling, or the anger of the dead whose bones I was walking over? Although I didn't regret going there, I wasn't sorry to leave. Three years ago I would have found it unbearable. Now I wondered if I was starting to become brutalized.

What I'd seen here – the skulls, the bones, the rags, the mud, the street kids begging for dollars from tourists – had left me with a cold sense of rage, and yet it hadn't shocked me. Although the scale was bigger, in character it was no more vicious, cruel or callous than what was going on today in dozens of other countries around the globe. This was the world that I lived in. This was what human beings did to each other, and this was what happened afterwards. The mass graves were being filled right now in Burundi, Congo, Burma, Iraq and Indonesia.

At the Killing Fields souvenir shop I picked up a copy of Jon Swain's book, *River of Time*. Jon had done a piece on Charlotte's case for *The Sunday Times* a couple of years back, and it was only later that I'd found out how well known he was for his coverage of the Khmer Rouge atrocities. When I unwrapped the book I discovered that the entire thing was a bootleg – and from an outfit so stingy that the reverse of the cover was printed with the design for the latest Harry Potter book.

We climbed back into the minivan that had brought us here. 'You wan' go shooting range?!', our driver asked, hopefully.

I wondered where those Khmer Rouge people were now, and how easy it would be to find them. Where were the big houses that they'd been given to live in, on comfortable government salaries, while so many Cambodian kids scratched out an existence on the streets?

I knew that I was raging, in part, because I was sure that what I'd seen here was the future of Burundi. A country not quite at war any longer, but not quite at peace either. An impoverished, brutalized nation ruled by a coalition of killers and people willing to do business with killers; a corrupt, self-serving government that wins elections by terrorizing people into voting for them; an angry, humiliated people, ready to lash out at any provocation, real or imagined.

I understood better now how a throwaway line in a fictional television series could have led to such an extraordinary outpouring of violence. Angkor Wat was one of the few reasons that Cambodians had to feel proud of their country – so much so that they'd made it the central feature of the national flag. Cambodia might be poorer, less stable, more messed up than any of its neighbours, but it had one of the wonders of the world. People came from all over the globe to see their magnificent temples, proud testament to the fact that Cambodia was once a great empire. And now these Thais, these same people who had sacked Angkor Wat back in the fifteenth century, these historic usurpers who'd denied Cambodia its place in the sun, were saying that they wanted to take even *that* away from them.

We visited the immense Angkor complex on our way back to the Thai border. A drunk police guard pointed out the many empty alcoves where statues had been stolen by thieves. No one will admit this, he said, but the statues are all in Bangkok, in the Thai national museum. I asked if there was any way they could get them back, thinking about the legal dispute between Britain and Greece over the Elgin Marbles. 'Maybe when Cambodia is an empire again', he told me. I laughed, but he wasn't joking.

I looked up Cambodia's history when I got back to Bangkok. Even before French colonial rule, the Empire had been in a slow, shrinking decline. Perhaps it was little wonder that the Khmer Rouge had wanted to erase the past, and start again from Year Zero. Perhaps this ambivalence towards their history was another reason why so many Cambodians would now prefer not to re-open old wounds by bringing the killers to trial. Yet what if the wounds never really closed? What if the killings are still going on? And what if the dead refuse to stay buried?

The second monk I met in Phnom Penh had told me that the essence of Buddhism was the doctrine of Karma. 'Do good, receive good. Do evil, receive evil.' There's no point praying for salvation if you've lived a life of evil deeds, he explained to me, somewhat sternly. But what of the Khmer Rouge killers? In Cambodia I'd got the sense of an unpunished injustice almost Shakespearean in its immensity. I'd felt so frustrated that I'd found myself willing the natural world itself to rise up in rebellion against it. If the Thai belief about the spirituality of nature was true, then there must be some angry, anguished spirits at Choeng Ek. Was it the dead who were refusing to stay buried, or the earth that was refusing to keep them hidden?

In mid-November, Burundi's President Ndayizeye met Pierre Nkurunziza, the head of the FDD rebel group, to finalize peace terms. I asked Kabonesho if this was good news. Now that the largest Burundian rebel group had come over to the government side, was there a chance that the FNL might find themselves high and dry? According to some reports, the FDD alone had 30,000 troops, while the FNL had just 3,000. Surely now they *had* to stop fighting?

Kabonesho's reply was downbeat. This was just the latest act in the the Bujumbura circus. FNL, Frodebu, FDD – there was no real difference between them. Ndayizeye and Nkurunziza were one and the same, and neither was much better than the FNL. The rebels were negotiating with themselves.

It was early December, and we would soon be leaving Thailand. In a few weeks it would be three years since the day Charlotte died. The boat was drifting a little further away from the shore. In Burundi, a new president was in power, one who openly admitted having been on the same side as the FNL. And the promises he'd given my mother when they met in London had come to nothing. Throughout the year I'd been trying, and failing, to get a story in the international media about the report that seemed to prove the FNL's involvement in the

Titanic Express massacre. All I'd managed was one solitary letter to the *Guardian*. Now we learned that President Ndayizeye, in addition to making peace, had signed a deal giving the FDD rebels cabinet posts and sweeping immunity from prosecution. With no apparent hint of irony, he had made Pierre Nkurunziza, a documented murderer, his Minister for Good Governance. How long now before Agathon Rwasa took the Ministry for Child Welfare? How long now before Charlotte's killers got their long-cherished amnesty?

There were still no answers from the Foreign Office on what they would do if the Burundian government tried to pardon the FNL, still no answers on whether they thought that the Titanic Express massacre was a war crime, a crime against humanity or just a rather appalling breach of etiquette. There was still no news from the Burundians, either, on the investigation that they now claimed to be carrying out into Charlotte's death.

I emailed the *Guardian*, asking if they'd be interested in an article to coincide with the third anniversary of the Titanic Express attack. To my surprise one of the editors got back to me, suggesting that I 'draft something up'. I spent three days manically hammering away at an 800-word piece, laying out the details of the last three years as best I could, angrily attacking the Foreign Office for their 'quiet forgetfulness' over Charlotte's case. I was exuberant when the *Guardian* got back to me sounding positive, and asking when I wanted it to run. I'd been keeping my powder dry for long enough. It was time for some fireworks.

— 14 —

It was the afternoon of the day before Christmas Eve 2003. We were back in Belgium and the snow began falling as we arrived at Heleen's parent's house, almost exactly a year since we'd left. So little seemed to have changed that it was as if we had stepped back out of the wardrobe and into the real world, only to find, like the children in the Narnia stories, that we'd been away just a few days.

I heard nothing more from my contact at the *Guardian*. Just after Christmas, sensing that things weren't going to go the way I'd hoped, I put together a more modest, 100-word letter to the editor and emailed it through. While Heleen stayed on in Belgium for a few more days, I flew home on 27 December, the day before the third anniversary of Charlotte's death. It felt like such a short time since we'd left – and yet I also felt that I'd been away much too long. While little may have changed at home, in Burundi, the wheels had been rolling inexorably towards a blanket pardon for the man with command responsibility for Charlotte's death.

The *Guardian* didn't run the comment piece, but printed my letter instead. My firework flare had fizzled out, but at least I'd lit a sparkler. Antoine Kaburahe, faithful to the cause as ever, sent up a rocket of his own on his news website, featuring an interview with my mother, recalling the promises that President Ndayizeye had made in July. I spent the third anniversary of Charlotte's death at my computer in the spare room of my mother's house, hammering out emails. I wrote to the Foreign Office, trying to pin down what they would do if Ndayizeye tried to give Charlotte's killers an amnesty. I wrote to Jon Swain at *The Sunday Times*, who'd done a piece on Charlotte a couple of years before, reminding him of the story and asking if he might be interested in the FNL report.

The next day, Monsignor Michael Courtney, the Vatican's envoy to

Burundi, was killed in an ambush in Bujumbura-Rurale. Courtney, who'd been dressed in his full priestly regalia, was specifically targeted. The three other people travelling in his car escaped unharmed. The Burundian government accused the FNL of being responsible for Courtney's killing. The FNL angrily denied it. The next day, Simon Ntamwana, Burundi's most senior Catholic bishop, made the same allegation. The FNL denied it again, then threatened to kill Ntamwana for accusing them.

It was one of the strangest sequences of events I'd seen since I first began trying to understand Burundi. The timing of the attack, three years and a day after the one in which Charlotte had died, seemed uncanny. There didn't appear to be any obvious motive. Courtney had, apparently, made concerted efforts to engage the FNL and listen to their grievances. He had generally been regarded as sympathetic towards their concerns, albeit not their methods. If anything, the Tutsi hardliners who opposed all negotiation with the rebels, and resented international mediation, had more to gain from his death than the FNL did.

A few days later, after a number of commentators had pointed out that the FNL threat against Ntamwana seemed to undermine their claim that they would never have had anything to do with Courtney's death, the FNL withdrew it, but the damage had already been done.

Picking up where I'd left off was so easy I was amazed I'd ever worried about it. I phoned Rory Beaumont to let him know I was back in town. I got a call back from Jon Swain at *The Sunday Times* – he was interested in doing a piece on the FNL report and wanted to know how we might authenticate it. I dropped a line to Laurent Ndayuhurume, one of a handful of Burundians working at the BBC World Service. He was the editor of the Great Lakes desk, and had met and interviewed Agathon Rwasa a number of times. Ndayuhurume was in such close touch with the FNL that some of my Burundian contacts had him down as an out and out fifth columnist.

I had tried to contact Laurent several times before, though I'd never had any replies to my emails. But my talk of an FNL report had caught his attention. He got back to me almost immediately, inviting me to his office for a chat. I arranged to meet Jon Swain straight afterwards, to relay whatever Laurent had said about the FNL report and hand him a copy, but I decided not to share this fact with Laurent.

While I was sceptical about the idea that the man was an FNL stooge, I didn't have any reason to trust him either, and I didn't want to take any chance that he might 'scoop' *The Sunday Times*.

Laurent's office was in the BBC World Service building at Bush House in Central London, just a couple of hundred metres from the intercollegiate lecture halls where, nearly a decade ago, I'd spent so many hours studying ethics and political philosophy. This felt like home territory – and in more ways than one. I wasn't at all sure I was doing the right thing by meeting Laurent, and sharing information with him – not because I suspected him, but because Kabonesho, the person who'd been most instrumental in getting me the report that I was about to show him, did. Ever since he'd first contacted me nearly two years ago, I'd worked more closely with him than anyone else. We'd supported and encouraged each other, we'd spurred each other on, and even though we'd never met face to face, even though I was on one side of the Atlantic and he on the other, I felt that we'd built up a kind of friendship. Now I was betraying that friendship. I was fairly sure that Kabonesho would be horrified if he knew what I was doing – and exactly for that reason, I was keeping this meeting secret. I hoped that he would understand – although I was sure I'd have to do some serious apologizing at some stage.

Of course in juicing Laurent for information, I was deceiving him as well. I was pretending that I was doing it simply because I wanted to understand the circumstances of my sister's death, when my main motivation was to test the authenticity of the evidence I wanted to use to discredit her killers. As I waited for Laurent Ndayuhurume on a cold January afternoon in the lobby of Bush House, on the Strand in Central London, I felt edgy and guilty.

From the moment I met him, I was struck by how different Laurent was from any of the other Burundians or Rwandans I'd known. It wasn't just that he was much older. This thin, reserved, well-dressed man didn't seem able to smile. As I shook his hand I wondered whether I was feeling uneasy because of his reserve, or the knowledge that this hand had, in all probability, been shaking Agathon Rwasa's not so long ago.

As Laurent led me to his small, cramped office, he did little to put me at ease, but he seemed quite happy to talk without wanting to know why I was so interested in what he was saying. Laurent made no secret of his sympathies with the FNL. All sides had done terrible things, he told me, matter-of-factly. 'You need to understand that Burundi is not like Britain, which is basically a *just* society', he told me. 'Burundi is basically an *unjust* society.' The FNL were fighting to change the balance and bring about equality, just as the RPF of Paul Kagame had fought to bring equality to Rwanda. 'Many people have compared them to the RPF, actually.' Just as Kagame's RPF had eventually taken power in Rwanda, so the FNL would inevitably take power in Burundi before long. I nodded as understandingly as I could.

The attack in which my sister died had been one of many, Laurent reminded me again. It took place in an area which bordered both FNL and FDD territory. In his view it could have been either group. There was no real prospect of ever seeing anyone prosecuted. The peace deal signed between the government and the FDD gave them 'provisional immunity' from prosecution, and it was only a matter of time before the FNL signed up for the same deal. The latest plan was for Burundi to have a South African-style Truth and Reconciliation Commission, which was another way of saying that everyone was going to get an amnesty except for those who had started the war by assassinating President Ndadaye.

Agathon Rwasa still denied responsibility for Charlotte's death. He had told Laurent that the persistence of the Titanic Express story was, in reality, the work of the Buyoyistes who still dominated the Burundian government, ruthlessly manipulating the media in their black propaganda war against the FNL. The Titanic Express case tended only to resurface, according to Rwasa, whenever Britain was about to take up the rotating presidency of the European Union. The assassination of Michael Courtney was no coincidence either. Ireland had been due to take over the EU Presidency two days after he was killed. Courtney had been a friend of the FNL, Laurent told me. They had no reason to kill him. It had been a stitch-up job.

What really surprised me was that Laurent seemed to have accepted Rwasa's conspiracy theories more or less uncritically. I nodded sagely as he explained that all the media coverage there had been about Charlotte's death was, whatever I might think, nothing to do with my family at all. I laughed inwardly at the irony that I'd be relaying all this to a *Sunday Times* journalist in about two hours time.

Rwasa was *angry* that the Titanic Express story kept on coming back, Laurent said. He was worried that the prominence of this case could damage his links with certain political groups in Europe who'd been giving him financial support. My ears pricked up – I asked what kind of groups Rwasa had meant. Laurent shrugged – 'Well, you know, far-right groups – in Belgium and Austria'.

It was interesting to see where the funding came from for the various groups fighting in Burundi, and who was providing the weapons, Laurent told me. Angola's UNITA rebels had supplied weapons to both sides. The FNL had certainly received arms from China and Korea. In fact, Laurent himself was writing a book about it all.

I explained to Laurent that I could show him the FNL report, but I'd need an assurance that he wouldn't do any kind of story on it. He looked at me as if I were mad. 'Who would be interested in it anyway?' I nodded sheepishly. But when I handed the report over Laurent's tone changed. He went quiet, studying it intently as he leafed through the pages.

'Yes . . . I have seen them make notes like this, at night . . .'

Laurent was silent again. I shifted uncomfortably in my seat, I was still reeling from what Laurent had told me. Rwasa was angry – *angry* that the Titanic Express case wouldn't go away. Angry that the dead were refusing to stay buried.

We'd got to Agathon Rwasa – our efforts to keep the case alive had *got to him*. The FNL had declared that 'there's nothing you can do', and we'd proved them wrong. We'd *annoyed* their leader. If I'd learned nothing else from having a big sister, it was how to be an annoying little bastard. I'd been bouncing my rubber ball against Rwasa's door for the last three years – and now I'd *got* to him. Not only that – Rwasa had no idea where the rubber balls were coming from, or who was throwing them. He was convinced that my family were, at most, pawns in a conspiracy led by the all-powerful Buyoyistes. A conspiracy which also involved, obviously, Antoine Kaburahe, the UK Foreign Office, Jon Swain, Alexis Sinduhije and the Letters page of the *Guardian* newspaper.

Most intriguing of all was the fact that Rwasa was worried that the publicity surrounding the case might jeopardize his links with far-right European groups. But what possible interest could the likes of Vlaams Blok or Jorg Haider have in a group such as the FNL?

As I sat and waited for Laurent Ndayuhurume to say something, I tried to think through the connections in my mind. Could it simply be that these groups wanted to sow chaos in the non-white world – get Africans to kill each other just for the sake of it? Or could it be something more subtle than that? The FNL's ideology seemed to view the course of human history as an epic struggle between competing races, and in this respect they were part of a long, albeit disreputable ideological tradition. It was a world view shared by Europe's Nazis and every copycat group that ever followed them – including many of the far-right groups now ascendant in Europe. Substitute 'Aryan' for 'Bantu' and 'Jewish' for 'Tutsi', and the match was almost exact.

After a good three minutes' silence, Laurent looked back up at me, with a little less contempt in his eyes. 'Just one question – was the person who gave you this document Burundian or Rwandese?' I told him as vaguely as I could that it was a Burundian.

'Well there are some words of Kinyarwanda here. I would say that the person who wrote this was either Rwandese or they had spent some time living there.'

I knew what was coming next – of course I'd known from the start that the FNL had links with the *genocidaires* who'd fled Rwanda in 1994 – but it was something different to know that the author of this report might have been one of them. Laurent told me that many ex-FAR – former members of the Forces Armées Rwandaises, the army of the genocidal government kicked out in 1994, had become military instructors for the Burundian Hutu rebels. Some had joined the FDD, as mercenaries. But many had joined the FNL, as it was an exclusively Hutu group, with ideology that matched their own.

Laurent Ndayuhurume had one more gobsmacking detail for me: Agathon Rwasa was coming to Europe. He would be meeting President Ndayizeye in the Netherlands in mid-January. So much for the President's protestations to my mother that the FNL leader was impossible to find. Laurent told me that if I gave him a copy of the document then he might be able to call the FNL and ask them about it upfront, see if they recognized any of the codes that had been used in the report. They still didn't trust him entirely, but if he could prove that he was onto something they would usually 'own up'. It was impossible to say right now whether the report was genuine, but if he could have a copy then he could go through it in detail and give me a thorough assessment. Laurent's offer took me by surprise and I wasn't quite sure what to do – and I wasn't going to give it to him before *The Sunday Times* had seen it. I lied and said that the copy I was showing was my only one, but if he could wait a few days I could get it duplicated. The truth was that having met Laurent, I now trusted him even less than before.

He shook my hand again and wished me a cold, courteous goodbye. Although I had no idea at the time, I would never see or hear from him again. I left Bush House, found a café and bought myself a sandwich. I sat for an hour and wrote down everything I could remember about what Laurent had told me. I found it hard to believe that someone with such a responsible job at the BBC would be so openly sympathetic to the likes of the FNL. This was the closest to Rwasa I'd ever come. And yet he had also given me a fascinating insight into the way the group operated, and the mindset of their leader. I'd read plenty of conspiracy theories in my life but I'd never been the subject of one before. Did Rwasa really believe what he'd told Laurent or was it just another tactic? Whatever the answer, I could be sure that if he was telling this to Laurent he'd also be saying the same thing to his own troops. Of course it made perfect sense that a man who sought to explain the entire history of Central Africa in terms of a global Tutsi-Nilotic Empire conspiracy would also see little conspiracies in the day-to-day events that affected him. A radio interview with the mother and brother of Charlotte Wilson condemning Rwasa over the Titanic Express attack could not possibly be a simple matter of a grieving family wanting justice. It had to be linked with an elaborately constructed Tutsi plot, cunningly timed to coincide with a grand shift in the power-balance of the European Union.

But it also seemed fascinating that the FNL leader would know more about the internal workings of the EU than most Europeans did. Was this guy a thug or a politician? And what of these 'far right groups'? The more I learned about the FNL, the more complicated things became.

I met Jon Swain at Holborn station a couple of hours later, and we went through the FNL report over a cup of coffee. This was the first time we'd met face to face. I told Jon everything I knew about the report, its author, Albert Sibomana, and what Laurent had told me. It felt mildly surreal to be talking to someone whose book I'd been reading just weeks before, bumping my way through the north of Cambodia.

Jon's piece ran in *The Sunday Times* on 11 January 2004. It had taken more than a year, but at last we'd been able to put our most damning piece of evidence into the public domain. Our firework flare had finally gone up.

I flew to Boston later that week. It was now more than a year since I'd last seen Catherine and Carl, nearly two years since my younger sister had emigrated to the USA. But it was the aftermath of our older sister's death, more than the physical distance, which had brought about a permanent and painful sense of separation. In Boston, amid the ice and snow of one of the coldest winters on record, I began to feel that my relationship with Catherine was emerging from the deep freeze. There were still moments when my obsession with Charlotte's murder clashed, as it had done so many times before, with Catherine's raw inability to talk about it, but there were many others when our old, easy friendship began to show itself again. And it was in Boston, during the days after Catherine and Carl had gone back to work, that I began to write this book, scribbling notes and tapping away on Carl's computer, trying to thread together the events of the last three years and make some sense of them.

Among the many questions that still lingered, there was one that haunted me above all. How had Richard Ndereyimana died? What could explain the horrific mutilations found on his body? How could I reconcile what Pierre had said with what the eyewitnesses had told me? I wanted to know partly for myself, but partly also for Jean-Bosco and the rest of Richard's family. For the last three years their grief over his death had been cruelly compounded by the belief that Richard had been brutally tortured in the last few minutes of his life. If this wasn't true – if Richard had died quickly – then it might at least be some consolation.

When I asked Kabonesho if he thought it possible that the injuries he'd seen were caused by bullets, he was dismissive. He'd seen bullet wounds before, and he knew the difference. 'I'm sorry to say that it wasn't the first time I've seen the body of someone who'd died through violence', he told me.

On 18 January, just twelve days after an FNL bus attack killed another seven civilians in the Democratic Republic of Congo,

Agathon Rwasa was welcomed to the Netherlands by the Dutch government. Less than six months after President Domitien Ndayizeye had told my mother that the Titanic Express attack was a crime against humanity, that Agathon Rwasa was responsible and that he'd love to arrest him but he didn't know what he looked like or where to find him, President Ndayizeye shook hands with the FNL leader and offered him a post in his administration. The British government made no attempt to intervene. The Dutch government hailed the meeting as a historic breakthrough, claiming that 'after 30 years of violence, peace is now within reach'.

The negotiations broke down within days. The delegation refused to recognize Ndayizeye's government because he was a Hutu, and the real power in Burundi was held by the Tutsis. It seemed that the FNL, had flown all the way to the Netherlands simply to tell Ndayizeye how uninterested they were in negotiating.

I sent Laurent Ndayuhurume a copy of the FNL report when I got back from the United States. I never received any acknowledgement, nor did I learn whether he was able to discover anything further about its authenticity. My phone calls and emails over the next two years all went unanswered. In the autumn of 2005 I heard a rumour that he was gravely ill. A few weeks later I learned that he had died.

In February, I phoned Rory Beaumont and told him I was writing a book about Burundi. 'Oh, fantastic!', he said. 'You *must* talk to Desmond Tutu.' Archbishop Desmond Tutu, the revered veteran of the anti-Apartheid movement, was coming to the end of a fellowship at King's College London, where he'd been lecturing on restorative justice. This had been the guiding principle behind South Africa's post-Apartheid Truth and Reconciliation Commission (TRC), and Archbishop Tutu was an enthusiastic advocate. Tutu had been advising the Burundians on how a similar system might be applied there, and Rory had met him briefly last year. I asked Rory why things seemed to be moving in this direction rather than towards the International Criminal Tribunal model that had been applied in Rwanda.

It was essentially a pragmatic issue, he told me. 'In Rwanda one side was very clearly much worse than the other – and that side also lost the war very badly. So when they picked up the guys who'd organized the genocide, no one was going to do anything about it. But in Burundi, both sides have been pretty terrible, and neither side lost.

Agathon still has all these people who are prepared to fight for him. It's like "How many divisions does the Pope have?"'

The TRC model wasn't ideal, but given how bad things were in Burundi, it was a start. I asked Rory about the meeting between Rwasa and Ndayizeye in the Netherlands. Surely Rwasa had been given enough 'last chances' by now?

'It's tough, I know', he said, 'but you've got to look at it from their point of view. They're trying to organize some kind of transition to democracy and all the time there's this rebel group still killing people and destabilizing everything.'

'The way they see it, it's better to have Rwasa inside the tent pissing out, than outside pissing in. So they have to keep trying – even if it means offering him immunity. I know it's an outrage given everything he's done, especially for someone in your position, but from their point of view it makes some sense.'

One of the peace process mediators, Nick de Vos, had recently been up into the hills to meet Rwasa in person. Led by a team of FNL guides, he'd had to travel on foot, through the night, dodging Burundian army patrols, until they reached Rwasa's camp. It had been a 12-hour trek uphill, and dawn was breaking by the time they arrived. 'These guys are tough – they're not going to be beaten easily', Rory told me. 'Nick's a fit man but in the end they had to carry him.' De Vos had been quite impressed with Rwasa, Rory told me, and came away feeling that there might be a way to bring him on board.

The following week I met up with another Burundi, human rights researcher in London. She had heard nothing to corroborate Laurent's suggestion of FNL links with far-right European groups, but was able to tell me a little more about Rwasa himself. Alexis Sinduhije and Burundi's former Human Rights Minister Eugene Nindorera had, like de Vos, travelled into the hills to meet Rwasa not long ago, hoping to find out what it would take to persuade him to stop fighting. They had not had much luck. While de Vos may have been impressed with him, Alexis and Nindorera were left in serious doubt about the FNL leader's sanity. Rwasa had refused to give straight answers to any of their questions, and launched instead into a series of rambling religious monologues. Alexis had apparently become so annoyed by this that he'd started getting argumentative with Rwasa, and Nindorera had to keep calming him down. Word had it that Rwasa's religious zeal was comparatively new, stemming, oddly, from a mystical revelation he'd had while attacking Bujumbura airport in 1999. When I asked her if she thought the FNL had any 'good points' she looked at me as if I was mad too.

I never managed to track down Desmond Tutu, but in early February I heard from Pierre that Maria Eismont was coming to London. I jumped at the chance to meet her. It was now more than two years since she'd last been in touch, and there were still many questions that I wanted to ask. I was also curious; this was one of the people who'd helped me most in the dark few months after Charlotte was killed, someone with whom I'd made an odd sort of connection, and yet I didn't even know what she looked like – nor had I ever discovered why she broke off contact so suddenly.

I met Maria Eismont one freezing February morning in the deserted streets above Pimlico tube station. Small, feisty, flame-haired and eloquent, Maria looked and sounded very bit the war reporter. She seemed a little prickly at first and I wondered if Pierre had cajoled her into seeing me. 'There really isn't much else I can tell you', she said. She'd never managed to find out anything more about Charlotte's death. An informant in Bujumbura-Rurale had given her the names of two people who he said had been involved in the attack, but the trail had led nowhere. 'I think he was just trying to make money out of us – and anyway, he's dead now. The rebels killed him'. I asked Maria if she'd ever heard anything about any of the passengers being tortured. 'There was a rumour, but the eyewitnesses said it didn't happen', she told me. 'There was this young boy who . . .' she made a face '. . . whose *penis* had been cut off – but in the end they decided it was because a bullet had caught him in that area.'

Maria seemed to soften when she told me about her family life in Moscow. She'd brought me some pictures of Pierre and their little daughter, Sophie. No one knew exactly how old Pierre was, she said. She told me, with dark amusement, how she had asked one of his sisters, who'd given it some thought and concluded that he'd been some time 'before the haricot bean season, after the genocide of the Hutu'.

We stayed in touch over email and met again when she returned to London the following summer. In late 2005 I finally asked Maria why she had broken off contact so suddenly four years earlier.

'Well there was nothing special . . . Just maybe I couldn't help much (like I hope I helped a little in the beginning of our virtual conversation) so I probably thought there is no point in disturbing you while I have no new information or update on the main topic (the ambush). That's it I think. Also of course I had a lot of problems to solve with me becoming a mother and moving continents and changing jobs all together (with Pierre being more as a child to be helped than someone to help me out). I was also a bit disappointed in my not being able to find out who did the ambush (in the beginning I hoped I could do more on that but I am a very bad Sherlock Holmes I have to admit.'

In March 2004, the UN set Agathon Rwasa a June deadline to begin negotiations or face political sanctions. In April, Rwasa and Ndayizeye met again in Tanzania, to agree a ceasefire, which was quickly broken. In June, the UN imposed a travel restriction on the FNL leadership, but failed to implement any of the other sanctions it had threatened. The deadline was extended by an additional three months.

In my own life, a semblance of normality was beginning to return. Heleen and I moved out of my mother's house, where we'd been staying since we got back from Thailand. I found a Press Office job in a breast cancer charity, and Heleen began work as an ethical investment researcher. Burundi, once again, had slipped out of the foreground. Charlotte's death was no longer the defining feature of my life.

One Friday evening in August, I took the train out of London to catch up with another old friend, Volker Dornheim. It was the first day of the Athens Olympics, and we sat eating pizza, watching the opening ceremony with the sound turned down, and listening to Indie music through Volker's whizzy, new stereo system.

Meanwhile in Burundi, the FNL were about to launch their bloodiest attack in more than five years. It was 13 August 2004, a day now infamous among Congolese Banyamulenge Tutsis. Human Rights Watch, in a report released soon afterwards, outlines what happened next:

The attackers came across the marsh from the direction of the border. At least one witness actually saw some of them cross the border; other attackers apparently joined the group on the Burundi side of the frontier. One of the attackers fired an initial shot at a distance, perhaps as a signal to others in their group. Then they moved towards the refugee camp, playing drums, ringing bells, blowing whistles, and singing religious songs in Kirundi. At least two local residents heard them sing, 'God will show us how to get to you and where to find you.' One other heard shouts of 'Ingabo Z'Imana,' '[We are] the army of God.' Many reported hearing attackers sing choruses of 'Allelluia' and 'Amen.'

Most of the attackers wore military uniforms, either camouflage or solid green, but a few were in civilian dress. Most carried individual firearms but they also had at least one heavy weapon. A number of the combatants were child soldiers. According to a survivor of the massacre, some attackers were so small that the butts of the weapons they were carrying dragged on the ground. There were women in the group, encouraging the others by their songs and shouts, and ready to assist in carrying away the loot.

When the policemen heard the songs and shouts, they began to fire at the attackers who returned their fire. When the policemen exhausted their ammunition, they fled, either to hide nearby or to report to their commanding officer at the police camp. Stopping some fifty yards from the tents, the attackers raked the tents with fire, mostly from small-arms. They had at least one heavy arm, however, 'so loud that it made its own echo,' said one witness. A Burundian who lived some distance down the road from the camp spoke of detonations of grenades that 'made the roof shake.'

Even in the midst of the noise and confusion of the attack some refugees did not immediately understand the danger. Some believed the attackers were bandits coming to steal the cows stabled nearby. Others believed those singing the religious songs had come to save them especially since some attackers were shouting 'Come, come, we're going to save you.' Anyone who stepped out the entry of a tent was immediately gunned down, as was one father who sought to save his two children by flight. The attackers, usually only two or three at a time, ripped open the tent flaps and slit the sides of the tent. Often they stayed at the entrance to the tent and either ordered people to come out or just began shooting into the tent. They then threw or shot incendiary grenades that caused the tents to catch fire.

Most victims died by weapons fire or by being burned to death. Fifty-one of the corpses of adults and fifteen of children had been burned. One survivor reported seeing an attacker stab a woman to death, probably with a bayonet, and several of the dead had received blows from machetes. But according to a survey of statistics collected at hospitals treating the wounded, only one person had been struck with a machete; all other injured persons suffered wounds from gunfire, explosion, or burns. These attackers were men 'experienced in killing,' as one observer remarked.

If the FNL had carried out the Titanic Express massacre seven times over, they still wouldn't have killed as many people as they massacred at Gatumba on Friday 13 August 2004. The victims were refugees, Congolese Tutsis who'd been desperate to flee the war in the east of the Democratic Republic of Congo, that they had asked for asylum in Burundi. One hundred and fifty-three people were shot, hacked and burned to death. Half of them were children. Of course the Gatumba massacre was, in character, no less brutal than the many smaller attacks carried out by the FNL and their allies in Burundi and the Congo. But it stood out for two reasons. The death toll was exceptionally high, dwarfing that of the Titanic Express massacre, which had been the rebels' record for the last four years. And the FNL took the extraordinary step of admitting responsibility for the massacre, saying that they had no fear of retribution, because they had become untouchable.

When I think about the viciousness of the FNL and what they represent, secular terms like 'crime', 'abuse', 'gross violation' or even 'terrorist' don't really seem adequate. There is something *biblical* about this kind of brutality, and the callous arrogance that goes with it. Gatumba and the FNL's bragging admission of responsibility reawakened my rage over Charlotte's death, the ongoing killings in

Burundi and the indifference of the UN and its member governments.

Over the past five years, Amnesty, Human Rights Watch and the Burundian human rights group Ligue Iteka had quietly and patiently recorded the FNL's crimes, and repeatedly lobbied the major world powers for concrete action. There was no excuse for not knowing. But despite the fact that the FNL had murdered one of its own citizens, the British government, my government, had done little more than wring its hands, claiming that to hold Rwasa to account would 'undermine the peace process'. Less than a month after the FNL had apparently killed another European Union citizen, Monsignor Michael Courtney, Agathon Rwasa was being welcomed to the heart of the EU by the government of the Netherlands.

Perhaps most dangerous of all, during the lead-up to Gatumba, the UN's member governments had given Agathon Rwasa one last chance after another, threatening sanctions if he refused to begin peace negotiations by a particular date – then, when the deadline was ignored, simply extending it with nothing more than a gesture in the direction of censure. Throughout 2004, the European Union and the United Nations pursued a joint policy that was all 'carrot' and no 'stick', when it had any coherence at all. It didn't take a PhD in psychology to see that it was a policy destined to fail.

Amid the smouldering consequences of this failure, a shocked-sounding Agnes van Ardenne, the Dutch Minister for Development Cooperation, denounced the FNL as 'terrorists', declared that her government had broken off all contact with them and urged that Gatumba be referred to the International Criminal Court (ICC). She was speaking after visiting the site of the massacre and meeting the survivors. On the day that the attack took place van Ardenne had been touring the region promoting her government's vision for Central Africa. The Netherlands had taken over the rotating presidency of the European Union in July, declaring that the Great Lakes Region was a key priority on their foreign policy agenda.

Witnesses reported that some of the attackers appeared to be Rwandan or Congolese, and a row immediately broke out over whether the FNL had carried out the attack alone, or as part of a coalition. The Burundian government claimed that Gatumba had been attacked by an alliance of Burundian FNL fighters, Rwandan

Interahamwe and ex-FAR, Congolese Mai-Mai militia and some elements of the Congolese army. Rwanda and Burundi threatened to reinvade the Congo in pursuit of the insurgents.

Van Ardenne's outrage was echoed around the world. European Union governments took up the call for Gatumba to be referred to the ICC. African governments declared the FNL a terrorist organization, and urged the UN to follow suit. The South African President Thabo Mbeki made a speech likening FNL ideology to that of the Nazis. The Burundian authorities issued arrest warrants for Agathon Rwasa and his spokesman Pasteur Habimana, on charges of 'crimes against humanity and war crimes'.

The group that killed Charlotte was now looking more vulnerable and isolated than ever. Whatever purpose the Gatumba attack had served, I couldn't help feeling that the FNL's defiant admission of responsibility had been a major error. For as long as they had kept up the pretence, however implausible, that they were not killing innocent people, the FNL's international negotiating partners could keep up the marginally less implausible pretence that they just didn't know how bad the FNL really was. But with the group openly boasting about their freedom to kill with impunity, this had become politically impossible.

Had the FNL finally pushed it too far? After four years of waiting, was this the moment when we would finally see some action against the group that had killed Charlotte? To press the point home, my mother asked for another meeting with the Foreign Office. It seemed clear that their attitude had changed. Gatumba had convinced them, and many other governments around the world, that Rwasa and the FNL were simply beyond the pale. They agreed that there could be no amnesty for a crime like the Gatumba attack. Although they were unsure that the arrest warrants issued by the Burundian government were anything more than a symbolic gesture, they supported moves to refer the case to the ICC.

As the weeks passed, the FNL tried to backtrack from their admission of responsibility for Gatumba, and then began to circulate a completely new version of events. An article on a pro-FNL website whispered that Gatumba had not, in fact, been a refugee camp at all. It had been a covert military base for the Rwandan-backed, Congolese, rebel group RCD-Goma. The FNL just happened to be passing when shots were fired at them from the direction of the camp. It was only then that they decided to attack it. When they did so, the 'refugees' pulled out guns and a shoot-out ensued. The reason so many tents were burned to the ground was that they had been housing stockpiles of ammunition.

It was a story completely at odds with the testimony of those who'd survived the attack, with the fact that the FNL had suffered no casualties and that most of the dead were women and children. But for some even this explanation was too hard on the FNL. Notwithstanding the group's admission of responsibility, rumours were spread in the eastern Congo that it was actually RCD-Goma who had attacked the camp themselves, killing their own people as a pretext for a renewed Rwandan invasion of the Congo.

I left my job in October to work on the book full-time. The following week I had an email from a contact in Parliament, asking if I'd like to meet Pierre Nkurunziza. The leader of the FDD, who had emerged from the bush only a year or so before, was visiting London in his capacity as Burundi's Minister for Good Governance, and was due to give a presentation to one of the Parliamentary All-Party groups.

After everything I'd read about FDD atrocities, the prospect of meeting him terrified me, but I was also fascinated. Not only was this man the leader of Burundi's largest rebel group, he was being hotly tipped to win the 2005 elections and become the country's first democratic president since Ndadaye.

I took along my friend Désiré Katihabwa, an outspoken young Burundian refugee who'd got in touch with me earlier in the year via a campaign website I'd set up. We had a chat over coffee before the meeting. Burundians were tired of fighting, Désiré told me. The FDD had ended their armed struggle and relaunched themselves under their full acronym CNDD-FDD. Nkurunziza had publicly apologized and asked for forgiveness 'for the war that was forced upon us', and some were minded to give him a chance. Désiré, for one, seemed hopeful that this might be the man who could finally bring peace.

The meeting was held in a small committee room in one the smart offices on Parliament Street. Nkurunziza came in with his entourage a few minutes after we'd taken our seats. Seeing this stocky, shaven-headed and besuited man, whose face I knew well from so many grainy images on Internet news reports, was a distinctly odd experience. Whatever Désiré's view of him, I knew that Kabonesho believed Nkurunziza to be every bit as bad as Agathon Rwasa, and that his shows of contrition were nothing more than a ruse. Was it just because of the things I'd heard that I seemed to sense a sinister air about him? Looking at Pierre Nkurunziza's eyes, I found it far easier to imaging him killing people than saying sorry for it.

Nkurunziza gave his presentation in French, while his spokesman translated it into English, and it was all quite reassuringly dull. At the end of Nkurunziza's talk, I forced myself to go over and speak to him. In nervous, stumbling French, I introduced myself and tried to explain who I was. I couldn't help wondering how many people had been killed by the hand that I was shaking. I handed over a letter that I'd brought with me, asking Nkurunziza to use his influence to see that the Titanic Express massacre was properly investigated, then hastily withdrew.

I'd spotted Rory Beaumont in the audience, and although we'd spoken on the phone it was the first time I'd seen him since I got back from Thailand. I was more than ready to leave and we decided to head to the pub in Parliament Square, I looked round to find Désiré, who I'd last seen engrossed in conversation with Pierre Nkurunziza, but he was nowhere to be seen.

In the pub, I asked Rory what he'd made of Pierre Nkurunziza, and the prospects for peace. 'Well, you know, he's saying all the right things but only time will tell. What really matters is the *economy*. If they can't find jobs for all these demobilized soldiers then the whole thing will flare up again in a few years.' Désiré phoned me the next day, and told me where he'd disappeared to after the meeting: he'd gone *shopping* with Pierre Nkurunziza. The CNDD-FDD delegation had wanted to bring home presents for their children, and Désiré had taken the entire entourage down to Oxford Street.

As the months rolled on, the furore over Gatumba slowly ebbed away. The UN declined to follow regional governments' lead in proscribing the FNL as a terrorist organization. Efforts to refer the case to the International Criminal Court stalled at the UN Security Council not long before the fourth anniversary of Charlotte's death, in part because of US opposition to the court's existence.

In mid-April I got a series of anguished emails from Antoine Kaburche asking if I'd given up the fight. Rwasa, he said, was about to be given an amnesty – shouldn't 'la famille Wilson' be trying to do something?

Soon afterwards I saw a photograph of the FNL leader for the first time. It had been taken in the Tanzanian capital Dar Es Salaam a few days before, and it was part of a news report on a French-language, Burundian news website. Agathon Rwasa, the man with command responsibility for the troops who murdered my sister, was tall, well-built, dressed in a blue suit and shaking hands with the Tanzanian President Benjamin Mkapa. Burundi's Ambassador to Tanzania was grinning broadly in the background. It was quite a small picture, so I couldn't be entirely sure what was going on, but neither President Mkapa nor anybody else in the picture *appeared* to be trying to place Rwasa under arrest for war crimes, or crimes against humanity.

A few days later, there was another picture of Rwasa wearing the same blue suit but this time shaking hands with President Domitien Ndayizeye, the same man who'd told my mother how sorry he was about Charlotte's death and how much he would love to be able to arrest Rwasa if he could only find him. 'Last rebels make peace in Burundi', proclaimed the BBC news website shortly afterwards. A few days later, the FNL resumed their attacks on Bujumbura. The UN's Burundi office condemned the attacks, declaring somewhat tellingly that 'the international community will not tolerate war crimes any more', and promising that 'any group responsible for war crimes will be held accountable for its acts'.

When my mother and I met the Foreign Office officials at the end of May, it was clear that the political landscape had shifted again. Less than nine months after Gatumba, the issue had been 'kicked into the long grass'. The Tanzanian government had quietly organized the meetings between Rwasa and Ndayizeye, then presented what they'd done as a *fait accompli*. Now, despite the fact that the ceasefire had been broken almost as soon as it was signed, the Tanzanians were heralding a breakthrough and urging everyone to stop saying that the FNL were terrorists. Other governments involved in the peace process were, for the most part, going along with it, in the hope that this time it might work. The UK government was still arguing against any amnesty for the FNL, and continuing to press for justice over Gatumba, but they were not actively pushing for Rwasa to be arrested. Relative to most other European nations this position was actually quite hardline, I was told. The Dutch, in particular, were now pushing for an even softer approach to the FNL, and seemed convinced that an amnesty for Rwasa was inevitable.

It was a useful meeting, albeit a disheartening one. When last I'd heard the Dutch had broken off all contacts with the FNL, branded them terrorists and demanded that Gatumba be referred to the ICC. And now they were the FNL's main champions in Europe.

I decided to try to find out more about the 'Dutch connection'. Going back through the news reports from the immediate aftermath of Gatumba, I found a tough-sounding article in the English-language, Radio Netherlands website. 'No mercy for Gatumba killers' blasted the headline. It was based on one of the interviews that the Dutch Development Cooperation Minister Agnes van Ardenne had given shortly after visiting the remains of the Gatumba camp. The text of the article was unremarkable, but the audio report which accompanied it was something special.

What they did now is totally different from all the attacks in the past. In Gatumba women, children, babies were murdered in a most cruel way, with machetes, guns, and some were burned alive. They didn't do that before. They attacked the Burundian armed forces until now, and are still doing, but they don't attack vulnerable people – women, children, etcetera, so it's totally new.

Every so often I go back to the Radio Netherlands website and listen to this interview again. You really have to *hear* those italics to get the full force. Ardenne sounds so confident of herself. 'What they did now is *totally* different from all the attacks in the past . . . They attacked the Burundian *armed forces* until now, and are still doing, but they don't attack vulnerable people – women, children, etcetera, so it's *totally new*.'

I've heard van Ardenne's slow, heavily-accented, italicized words so many times now that they've been seared into my brain – and they still make me angry each time I think about them. But they also fill me with a quiet kind of wonder, because alongside those crisp Northern-European dipthongs and phonemes, I can hear the quiet creaking, shifting and reforming tectonic plates of history. All the reports I've read of FNL atrocities over the last four years, the seemingly endless killings and reprisal killings. All the accounts I've seen about the Titanic Express massacre, the eyewitness statements, the FNL report recording in cold detail how they did it and what they stole. All the people I know who have lost friends or family at the hands of Agathon Rwasa's forces. Richard's eyeless, noseless corpse, and the bodies of the children. Charlotte's body, her face blackened, lips slightly parted, forever frozen in time behind the glass at the Harringay mortuary in January 2001. None of these things are real. None of it ever happened. Charlotte didn't die, and neither did any of the others.

When I first heard van Ardenne's interview I thought how extraordinary it was that a minister who'd been representing the European Union on a mission to Burundi wouldn't have known about the vicious track record of the only rebel group still fighting. It seemed to me to characterize the haphazard nature of international involvement in Burundi. It seemed also to say something about the internal workings of the Dutch government. I knew that Agathon Rwasa had actually been invited to the Netherlands in January 2004, just eight months before the Gatumba attack. I knew from Foreign Office documents that Dutch officials knew that the FNL were the prime suspects in Charlotte's case, and had even offered to ask the group about it when they met. So it seemed especially bizarre that the Dutch Minister for Development Cooperation, who'd been in the job more than two years, would be so completely convinced that this group had never attacked civilians before.

Of course government ministers are active people with lots of things to think about, and none of us is infallible. Maybe this was simply a case of a busy politician not having time to read through her brief before going on the air. But then I found something that made me doubt even this charitable explanation. Like all good politicians, Agnes van Ardenne has a presence on the Internet. The Dutch Foreign Ministry website publishes regular extracts from her diary. I discovered this when I looked up 'Rwasa', 'Ardenne' on Google, and immediately found a reference to 'de legendarische Agathon Rwasa' – the *legendary* Agathon Rwasa. It was van Ardenne's diary entry from the day she heard that Rwasa had signed a peace deal in Tanzania.

Fred Racké, ambassador in special service, calls me from Dar Es Salaam . . . He has good news. I have to go and sit down. An agreement has just been signed . . . I still remember Fred's first trip through the hills in Burundi for his first nocturnal meeting with the legendary Agathon Rwasa. My letter to this rebel leader, who until then had had absolutely no contact with the outside world, was answered by him with a reference to Galatians Six: 'He who sows, will reap'. Following this the first discussions were held in the Netherlands in January 2004, but the peace process was later disturbed by the attack on refugee camp Gatumba. This is a real breakthrough.

The tone of the diary entry seems quite puzzling. Van Ardenne wrote it only nine months after visiting the devastated aftermath of the Gatumba massacre, nine months after denouncing the FNL as 'terrorists', and demanding that the case be referred to the ICC. And yet now, in her one reference to Gatumba, she simply comments that 'the peace process was disturbed'. By using the passive tense, van Ardenne avoids having to say who actually carried out the killings.

What's surprising is that when van Ardenne claimed the FNL had never attacked civilians before, she wasn't doing so from a position of ignorance. According to her diary, she had been actively involved with Burundi since long before Gatumba. She'd sent her 'ambassador in special service' to meet Agathon Rwasa, and struck up a written correspondence with him. She had helped initiate the January 2004 talks in the Netherlands, and she'd taken an active interest in ongoing efforts to bring the FNL to the negotiating table. It seems inconceivable that she wouldn't have known about the group's record.

I can't help but feel that in their desperation to draw Rwasa into the peace process at any price, the European Union and the UN might have made things worse. Of course it made sense to try to persuade the FNL to stop killing people. But inasmuch as they took Rwasa seriously primarily *because* of his willingness to kill, they were starting down a very dangerous road. For a figure like Rwasa, simply being taken seriously internationally was a reward in itself.

The more outrageous Rwasa's atrocities became, the more urgent became the need to persuade him to stop. And however many people Rwasa killed, no international body was ever prepared to impose sanctions on him. Rwasa was being offered one carrot after another. Simply by hosting him in Europe in January 2004, thereby according him all the trappings and status of an international statesman, the Dutch government was giving him a significant reward, and doing so just two weeks after one of the most high-profile, apparently FNL atrocities in years – the 29 December assassination of Michael Courtney. From Rwasa's point of view he had every reason to keep on killing, and very few reasons to stop. One explanation of the Gatumba attack might be that Rwasa was trying to maximize rewards.

Although the UN had solemnly vowed that it wasn't going to tolerate war crimes any more, they spent the rest of 2005 trying their hardest to do just that. When, during the first round of elections in June, the FNL attacked polling stations, mortally wounded a UN peacekeeper and massacred six churchgoers in Bujumbura-Rurale, the UN did nothing about it. When on 31 June, CNDD-FDD accused their electoral rivals of paying the FNL to kill and intimidate voters, the UN did nothing about it. On 7 July 2005, four suicide bombers blew themselves up in Central London, killing 52 people. The attack caused outrage around the world and was vigorously condemned by the UN Security Council. But when, at the end of July, Burundian radio reported the discovery of several *hundred* bodies in recently dug mass graves on FNL territory, the UN did nothing about it.

Despite the disruption, the CNDD-FDD won the elections by a landslide, and in August 2005, as had been widely predicted, Pierre Nkurunziza became Burundi's first democratically elected president in 12 years. One of the first things he did was to offer posts to the FNL.

In September, a group of dissident FNL officers split with Rwasa over his continued refusal to negotiate. They condemned his killings not only of Tutsis but also of hundreds of Hutu civilians he'd killed on suspicion of disloyalty, and a fairly long list of his own lieutenants. The dissidents, led by the FNL's former Vice-President, Jean-Bosco Sindayigaya, wrote to the UN's office in Burundi alleging that:

> When Rwasa tells Burundians and the international community that he will start negotiations, we who are in meetings led by the secretary general of the FNL, Jonas Nshimirimana, are told that the negotiations will serve nothing, that we must continue combat and take the country by force.

Seven of the dissidents were reportedly murdered soon afterwards. In October, the Sindayigaya faction declared that Rwasa had been sacked as FNL leader over his 'gross human rights abuses', and his ongoing refusal to negotiate with the new Burundian government.

In November, a week after the expiry of another 'final deadline' for the FNL to begin negotiations, Burundi's new government arrested a senior FNL member, Aloys Nzabampema. Bizarrely, Nzabampema was wearing a UN peacekeeping uniform when he was captured. The UN office in Burundi lashed out at the local independent media for making 'unfounded allegations' of complicity between them and the FNL, but admitted that the uniform belonged to them.

On 28 December 2005, the fifth anniversary of Charlotte's death, I received a copy of a statement from the FNL's Sindayigaya faction admitting that the Titanic Express attack had been carried out by FNL forces, and accusing Agathon Rwasa of being responsible.

— 15 —

Charlotte still appears in my dreams from time to time. 'If you ever want to reach me, pray to Saint Quinton', she told me a few months ago. For days I was obsessed, hoping to discover a meaningful connection between the life of this third-century Christian saint and some aspect of Charlotte's life and death. I found only a reference to Saint *Quentin*, a Roman missionary to Gaul martyred by the Imperial authorities in 287 AD, now the patron saint of coughs (an honour he shares with Saints Blaise and Walburga).

Among the portents, signs and strange connections that seemed to present themselves in the weeks and months after Charlotte was killed, I'm not sure there was anything that couldn't be explained either in terms of coincidence or the wishful thoughts of a traumatized mind. But I have no doubt that by succumbing to the desire to believe, I helped ensure my survival during that most difficult of times. My comfortable agnosticism may have sufficed when life was going well, but in the face of a real tragedy it was completely inadequate.

The questions raised by my dream in January 2001, the first dream in which Charlotte appeared to me after her death, *have* been answered. More than three of the attackers were firing guns. Richard, almost certainly, was not the second person to die. The 'verifiable conditions' have not been met.

My will to believe and my fear of irrationality seem equally strong, and I have not yet found a way to reconcile them. Time and again I find myself struggling with the same paradox. Even if we are just 'monkeys with car keys', destined for oblivion, why should we assume that knowing the truth about ourselves will do us any good? What if the blind, uncaring forces of evolution have produced an animal that needs to delude itself in order to survive? It seems quite possible to me that there is no life after death, that faith is a wilful delusion and that human life is a meaningless, accidental product of blind, evolutionary forces. It also seems possible that there is a spiritual aspect to life, unprovable but real nonetheless, which makes suffering meaningful, and which can carry us through adversity when all else has failed. If religious faith is nothing more than a delusion, then it seems like a profoundly useful one.

In my life I've known few as gregarious, compassionate, generous or principled as Charlotte Lucy Cameron Wilson, and none so focused or driven. I think I knew that this energy and drive stemmed, at least in part, from my sister's need to drown out the inner noise of the restless spirits that still haunted her – the calamitous loss she had suffered as a child, and the brutal, turbulent school years that followed. At times she could display a lack of caution which seemed to verge on recklessness, and a lack of self-awareness which I found in-furiating. I often felt that in drowning out her demons she was also drowning out her 'still small voice of calm' – her sense of reason and proportion and common sense. Even when we had grown up and become good friends, even when I knew I was being harsh and hypo-critical, even when I suspected that I was only hurting her, I never stopped kicking against this side of Charlotte's character.

But although we were still capable of bickering like infants on occa-sions, the last time I saw my sister I felt that our relationship had reached a new level of maturity. In Rwanda, more than anywhere else, I saw how Charlotte had managed to transform her weakness into a strength, channelling all of her manic intensity into the most chal-lenging task she'd ever faced. She spent the last year of her life helping to educate a new generation in a country that had been torn apart by genocide, and it was clear from the warmth shown to her in Shyogwe how much her efforts were appreciated.

From Charlotte's letters and emails during the last weeks of her life, and from the accounts of those who knew her in Rwanda, it was clear that she and Richard Ndereyimana were very much in love. 'I'm happier than I've ever been in my life', she told me in the last email I ever received from her.

As I made my way to my mother's house on 29 December 2000, reeling from the news that Charlotte had been murdered by Burundian Hutu rebels, I felt an urge to go to Burundi and kill some of them. By *some of them*, I was thinking, ideally, of some actual Hutu rebels. But really any Hutus would have done. I already had a pretty dim view of *them* from the books I'd read about Rwanda, where Hutus seemed, for the most part, to be vicious bullies – and even the ones who didn't actively participate in genocide were complicit in some way. Now that 'the Hutus' had killed my sister, I felt like going and murdering a few. I knew it was racist, and wrong, and irrational – but that was how I felt.

Charlotte's death brought out a side of me that I had never seen before. I find it all too easy to understand the actions of the grief-stricken Burundian army officer, who, after his son was killed and dismembered by Hutus, went out into the street and shot as many as he could find. I am as certain as I can be that, in similar circumstances, I'd have done the same. The impulse to seek sadistic revenge runs deep. And yet, paradoxically, it is this impulse that has helped me to understand how Charlotte's killer could have done what he did.

I don't know what personal horrors the man who killed Charlotte thought he was avenging, but I do know that Burundi's Tutsi-extremists have tortured, raped and killed many thousands more civilians than the FNL – and that most of Burundi's victims have been Hutu. For much of the last century, Hutus have been treated like second-class citizens in their own country, discriminated against, humiliated and excluded from power. In 1972, more than 150,000 educated Hutus were systematically killed by Burundi's Tutsi-dominated government, in an attempt to end Hutu political aspirations for good. In October 1993, seven years before Charlotte's death, Burundi's Tutsi-led army assassinated Melchior Ndadaye, the country's first democratically elected Hutu president, just months after he and his Front pour démocratie au Burundi (Frodebu) took office. During the vicious fighting that followed, thousands more Hutus were massacred by the army and by Tutsi militia groups. Yet most of these crimes were never even officially acknowledged, still less investigated and punished.

When Charlotte's killers told her, 'It's the white people selling the weapons in Africa. Now you're going to feel what it's like', I don't know whether they were speaking from personal experience – whether or not the FNL had itself bought guns from one of the many European dealers who have profited from the Great Lakes tragedy and helped to flood the region with small arms. But I do know that such dealers have supplied weapons, illicitly and illegally, to armed groups even more vicious and murderous than the FNL – some of whom have known links with Charlotte's killers. I do know that many of these dealers, like Avient's Andrew Smith and John Bredenkamp, are either British or resident in Britain. I know from Charlotte's autopsy that the gun that killed her was manufactured in Eastern Europe. And I know, too, that the army of Paul Kagame's Rwanda, an army implicated, at least in part, in the deaths of thousands of Rwandan Hutus and more than 3,000,000 Congolese, has received training from my own country.

Whether or not angry, anguished Charles Nzeyimana, the Netherlands-based FNL man who sent me outraged threats in December 2002, was telling the truth when he said that his family had been 'decimated by the monoethnic Tutsi army', there are many that were. I know there's a very good chance that Charlotte's killer came from such a family.

There is nothing so natural, nothing so universally human, as the impulse to seek indiscriminate revenge – the impulse to punish the crimes of one member of an ethnic, religious or social group by attacking other members of that group. Like most human impulses, it finds expression in an ideology of 'collective guilt' which attempts to give it a moral justification. The man who killed Charlotte wasn't *simply* indulging his impulses when he killed Charlotte. This wasn't a whimsical lashing-out for which he later felt remorse. The man who killed Charlotte was convinced that killing her was *right*.

What isn't true, in any important sense, is that 'they do things differently in Africa'. They do things in Africa just the same way that they do them in Europe, Asia, America and Oceania. When US soldiers tortured and killed Muslim civilians at Abu Ghraib prison during 2003, they were, at least in part, avenging the thousands who had died in the Twin Towers attacks. When the London bombers murdered 52 people on 7 July 2005, they were avenging the Muslims killed and tortured by British and US forces in Iraq. When, three days later, far-right extremists attacked mosques and murdered a Muslim man outside a corner shop in Nottingham, they were avenging the dead of the London bombings.

At the moment Charlotte's executioner pulled the trigger and fired seven bullets into her back, he was doing more than just blowing away a *msungu*. He was avenging hundreds of thousands of cruel, brutal murders, over decades of injustice and exclusion. He was avenging the international community's indifference – and complicity. He was avenging the 'white people who supply the weapons in Africa'. And he was, in all probability, avenging some very private, personal injustice – some quiet, vicious, unreported horror that the world had ignored and then forgotten. Burundi's Hutus have plenty of reasons to feel aggrieved. To say that those grievances were, almost certainly, the primary motivation for the massacre in which Charlotte died is not, in itself, 'justifying terrorism', it's simply stating the facts.

By killing Charlotte and her fellow passengers, the FNL were not simply trying to *punish* an injustice, they were fighting to bring such injustices to an end. By carrying out such a vicious and audacious massacre so close to Burundian government positions, the FNL were enhancing their credibility as an effective fighting force, and exposing the weakness of their enemies, putting further pressure on the Burundian government to meet their political demands. The FNL's systematic ambushes of civilian vehicles on the roads in and out of Bujumbura, were a key part of their military campaign. The Titanic Express massacre, though only one among many, was the largest and most high-profile of these attacks.

The chain of events which led to Charlotte's death began the year before she was born. Antoine Kaburahe, a Tutsi, was sitting in his primary-school class when the soldiers came to take away his Hutu teacher. 'Some say it wasn't a genocide', he told me as we sat together in an Antwerp café, 33 years later, 'but I know what I saw'. One of the many thousands of children left fatherless was seven-year-old Pierre Nkurunziza, later the leader of the Hutu rebel group CNDD-FDD, and now Burundi's president. Another was the young Richard Ndereyimana.

The Partie pour la libération du peuple Hutu (Palipehutu) was created as a direct result of the 1972 genocide. The movement's most radical faction, Palipehutu-FNL, formed and flourished in the aftermath of the 1993 assassination of Melchior Ndadaye. Throughout the 1990s, the continued suspension of democracy, the slow genocide of Hutu by the Tutsi-dominated army, the West's apparent favouritism towards the Tutsi-dominated dictatorship in Rwanda, and the rest of the world's indifference to what was going on, did nothing but strengthen the FNL and help it justify its existence – and its methods.

The Burundians who had gained most from the 1972 genocide were not the Tutsi ethnic group as a whole, but the small group of Tutsis, mostly from the southern region of Bururi, who had dominated Burundi since a young army officer, Michel Micombero, seized power and overthrew the monarchy in 1966. The death or exile of hundreds of thousands of successful Hutus left large areas of land available for appropriation, and those who profited most were members of the Bururi elite. When Micombero was overthrown in 1976, it was another Bururi Tutsi, and a distant cousin of his, Jean-Baptiste Bagaza, who deposed him. When Bagaza was deposed in 1987, it was *his* cousin, Pierre Buyoya, who took power.

When Ndadaye defeated Buyoya in the 1993 election, he became not only the first Hutu president, but also the first non-Bururi president. Yet Bururi Tutsis still dominated most other institutions, including the army. Economic issues soon came to the fore, particularly the issue of land. With the accession of Ndadaye's Frodebu, many Hutus who had fled in 1972 felt confident enough to come home – and to lobby for the return of the land they had lost 20 years earlier. At the same time, Frodebu set about reforming the institutions that had for so long been dominated by nepotism. For the Bururi elite, this was a step too far. With their commercial interests threatened, a small number of powerful individuals set about planning to depose the government.

In his essay 'Speaking the truth amidst genocide', Alexis Sinduhije, the Burundian journalist who'd worked on the 'Breaking the Codes' documentary, gives a compelling account of the coup that began on the night of 21 October 1993:

At around two o' clock that morning, mortar shelling and automatic weapons fire woke the entire city of Bujumbura. I got out of bed and began making phone calls. Nobody knew what was happening . . . When I turned on the radio, there was no sound. I knew then that it was a military coup. With great difficulty, I convinced my wife that I had to go to cover the story. As I left my house, I saw that our Hutu neighbours were also awake, and tense with anger. Many looked at me full of hate. I understood that the situation was going to degenerate into violence, but I didn't know how bad it was going to be. The soldiers going back and forth in their tanks were Tutsi like me, and they had attacked a Hutu president whose fate was unknown . . .

One of my childhood friends, a Hutu named Gashira, saw me and asked, 'You Tutsis, why are you so arrogant? We elected our president and your soldiers killed him.' The question troubled me. It is true that I had brothers in the army, but I wasn't responsible for their actions. I was surprised and afraid at how ready he was to include me among those who were responsible.

Thanks to a soldier I knew, I got access into the palace court-yard, where I found a group of soldiers pillaging the house. They had already emptied the presidential refrigerator, and were drinking and celebrating. They asked me if I wanted some champagne. I replied that I never drank before sundown and it wasn't yet midday. One of them told me that I was missing a unique opportunity to taste champagne. We all burst into laughter. Champagne is the drink of the rich in Burundi, and then only the extremely rich.

The palace roof was riddled with holes, windows were shattered, and the southern walls surrounding the palace were destroyed. 'That was from a shell fired from a tank,' the soldiers explained to me, laughing. I asked if there were any dead among the president's bodyguards, and they burst out laughing again. They replied that the bodyguard was comprised of soldiers, and that they wouldn't fire upon their colleagues, but that they had wanted to capture the president. They confirmed that they had done so and that the president had died at 10 A.M. in a military camp in Musaga, 6 kilometers south of Bujumbura.

I knew that the president's death would have grave consequences. I remembered what Gashira had said to me, but now I pretended to support the soldiers' act. In reality, deep down inside, I hated them because I thought of the thousands of Tutsis who would end up paying for it. I was convinced that the Hutu officials in the countryside would pit the Hutu peasants against the Tutsis. Then soon after, I learned from military sources that the situation was, in fact, turning catastrophic. Hutus were massacring Tutsis in several provinces of the country.

It's difficult to overestimate the role of conspiracy theory in Burundi's conflict, where competing versions of the truth can be as deadly as bullets and machetes. In the wake of Ndadaye's murder, hardliners with links to the conspirators claimed that the Frodebu government had been planning a genocide against the Tutsi population, and that the murder of Ndadaye was a desperate attempt to stop it. Many Hutus feared, conversely, that the Tutsi elite was trying to repeat the genocide of 1972. Some Hutu politicians, including some from Ndadaye's own Frodebu party, urged Hutus to 'resist' by attacking and killing their Tutsi neighbours. Tutsis, particularly Tutsi youths, were encouraged to form self-defence militias. 'Self-defence' often meant launching attacks against Hutu civilians, aided by the Tutsi-dominated Burundian army. Hutus saw this as further evidence of the 'Tutsi conspiracy' against them. In reality, the prophesies of genocide became self-fulfilling.

Those who bore the brunt of the punishment were those who were easiest to get to – the poor, the powerless and the vulnerable – the Tutsis in the outlying districts of Bujumbura, the Hutus of Bujumbura-Rurale and, especially, those who didn't fit neatly into one ethnic category or another. In 'revenge' for Ndadaye's killing, Hutu-extremists attacked and burned down Richard Ndereyimana's family home in Bujumbura, forcing them to flee to a predominantly Tutsi area. Burundi's capital quickly became a divided city.

In the midst of the chaos, a further, even more sinister factor emerged. When the Tutsi self-defence militias were given hit lists of suspected Hutu 'genocide planners' to hunt down and kill, these lists were not drawn up at random. The members of the elite who drew up the lists were deliberately manipulating the Tutsi youths, who'd been led to believe that murder was a matter of survival. Many of the targets were Hutus with whom the elite simply wanted to settle a grudge, or a business rivalry.

Under international pressure, the army officers who had orchestrated the coup attempt partially reinstated Burundi's Frodebu government, but the party had been severely weakened by the killing of so many of its leaders. Many Hutus concluded that a true restoration of democracy would be impossible until the Tutsi elite had been defeated militarily. Meanwhile in Rwanda, Ndadaye's assassination by Tutsis was seized on by Hutu-extremists seeking to inflame anti-Tutsi sentiments there. The 1994 Rwandan genocide began less than six months after Ndadaye's murder.

In 1995, a hardline faction split away from Frodebu to form the Conseil Nationale pour la Défense de la Démocratie (CNDD), with an armed wing, the Forces pour la Défense de la Démocratie (FDD). The ranks of the FDD were swelled by thousands of Rwandan Hutus, many of them soldiers of the former Rwandan army and the Interahamwe militia, who had fled after genocidal government was deposed. Others joined forces with the more overtly ethnic Partie pour la libération du peuple Hutu. In Burundi, the FDD began attacking both the Burundian army and Tutsi civilians.

Tutsis, in turn, retaliated by attacking Hutus. At the University of Bujumbura, Richard Ndereyimana was forced to abandon his studies, under threat of death, after Tutsi-extremists discovered his Hutu lineage. Soon afterwards, Pierre Nkurunziza, now a sports lecturer at the university, narrowly escaped death on campus after his car was ambushed and torched. Ndereyimana fled to Rwanda and became a monk, then a teacher and then, finally, one of the better-known victims of the Titanic Express bus massacre. Nkurunziza fled to Tanzania and joined the FDD, going on to become the organization's chairman, then its presidential candidate, and finally, in August 2005, Burundi's first democratically elected president since 1993.

It's sometimes said that there are 'no clear moral answers in Burundi's terrible conflict'. I think that this is a cop-out, largely inspired by the flimsy moral relativism that fiddled with semantics while Rwanda went up in flames in 1994. Whatever else the Titanic Express massacre was, it wasn't morally ambiguous. The FNL were pursuing a political cause by attacking civilians, and either this was OK, or it wasn't.

The most detailed attempt I've seen explicitly to justify the Titanic Express massacre was from an anonymous rebel sympathizer commenting on an interview I gave to a Burundian news website in 2003. It ran roughly as follows:

1. The passengers of the Titanic Express knew the risks that they were taking in entering an FNL 'zone rouge', and were therefore a legitimate target for attack.
2. 'C'est la guerre' – attacks on civilians are an inevitable part of warfare.
3. The FNL killed far fewer civilians in the Titanic Express massacre than died at the hands of the Burundian government. The attack was therefore a proportionate, perhaps even a restrained response to a much greater crime.

One of my former university professors, Ted Honderich, has argued that killing civilians *can* be acceptable if those killings help to stop an even greater injustice. The 'end' can always justify the 'means'. Honderich argues that the firebombing of German civilians by Allied forces during the Second World War was justified on the basis of this principle, as was the terror campaign waged in favour of the creation of the State of Israel. He has also earned notoriety by suggesting that Palestinian suicide bombings against Israeli civilians might be justified if they helped deter attacks by the Israeli army. Unsurprisingly, Honderich has been heavily criticized for putting forward this view. But the argument could also work the other way. If massacring Palestinian civilians might deter suicide bombers, and if the total number of Palestinians killed was less than the total number of Israeli lives thus saved, then that might be justified too.

Some such 'ends and means' argument has been used to justify many a terrorist campaign, and a great many counter-terrorist campaigns waged in reprisal. Very often, the debate centres on whether the objective behind the attacks is just, or whether the civilians coming under attack are genuinely innocent, rather than on the wider question of whether, as human rights groups argue (and international law demands) there should be an *absolute* prohibition against such attacks. But to me at least, this question seems like a rather important one, because if attacking civilians is *sometimes* OK, then I have to accept that Charlotte's murder might also have been OK.

On the day that Charlotte was killed, and just a few miles from where the Titanic Express massacre took place, thousands of Hutu peasants were being held in 'regroupment camps', ostensibly for their own protection, in reality to prevent them from supporting the rebels. For many Hutus, the regroupment policy epitomized everything they hated most about the Tutsi-led government. There were widespread reports of rape and torture by government soldiers. Unable to feed themselves, and lacking adequate care from the people who were holding them, the camp's Hutu detainees, whether by accident or design, were dying in their hundreds. Some believed that this was a deliberate attempt to exterminate those suspected of rebel sympathies.

If attacks on civilians can ever be justified, then, in my view, on 28 December 2000, the FNL would have had a pretty good case. At the time of Charlotte's death, both the FDD and the FNL were refusing to negotiate with the Burundian government until a series of preconditions had been met. One of those preconditions was the dismantling of the hated system of regroupment camps. There is some evidence that this hardline position, and the military campaign that backed it up, helped to hasten the regroupment policy's demise. It's therefore possible, though by no means certain, that the Titanic Express attack played a part in bringing the regroupment system to an end – and that lives were saved as a result.

Burundi's rebels also had a wider cause that many would agree was just. They were fighting for the restoration of democracy, and the dismantling of the Tutsi domination of Burundi's political institutions which had made democracy unviable in 1993, and which had led to so many deaths since. It's arguable that the campaign of violence against civilians by both rebel groups forced Burundi's Tutsi elite to accept that such reforms were inevitable. Many observers have compared the system of exclusion in Burundi to that of Apartheid, although of course far fewer South Africans have died at the hands of their government than were killed in Burundi. Clearly many in the rebel movement believed that the violence, regrettable though it was, ultimately saved lives – and was therefore justified.

But the fact is that attacking civilians almost always makes things worse in the long term. It's now estimated that 300,000 people, mostly civilians, have died in Burundi since Melchior Ndadaye was murdered in October 1993. Most lost their lives during the frenzied descent into hell in the years immediately following his death. Many others died in the slow, brutal, grind of ethnic killings that has continued ever since.

Burundi's tragedy is that the hardliners on both sides believed that theirs alone was the just cause, and that this gave them an exclusive and absolute justification for attacking civilians. In doing so, each side believed that they were punishing the injustices of the other, and helping to stop further such injustices. Instead, the readiness of both sides to attack civilians, combined with the all-too-human impulse to seek indiscriminate revenge, only inflamed the situation and led to an interminable cycle of massacres and reprisal massacres.

Nothing, to my mind, better epitomizes the absurd reality of 'collective guilt' in Burundi's conflict than the life of Richard Ndereyimana, the son of a Hutu father and a Tutsi mother. In 1972, Richard's father was murdered in the Tutsi-extremist genocide of educated Hutu. In 1993, his family home was attacked and burned down by Hutu-extremists in revenge for the assassination by Tutsis of Melchior Ndadaye. In 1995, he was driven out of university by Tutsi-extremists, in revenge for the massacres carried out by Hutus. Then, finally, on 28 December 2000, Richard Ndereyimana was murdered by Hutu-extremists, avenging, among other things, the genocide in which Richard's own Hutu father had been killed, and the institutionalized exclusion of Hutus of which he himself had been a victim.

Richard Ndereyimana, like the thousands of other Burundians of mixed parentage, spent his whole life being punished for the collective crimes of both ethnicities.

Many observers believe that the restoration of democracy, precarious though it is, would have been impossible without the armed rebellion. What's far less clear is whether the deliberate targeting of civilians helped or hindered this goal, and whether the same result could have been achieved if the rebels had attacked only military targets.

In terms of 'ends and means' morality, the rightness or wrongness of the rebels' scorched-earth policy comes down to whether the justice it achieved was outweighed by the injustices it caused along the way. But it's impossible to know how we could ever judge this. Perhaps the most unpredictable question of all – and one of the key challenges now facing Burundians – relates to the long-term effect of the violence carried out since 1993. Burundians, more than most, live amid a myriad knock-on-effects. The bitterness of the conflict between Hutu and Tutsi has its origins in the injustices committed by Tutsis against Hutus under Belgian rule from 1918. Yet the Belgians were only exploiting and exacerbating a rivalry that probably stretches back much further. The violence of the last ten years may have helped to bring about a restoration of democracy, but it remains to be seen what the long-term consequences will be.

I've often wondered how much time passed between the moment that Charlotte realized she was going to die and the moment that she was killed. How long she was lying there on the ground before they shot her, and how long she remained conscious after that. And I've often wondered what she was thinking during those last moments of her life. Of course I can never know, but it seems likely to me that one of her first impulses, as it often was during times of immense stress, would have been to pray – and that the religion she spoke of as her 'crutch' was able to support her when she needed it most.

In one of her letters from Rwanda, Charlotte told me the harrowing story of a Rwandan Hutu man and his Tutsi wife during the 1994 genocide. The couple were on the run and the killers were closing in, Charlotte told me. They knew that if they were caught together they would both be murdered – she for being Tutsi, he for being married to her. She would be raped, and they would both, almost certainly, be horribly tortured before they were killed. In the face of certain death, the Tutsi woman asked her husband to kill her, so that she might die quickly and that he might escape with his life. Seeing no other way, he agreed. But before this Hutu man killed his Tutsi wife to save her from a fate worse than death, they sat together and prayed for forgiveness for what they were about to do. 'How can I judge that?' Charlotte asked me.

I know that this story in particular stuck in her mind, but there were many others. In the last year of her life, Charlotte seemed pre-occupied with ideas of violent loss, judgement, prayer and forgiveness. And it seems quite possible to me that some of these stories might have been in her mind during her last moments.

I like to think that Charlotte was able to face death by sticking to the principles by which she had lived. Central among these was her Christian faith – and central to Christianity is the ideal of forgiveness. It is an *ideal* because Christians recognize that the principle isn't always easy to live up to. While all sins are forgivable in principle, some sins, in practice, are far more forgivable than others. One of the hardest of sins to forgive is the sin of murder – and yet, Christians believe, Jesus forgave even those who crucified him.

It seems possible to me – likely in fact – that during the last moments of Charlotte's life she was able to compose herself enough to say a prayer, and that doing this might have brought some comfort. And if I know my sister in the way that I think I do, I think she might have prayed for her killers to be forgiven. This is not a question that can ever, in practice, be subject to empirical proof. It's a question about the silent thoughts in the last moments of the life of a woman who, as I write, died nearly five years ago. But neither is it a mean-ingless question. It's a question that has an answer, even if it's an answer I can never know. It is, in fact, a question of faith.

Did Charlotte muster the same strength of will, at the moment of death, that she had shown throughout her life? Was she able to uphold the principles she had lived by, even in the face of such terror? Could she find a way, at the last, to extend her compassion and gen-erosity of spirit even to those who sought to destroy her? All I know is that if she did, then the victory was hers.

And if Charlotte *might* have been able to forgive her killers, should I? What would forgiveness entail? On the one hand I can't shake the conviction that Charlotte's killers must face justice for what they have done – that to accept anything less would be a betrayal. And yet on the other, and without fully understanding why, I've lately started to feel that I should try to forgive, or at least try to understand what forgiveness might mean.

Forgiveness is at least as much about cultivating a particular state of mind as it is about action. It's not enough to *say* that you forgive someone – it's not even enough to *act* as if you forgive them, although this is important too. Forgiveness is something internal. When we forgive people, we sometimes say 'no hard feelings', by which I think we mean 'no feelings of anger'. To forgive somebody is, at least in part, to stop being angry with them. My dictionary defines forgiveness as to 'cease to blame or hold resentment against' someone. Resentment is defined in terms of 'indignation'. To be indignant is to be 'angered by a sense of injury or injustice' – and this is, in fact, a fairly precise description of how I have felt towards Charlotte's killers for the past five years.

So in order to know whether I can, and should forgive them, I need to think about whether I can, and should, stop being angry with them. One of the problems I have is that the anger I feel over Charlotte's death, and the injury that it did to me and my family, is tied up with a much wider 'sense of injury and injustice'. From the start, my knowledge that Charlotte's death was only 1 among 21 injuries and injustices – that this wasn't just a murder but a massacre – sickened and angered me even more. And my anger was compounded further as I learned more about the attack and its consequences – the fact that the killers crowed that 'we're going to kill them all and there's nothing you can do', the fact that a number of little children were among the dead, fears that some of the victims may have been tortured, and the glimpses I have seen of the terrible grief borne by others – not only members of my own family, but also people like my friend Jean-Bosco, the brother of Charlotte's fiancé Richard Ndereyimana.

My anger has been further exacerbated by the fact that the FNL has shown no remorse for what they did, and that they have killed many hundreds more people in the months and years since she died, and perhaps even more so, the callousness and disgusting brutality of these killings. Perhaps most of all I've been sickened by the murders of the 153 Congolese Tutsis, half of them children, who were shot, hacked and burned to death at the Gatumba refugee camp in August 2004.

At every stage, my anger over Charlotte's death has been my reference point for the anger I feel over the FNL's other injustices, to the extent that it's now sometimes quite difficult to separate the two. Another problem I have is that there's a vagueness in my mind about *who* I should stop feeling angry with. Strictly speaking, Charlotte was killed by just one person, probably a relatively junior member of the FNL. If all I had to do to forgive Charlotte's killers was to stop feeling angry with *this* man then the task would be much easier. He had almost certainly himself been a victim of many terrible crimes during his life. He may well have joined the FNL as a child soldier, even if he wasn't one on the day he killed Charlotte. The life of the average FNL foot soldier is nasty, brutish and short. The ideology with which he had been indoctrinated could arguably be described as brainwashing. He likely gained little from his involvement in the Titanic Express attack. A defence lawyer could make a pretty good case for 'diminished responsibility' – assuming of course that this man isn't already dead.

I still believe that what he did was an appalling crime – and that, like any criminal, he must be held to account for it, and do something substantial to make amends. But that is not the same as being angry with him. The truth is that the more I learn about the life of the average FNL foot soldier, the easier it is to feel compassionate towards him. It can never be my place to forgive on behalf of a third party, but if Charlotte could have forgiven her killer for what he did to her, then I can forgive him the grief and pain that he caused me through what he did to her.

But Charlotte's death was just 1 among 21, and the Titanic Express massacre was carried out not by one man but by an entire FNL unit, consisting, according to the group's own records, of 40 soldiers. In carrying out the massacre, these soldiers were implementing a policy of deliberate attacks on civilians which the FNL senior leadership had ordered and approved. The unit which ambushed the bus was part of a battalion under the command of Albert Sibomana, who in turn was acting under the orders of the Bujumbura Chief of Operations, Agathon Rwasa. In overall charge of the FNL at the time, although there is some evidence that he had only nominal control, was the then president of the organization, Cossan Kabura.

I still find it impossible to believe that it's wrong to get angry about what happened on 28 December 2000, and everything that followed. In fact, I think that we need to get *more* angry about such injustices, rather than less so. Anger certainly seems preferable to indifference. Part of me thinks that if you don't get angry about such an injustice then you haven't truly understood it. I still believe that justice must be done over the Titanic Express massacre, and that we won't get it if we don't keep fighting for it. At every stage of this fight, it has been my anger that has kept me motivated.

And yet, at the same time, this anger, which on occasions has been almost uncontrollable, has turned me into someone that I'm not sure Charlotte would recognize. At various turns I have been unreasonable, selfish, self-absorbed, endlessly needy, obsessive, rage-ridden, insomniac and, more often than seldom, a downright bore to be with. It's not the killers who have borne the brunt of this, it's my family, my friends and, perhaps most of all, the woman I love. If I could forgive Charlotte's killers and, in doing so, let go of just a fraction of this rage, then my life, and the lives of those I love, would be much improved.

At heart I believe that forgiveness is an ideal, and an important part of what it means to be human. I've admired others who have been able to overcome their rage at the great injustices committed against them, and pitied those who couldn't. At heart, I do not want to be an angry relative, baying for blood.

One way of trying to navigate through this might be to focus on the distinction between anger at an injustice and anger at the people who committed the injustice. The distinction has sometimes been expressed as 'love the criminal, hate the crime'. I can still be angry over what happened to Charlotte, and I can still fight for her killers to be held accountable, but I don't have be consumed by rage against them. Looked at in this way, it doesn't seem so difficult to stop being angry with my sister's killers, even Rwasa.

The essence of how I now feel about Charlotte, her life, her death and everything that followed is an idea put forward by Plato more than 2,000 years ago: 'To know the good is to love the good'. When Charlotte first began to show kindness towards me as her younger sibling, I neither understood nor trusted it, and even when we started to have a more normal relationship there were lapses. But gradually I began to see her in a completely different light. One of the thoughts that I held on to in the days following Charlotte's death was how miraculous it had been that such a difficult brother–sister relationship in childhood had been so transformed as we grew into adults. It was a good thing that came out of a bad thing – and in that cold, dark time, I desperately needed to remind myself that the good and miraculous can emerge from the bad.

Perhaps the hardest thing to accept and understand is that Charlotte's killers, like all human beings, must have had some good in them. But to accept this is, I believe, the key to forgiveness. I know now that the people who carried out the Titanic Express attack were not evil monsters. Zealous, hate-filled, misguided and brutalized though they were, they were every bit as much 'living, breathing human beings' as their victims.

Not long ago I found a recording on the BBC news website of a radio interview that Anicet Ntawuhiganayo had given in 2001. It was the first time I'd ever heard the voice of an FNL member, let alone one rumoured to have a direct connection to Charlotte's death. It was eerie to listen to the words of this man whose gruesome death I had rejoiced over just a year after the interview was made. What shocked me most was the warmth and humour in his voice. He spoke fluently in English, and I was struck by how similar he sounded to my friend Kabonesho. It was suddenly impossible to hate him.

Charlotte's killer was able to do what he did because he couldn't see the good in her. He couldn't see the dedicated teacher, or the masterful cook, or the mischievous joker, or the complex, loving sister. Instead he saw a *msungu*, a friend of the Tutsis, one of the white people selling the weapons in Africa. Her murder was, in a sense, a case of mistaken identity.

In October 2005 a dissident faction split off from the FNL and issued a statement accusing Rwasa of leading a 'descent into hell'. The dissidents, led by Rwasa's former deputy Jean-Bosco Sindayigaya, accused Rwasa of 'gross human rights violations', including the beheading of Hutu civilians and the killing of many of his own lieutenants. An earlier statement had given a long list of FNL officers that Rwasa had killed for suggesting negotiations with the government. I saw two names on the list that I recognized. One was Anicet Ntawuhiganayo.

Albert Sibomana, commander of the FNL's RUK battalion, the man whose name proudly adorns the covering note, dated 12 January 2001, of the FNL's December 2000 activity report. The man whose handwriting matches that of the page detailing how many 'mils' attacked the 'Titanic, au provenance du Rwanda'. Albert Sibomana, the man for whom the '21 dead' of the Titanic Express were worthy of just one line on that page, a mere note above the long and detailed list of everything that he stole from them, down to the last bottle of vegetable oil.

Seeing Sibomana's name on that list, I actually felt quite sad. I really had hoped that I might one day see him on trial, see him confront the reality of what he had done, and perhaps even be able to forgive him. And although I'd always known that, given the brutal nature of Burundi's conflict, this was one of the most likely outcomes, it just hadn't occurred to me that it would happen so soon.

Charlotte has been dead for just over five years, but already two of the most senior FNL officers implicated in her murder are rumoured to have joined her. And while Agathon Rwasa appears to have a remarkable talent for surviving attempts on his life, he now seems more isolated and exposed than ever before. I can not say with any confidence that he will live to see the end of this year, let alone the next. The more I learn about Charlotte's killers, the more I feel that these are not *evil* people, but profoundly foolish ones. I'm not sure that there ever was a more vivid or tragic illustration of the old Biblical proverb that 'those who live by the sword, die by the sword'.

And yet I hope that Agathon Rwasa *does* live to see the end of this year, and many more. His death will serve no purpose that justice, with mercy, could not have served better. For me, the most profound and comprehensive rejection we can give to the FNL's twisted ideology is to overcome our natural, normal, all-too-human impulse to revenge.

But this is not the same as rejecting the principle that those who kill others must pay a price for what they have done. If someone steals five pounds from you, then you can forgive them for thieving but still insist that they have to repay the money. And while forgiveness without justice may be possible in theory, it is far easier in practice to forgive someone who has been forced to confront the consequences of their actions, make some gesture of atonement and who, crucially, is no longer in a position to commit the same crime again.

The reason it seems so important to try to explain Burundi's conflict is that without such an explanation, this story, like so many others, becomes just one senseless massacre after another – and stops seeming real. Maybe it's not such a surprise, therefore, that we so often fall back on clichés like the 'ancient tribal hatreds' mantra. In the absence of any better explanation, our stereotypes are all that we have to go on. But the problem with these stereotypes is that they stop us from *identifying* with the people we are applying them to. By telling ourselves that 'these people are killing each other all the time', and 'maybe there just isn't a reason' we are saying that 'these people' are fundamentally unlike us. It's very difficult to empathize with people who we see as fundamentally unlike us.

The single most widely held stereotype I've heard about Africans in general and Burundians in particular, is that *they* don't have a concept of justice remotely comparable to our own. A great deal follows on from this, notably that if *they* don't share our concept of justice, then who are *we* to try and impose it on *them*? By trying to impose our cultural concepts on others, are *we* not simply repeating and continuing the mistakes of the colonial era? Through such efforts, well-intentioned though they may be, do we not risk the same disastrous consequences?

One reason that the argument is so effective is that it is founded squarely in the discourse of cultural relativism, which still dominates large areas of academia, particularly in European countries still struggling to come to terms with their colonial legacy.

In its strictest sense, cultural relativism is simply an anthropological theory describing the diversity of values between different human societies. But the danger comes when we try to draw *moral* conclusions from such a theory. Cultural relativists might begin with the assertion that the application of moral values varies, in practice, from culture to culture, but often such arguments seem to collapse into a claim that morality itself is completely subjective and culturally relative. The conclusion that many relativists then draw is that it's morally wrong to apply our own values outside our own society.

While organizations like Amnesty International and Human Rights Watch premise their existence on the objectivity and universality of human rights – many of the national governments and UN agencies involved in Burundi seem to see things very differently. Perhaps the phrase 'culture of impunity', which has so often been used to describe Burundi's state of lawlessness, is part of the problem. In reality, the mass killings that began at the end of the colonial era were just as much a corruption of indigenous values as the atrocities in Nazi Germany and the Soviet Union. In Burundian culture, like every other culture I've ever had contact with, the murder of innocent people is morally abhorrent.

One of the first things I learned about Richard Ndereyimana, following his death, was that he had once challenged President Pierre Buyoya to set a better example to his people and been told 'Say that again and I'll arrest you myself'. Not long ago I asked Kabonesho if he'd heard this story.

'I didn't just hear it, I was there!' he told me. The incident had taken place not, as I had thought, in the mid-1990s, when Richard was at university, but in the early-1990s when he was still at school. It was during Buyoya's first term in office, before the first transition to democracy, before the election of Ndadaye, before the 1993 assassination and all that came after. And the issue that Richard Ndereyimana felt so strongly about, to the extent that he was willing to risk being arrested, was the fact that Buyoya was proposing to give an amnesty to the members of the Partie pour la libération du peuple Hutu who had massacred hundreds of Tutsi civilians in 1988.

On the first anniversary of the 13 August 2004 Gatumba massacre, more than 2,000 people gathered at the site of the attack to remember the 153 Congolese Tutsis who had been shot, hacked and burned to death a year before. Many had travelled into Burundi from across the Congo border to be at the service. After the hymns had been sung and the prayers had been said, community spokesman Binagana Amon addressed the media.

'What happened on August 13 was a genocide', he said. 'We demand that justice be done . . . We condemn the silence of the United Nations.'

Article 8 of the Universal Declaration of Human Rights, the document which underpins international law, states that:

Everyone has the right to an effective remedy by the competent national tribunals for acts violating the fundamental rights granted him by the constitution or by law.

To deny this right to Rwasa's victims is therefore, in itself, a further abuse of human rights. For those who believe that human rights are absolute and inviolable, the case against any blanket amnesty is thus pretty clear-cut. For those who don't, there is only one good argument that *might* justify giving Rwasa an amnesty, and it's tenuous at best.

Like the argument that says it's OK to kill civilians, the argument that says it's OK to let killers go unpunished is an 'ends and means' argument, i.e. if we don't let Rwasa off, distasteful though this may be, then the FNL will kill even more innocent people.

While Rwasa's forces may be small in number, some claim he still commands respect among a much wider constituency. Many, it is said, who fear Palipehutu-FNL still admire their resilience, and the sacrifices that they have made. Many who differ with Rwasa over his politics and methods nonetheless see him as a worthy heir of Remy Gahutu, the revered Palipehutu founder who first 'awakened' the majority – and began the struggle for Hutu liberation – long before CNDD-FDD or Frodebu even existed. A further complication is the very real grievance among Hutus over the historical bias against them within Burundi's judicial system. If Rwasa alone was arrested, his sympathizers would try to portray the arrest of such a totemic, Hutu leader as a further injustice against Hutus as a whole.

Rwasa's enduring power and popularity may be unfortunate, but, so the argument goes, for as long as he retains it, any political process that excludes him is more likely to fail than one that can draw him in. Given that the objective of the current political process is a stable and democratic peace, there is a clear argument that accommodating Rwasa, at least for now, will save lives and bring about a greater long-term good than putting him on trial.

This as I understand it, is the current position of the UK government, along with the UN and most of the other governments who've been involved in the peace process. Many, though not all, agree that Rwasa has a serious case to answer, especially in the aftermath of Gatumba. Most agree that this is at the level of crimes against humanity, war crimes and, perhaps, even genocide. But so long as there's a significant risk that moving against him would disrupt the political process, and might trigger off an upsurge in violence, the argument goes that we have no choice but to wait him out. Rwasa's FNL is, in a sense, holding Burundians hostage.

Yet Rwasa is not simply holding Burundians hostage – he's killing his hostages one by one. So if we're applying the logic of 'ends and means', then we need to think seriously about the number of people the FNL would likely kill in retaliation for any move against Rwasa, compared to the number that they would likely have killed over the longer term. In the 18 months since I began writing this book, several hundred FNL killings have been reported. But given the under-reporting of such things, it's likely that the real figure is higher. If Interpol had swooped at the moment that Rwasa stepped off the plane in Amsterdam in January 2004, there may have been some upsurge in violence in Burundi. But I'm not at all sure that the overall outcome would have been any bloodier than the one we have seen as a result of *not* moving against Rwasa.

Furthermore, many Burundians I know deny that Rwasa retains any significant support, or has anything to contribute to the political process. During the July elections, Rwasa's militants backed Frodebu, and used violence and intimidation against CNDD-FDD voters. Frodebu lost, and CNDD-FDD won by a landslide. Burundi now has a democratically elected government for the first time since 1993. And yet Rwasa's forces continue to fight against that government, allegedly with support from Frodebu.

'Any Burundian will say, if he is honest, that he lives in constant fear of the spirits of his ancestors', Kabonesho told me not long ago, and this seems to have a wider, metaphorical resonance. The 200,000 uneasy spirits of 1972 still haunt Burundi. The violence after 1993 was, to a considerable degree, driven by a determination among Hutus to avenge those deaths, and avoid a repetition of them.

A 1996 United Nations report into the assassination of Ndadaye implicated the army Chief-of-Staff Jean Bikumagu, and another senior officer, Lt Colonel Pascal Simbanduku. But despite the many changes of government and the return to power of the Hutu majority, neither has been brought to justice. Simbanduku remains one of Burundi's most powerful and feared men. There is no sign of any end to the 'provisional' immunity from prosecution that the Hutu and Tutsi elites agreed between themselves in November 2003. Few that I know hold out any great hope that Burundi's much talked about Truth and Reconciliation Commission will ever materialize.

It seems impossible to say how many more killings there will be before the 300,000 dead of this last decade have been avenged, but it seems inevitable that their consequences will continue to play out far into the future. Whatever the rebels have managed to achieve today through unjust and indiscriminate killing could be undone tomorrow unless justice is done. Without forgiveness, the cycle of revenge will never end. Without justice, forgiveness will be impossible, and the dead will refuse to stay buried.

In many ways, our moral universe now seems very different from the one in which Charlotte lived and died. We were told that 'the world changed' following the attacks of 11 September 2001 and that the 'rules of the game have changed' after the London bombings of 7 July 2005. In practice this has meant the rise of the doctrine of pre-emptive war, the indefinite detention without trial of alleged terror suspects on the basis of secret evidence, limitations on the right to protest, efforts to constrain the independence of judiciary and a growing acceptance of the use of torture.

The ideal of universal, non-negotiable human rights has taken a battering in recent years. It had already been under attack by left-wing relativists, but in the aftermath of 9/11 it has been criticized by conservative critics who see it as an obstacle to the effective pursuit of the War On Terror. We've been told that individual rights must now be weighed up against security concerns. Tacit in this seems to be an acceptance that innocent people may end up getting imprisoned, tortured or killed in the course of efforts to root out and defeat the terrorists. A less charitable way of describing this is that the British and American governments have decided to fight terror with terrror.

But what seems striking to me is that our new, changed Western world has, in some ways, become more similar to the developing world in which Charlotte died. The government of Pierre Buyoya routinely imprisoned, tortured and killed Hutus suspected of involvement with the FNL or FDD. Hundreds of thousands were rounded up and held in regroupment camps, ostensibly for their own protection – in reality to ensure that none could give succour to the terrorists fighting to overthrow Buyoya.

The problem was that it just didn't work. The injustices of the Buyoya regime served only to fuel Hutu anger, driving people into the arms of the groups that the government was trying to defeat, creating grievances which the extremists ruthlessly exploited and perpetuating the violence. The injustices also defined the norm – if the government was going to attack innocent civilians, what reason was there for the rebels to hold back? In Burundi, fighting terror with terror only led to more of the same. In Britain and the United States, I find it hard to believe that following Burundi's lead can do anything other than store up trouble for the future.

The consequences of the Titanic Express massacre continue to affect its victims. Richard Ndereyimana had a close, loving family – two brothers, a sister and a mother who, five years on, still grieve deeply over his loss. For Richard's widowed mother, Catherine, the murder of her second son inevitably compounded the grief she felt over the killing of his father, her husband, by Tutsi *genocidaires*, in the 1970s. Richard Ndereyimana had been the pride of his family, the most naturally gifted academically, the most avid reader. Others went without so that they could afford to send him to university. And it was an investment that began to pay off. When Richard got a good job working for World Relief in Kigali, he was able to send extra money home to help support his ageing mother. For an impoverished widow living in the war-ravaged capital of one of the poorest countries in the world, having a son who worked for an international organization was not only a source of pride – it was a financial lifeline. When Richard was killed, on top of everything else, that financial lifeline was taken away.

Catherine is just 1 of 21 mothers whose children were killed on 28 December 2000. The Titanic Express was just one among hundreds of similar attacks. When I think about all the people who have lost loved ones, as I have, at the hands of the FNL, or the FDD, or the Tutsi-militias, or l'armée monethnique Tutsi, it seems distasteful to consider that the rightness or wrongness of their personal tragedy might come down to a simple matter of mathematics – a question of whether or not this particular murder of this particular son or daughter, or wife or husband, or brother, or sister, helped save lives overall. But if we accept the logic of ends and means, this is what we must embrace.

One of the things that has surprised me most since the day I found out that my sister was dead is how many people do accept the logic of ends and means, at least in some circumstances. Comparitively few people, in my experience, support the absolute prohibition against the deliberate killing of civilians which is enshrined in international law.

But if we don't support this prohibition, if we accept that, in principle, attacking civilians is sometimes OK, we have to accept that the principle applies universally. And that means accepting, if we are not to be hypocrites, that we ourselves, and those we love, would, if circumstances demanded it, be a legitimate target for murder in pursuit of the greater good. If I agree, as does Ted Honderich, that the policies of the Israeli government can justify the indiscriminate murder of Israeli civilians, then I must also agree that, if the British government engaged in similar policies, I could have no complaint when my own family was killed by suicide bombers. If I agree that the crimes of the Nazis justified the firebombing of German civilians during the Second World War, then I must also accept that, if a similar regime ever seized power in Britain, the firebombing of my home town, with me in it, would also be OK.

To give Ted Honderich credit, I think he does accept this consequence of his theory, but in doing so I feel that he is turning his back on a fundamental part of his own humanity. To me at least, the conviction that my own life, and the lives of the ones I love, have an absolute, inviolable value, is central to my idea of who I am and what it means to be human.

When I think about Charlotte and the life she lived, and the hopes she had for the future, when I think of my earliest memory of her, sitting on my mother's bed eating apples in May 1978, when I think about the last time I saw her, eating tinned peaches in the cool air of Kigali airport on 21 July 2000, when I think about the last time I hugged her and said 'See you soon', when I think about the last email she sent me, when I think about the moment I heard that she was dead, when I think about what I saw in the morgue on January 2001, when I think about the dark, sickening days and weeks that followed, when I think about everything that has happened since, when I think about the bond I still feel with my sister, when I think about this book and the tears I have shed in writing it, I find it simply impossible to accept that Charlotte's cruel, callous, bloody murder was, or could ever have been, OK. I find it impossible to accept that my big sister's life was simply a token to be held or thrown away as part of a political game, a token life to be weighed up against other token lives. I find it impossible to accept that Charlotte was a 'means to an end', however noble that end, however great the injustice that her death was supposed to avenge.

I believe this knowing that Charlotte's was just one among 300,000 deaths in Burundi, and knowing that her life was no more or less valuable than any other. I believe this knowing that if Charlotte's life had an absolute value, then so too did the life of Richard

Ndereyimana, Arthur Kabunda, Ibrahim Mugabo, Judith Nduwayo, Rugenerwa Hakizimana, Simon Nkundabantu, Magambo Kabika, Laetitia 'Titi' Mbeyeyinzima, Georgette Mukankubito, Audace Ndayisaba, Innocent Kamatari, Aline Umulisa, Innocent Mukila, Flora Nzeyimana, Béatrice Benecaza, Eugène Mantore, Rwego Cyaka, Fredy Mitima, Ally Nzeyimana, Marie Agatore, Mwamire Ingabire, Jean-Jacques Marango, Rusine Girimana, Rwaka Wakana, and Donatien Ruberintwa, the victims and survivors of the 28 December 2000 Titanic Express massacre, at Mageyo. So too the 173 Hutu civilians massacred at Itaba by the Burundian army on 9 September 2002, and the hundreds more killed since. So too the dozens of FNL boy soldiers whose battered corpses littered the streets of Bujumbura in July 2003, childish hands still clutching the amulets they'd been told would protect them from bullets. So too did the lives of the 153 Congolese Banyamulenge Tutsis massacred by the FNL on 13 August 2004 at the Gatumba refugee camp. So too the six Bujumbura-Rurale churchgoers massacred by the FNL at Muhuta in June 2005, and the South African UN peacekeeper shot and fatally wounded as he guarded a polling station during Burundi's first democratic elections in 12 years. So too the 300 whose bodies were uncovered in mass graves during August 2005. So too the 20 'government collaborators' killed by the FNL, and the 11 'FNL suspects' killed by the Burundian army during September and October 2005.

Most of these deaths were not reported on CNN, and most of these lives will not get books written about them. Few, had they lived even another 50 years, would ever have travelled far from the hills where they were born. But all, like us, were human beings with hopes and fears and ambitions and regrets. All, like Charlotte, had brothers and sisters and mothers and friends who will spend the rest of their lives grieving for them.

Heleen and I got married on 4 September 2005, 10 days before my 30th birthday. I chose as my 'best man' my younger sister Catherine, and she made a speech remembering Charlotte, just as I had done at her wedding three years before. The barrier that existed between us for so long has dissolved. The sadness endures, but the shock and trauma have receded, and we can talk to each other again. Life continues, for all of us.

The small charity we established in Charlotte's name has now helped more than 20 students at the school where she taught, funded

AIDS-education programmes across Rwanda and supported a new peacebuilding project in Burundi. We believe, as Charlotte did, that Africa's problems can only be solved by Africans themselves, but that our solidarity can help. A week after the August 2004 Gatumba massacre, a multi-ethnic group of Burundian volunteers from 'Youth Intervention for Peace' took food and clothes to the survivors, paid for in part by the Charlotte Wilson Memorial Fund. It was only a small gesture, but it was *something they could do.*

At the end of 2005 I found an interview, published earlier in the year, on the website of a Swiss-based Christian organization. In the interview, a man by the name of Dieudonné Niyonzima, who had previously been listed among those killed in the Titanic Express massacre, describes his narrow escape from death more than four years earlier, in December 2000, following a bus ambush by the Burundian rebels on a return journey from Kigali to Bujumbura. Twenty-one of his fellow passengers had been shot, but the attackers released him unharmed. 'I saw the hand of God', Dieudonné said.

But one seemingly mundane detail stood out above all the others. The purpose of Dieudonné's trip to Kigali, he said, had been to pick up a projector for use in his church group's New Year celebrations. I immediately remembered the FNL's inventory of 'butins' from the Titanic Express. '3 NOKIA, 2 ERICSSONS, 1 télé, 1 *projecteur . . .*'

With help from an old friend in Germany, I contacted the Swiss journalist who had written the article, and within days I had an email address for Dieudonné. He wrote back almost immediately, confirming that the attack he had survived was the Titanic Express massacre, and offering his condolences for Charlotte's death. The following week, Dieudonné sent me his own account of what he had seen:

It was around three in the afternoon and the sky was overcast. The rain had lessened but there were still streams and puddles on the road. We were between Bugarama and Kinama (Mubimbi Commune), in the mountains and the road had many twists and turns.

Charlotte and Richard were sitting next to me throughout the journey, Richard to my left and Charlotte on the left of Richard, by the window. I remember that some time before the attack, Richard was explaining to his fiancée that we were passing through some beautiful valleys, but unfortunately the view was obscured by the rain and mist.

When the attack began, I heard a loud noise and my first impression was that it was thunder. Then I realized that it was gunfire. The bus crashed and turned over onto its right side; the wheels on the left side of the bus were in the air.

A group of young men, armed mostly with rifles, converged on the bus. Some were in military uniform, some in civilian clothes. Some came in through the doors and some through the broken windows. They demanded that we give them our money, our watches, and jewellery; some were saying at the same time that they were going to kill us, while others were promising that we would be massacred.

We were all afraid. Richard and Charlotte were almost motionless with fear. One of Richard's arms was resting on me. Because they were asking us for money, I told myself that perhaps they would spare our lives. When I saw the attackers approaching us, I emptied the money from the pocket of my shirt and put some of this into Richard's hand, so that he would have something to give them (when they took money from someone's hands, they said – 'for you it's OK').

After that, they ordered us to leave the bus slowly and leave the rest of our belongings inside the bus. They said 'We're not going to hurt you'. While I was getting out I heard one of them say 'We, we are the FNL, we are not your FDD'. Another said 'Where are your Tutsi soldiers? Why aren't they coming to save you?' Others hurled insults at us.

They told us to sit down on the road, and called a group of youths, who'd been hiding in the woods, to come and take everything that was left in the vehicle. There was a man who was older than the rest of the group and in civilian clothes, who took charge of gathering together everything that was stolen.

They asked me to take off my shoes. Another demanded, with a lot of threats, that I remove my shirt. A third made me take off my trousers. So I was left with only my shorts and socks. Then they started telling everyone to gather together next to the back wheels of the bus. I was on the other side of the bus, with a man who was hesitating to take off his trousers, a woman who was with her three-year-old child, and a young girl injured in the thigh. I was lying on my back. They told us to get into just one group.

The woman with the child was asking them again and again to spare her, and they let her go with her child, and the girl who was seriously injured in the thigh. I could hear the others crying for mercy, saying that they'd given all they had.

I was still lying on my back, and one of the attackers came up, pointed his gun at me and said: 'I'm going to kill you, son of a bitch!' Suddenly, my blood cooled. I raised my head and I said to this young man: 'Why must you kill me?' He stared at me for a few seconds and then kicked me and told me to go. I was afraid to get up and he repeated it – 'Go on!'

I got up and I left but after some five metres one of them stopped me – but the first told him that he'd let me go. I started to fear that they were going to shoot me in the back. I looked back to see if they were going to release any others but they weren't. At that moment I could see Charlotte in the group asking them to have pity.

I continued along the road and caught up with the woman who was with her child and the wounded girl, and another injured girl who'd been in a lorry that had been ambushed in the same place some minutes after us. I had to help Eugénie, the injured girl, to walk. After some minutes we heard gunshots and we thought that they were firing at us; they were already massacring the people who'd been with us in the bus.

Some minutes later, someone in the rebel positions fired over us to stop us from continuing. We dropped to the ground beside the road for several minutes before continuing. One person who had abandoned his bicycle to hide saw us passing and joined us. He took us to a health centre, nearly three kilometres from the scene of the attack. The nurses gave first aid, and we spent the night there. There was a military position nearby.

In the morning we talked to the soldiers who'd gone to see the situation and attend to the dead, and they told us that they had counted twenty-one bodies and fifteen injured, who were taken to hospital. I asked if they had noticed a European among the corpses, the soldier replied 'There was a person who looked like an Arab'. Then I knew that the white girl had also been killed . . . They took us back to Bujumbura in a military lorry. When I arrived home, the mourning had already begun. When they saw me, everyone started crying. I must tell you that this is one of the worst experiences that I have known.

In January 2006, in the final stages of writing this book, I received an email from someone who claimed to be a member of Palipehutu-FNL's Sindayigaya faction, offering to 'shed light on the barbarous acts of Agathon Rwasa'. I've yet to see whether this will lead to more answers or turn out to be another false trail.

As I write, Jean-Bosco is still waiting to be allowed to be reunited with his family, nearly four years after arriving in Britain. The enormity of suffering endured by the Burundian asylum seekers I count among my friends defies all my attempts to make sense of it. My sadness over these individual tragedies is matched only by my admiration for the courage, forbearance and heroic human dignity with which they are borne. There is nothing bogus about the terror that they have fled, or that which they would face if they returned home. They seek protection in my country because they are forced to, not because they want to. Yet few Burundians are granted anything more than the meagre, precarious, security of 'exceptional leave to remain', while some are denied even that. For many I know, the well-founded fear of being catapulted back into the horrors they had hoped to escape further exacerbates the suffering already endured.

And yet even in the midst of compounded tragedy, the story of Burundi is also one of endless, ludicrous hope. At the very moment that the Titanic Express bus was attacked, a chain of events had begun that led, through the cold, dark days that followed, and the anguished years that came after, to the birth, in 2002, of a new life. Pierre and Maria met just a few days after the Titanic Express attack. He was recovering in hospital. She had been sent by Reuters to interview him. They became friends, fell in love and a baby girl, Sophie, was the result.

'She's nearly three years old now,' Maria tells me, as we sit by the Thames, chatting in the sunshine. 'But she's so precocious already. Such a little flirt, you know? She has this boyfriend. I was listening to them talking the other day. 'Look!', she was saying. 'Look at the stars'. Aren't they beautiful?"

Acknowledgements

This book would not have been possible without the tireless commitment of my agent Louise Greenberg, the advice and encouragement of my uncle, James Wilson, and the love and support of my wife, Heleen Bulckens. I am especially indebted to Robin Baird-Smith for giving me the opportunity to write it.

I am also particularly grateful to my mother Margot Wilson, my sister Catherine Erdly and my hypnotherapist Tanya Colley for their assistance in piecing together the events of the last five years, to Annarita Ferreri, Clara Arbizu and Greg Till for their friendship during the darkest of times, and to Rory Beaumont, Jean-Bosco Nsengyumva, Kabonesho Kagoongo and Désiré Katihabwa for their role in helping me to understand Burundi's complex history. Without the courage of Pierre Nzeyimana, Xavier Hitimana and Dieudonné Niyonzima, who dared to speak out about what they saw, there would have been no story to write.

Without the work of Amnesty International, Human Rights Watch and Ligue Iteka there would have been far less to say. Thanks are also due to Alexis Sinduhije and the staff of Radio Publique Africaine, Jean-Claude Kavumbagu and the Netpress news agency, Maria Eismont, Bryan Rich, Jon Swain, Will Woodward, Alison Des Forges, Alison Dilworth, Tony tate, Godfrey Byaruhanga, Arnaud Royer, Andrew Walby, Carina Tertsakian, Emmanuel Nkurunziza, Antoine Kaburahe, Lydia Zacharias, Joanna Rowelle, Lewis Tasker, Dick Bird, Ben Pollitt, Karen Aylward, Mine Bolgil, Amanda Liddle, Laurent Ndayuhurume, Mike and Collette Hughes, Mark Pallis, Nicholas Howen, Wesley Gryk, Alex Ntung, Rosana Lorente, Justine Greening MP, Robbie Hudson, Gina de Ferrer, Lisa Gee, Simon Baker, Suresh Ariaratnum, Sarah Manson, Nazish Khan, Sue Cope, and Messrs Lynham, Oxley and Taylor.

My family and I are particularly grateful to Andy Love MP, and to the staff of the British Embassy in Rwanda, for their persistence in maintaining the profile of the Titanic Express case.

Further information

http://news.amnesty.org – General human rights news from Amnesty International.

http://web.amnesty.org/library/eng-bdi/index – Amnesty International on Burundi.

www.hrw.org/doc?t=africa&c=burund – Human Rights Watch on Burundi.

www.ligue-iteka.africa-web.org/ – News from Burundian human rights organization *Ligue Iteka*.

http://allafrica.com/burundi/ – Burundi news from mainstream sources across Africa.

www.globalvoicesonline.org/ – Collating weblogs from around the world, with a particular focus on development issues.

http://agathonrwasa.blogspot.com – Campaigning for the prosecution of Agathon Rwasa.

www.cwmf.org – The Charlotte Wilson Memorial Fund.